W9-ASM-672

The Closed Commercial State

Discard

HIN 15 23

SUNY series in Contemporary Continental Philosophy

Dennis J. Schmidt, editor

The Closed Commercial State

J. G. Fichte

Translated and with an Interpretive Essay by
Anthony Curtis Adler

Library St. Vincent de Paul
10701 S. Military Trail
Boynton Beach, Fl 33436

SUNY PRESS

Published by State University of New York Press, Albany

© 2012 State University of New York

All rights reserved

Printed in the United States of America

No part of this book may be used or reproduced in any manner whatsoever
without written permission. No part of this book may be stored in a retrieval
system or transmitted in any form or by any means including electronic,
electrostatic, magnetic tape, mechanical, photocopying, recording, or otherwise
without the prior permission in writing of the publisher.

For information, contact State University of New York Press, Albany, NY
www.sunypress.edu

Production by Kelli W. LeRoux
Marketing by Anne M. Valentine

Library of Congress Cataloging-in-Publication Data

Fichte, Johann Gottlieb, 1762–1814.
  [Geschlossene Handelsstaat. English]
  The closed commercial state / J.G. Fichte ; translated and with an
interpretive essay by Anthony Curtis Adler.
      p. cm. — (SUNY series in contemporary Continental philosophy)
  Includes bibliographical references and index.
  ISBN 978-1-4384-4021-7 (hardcover : alk. paper)
  ISBN 978-1-4384-4020-0 (pbk. : alk. paper)
  1. State, The.   2. Commercial policy.   I. Adler, Anthony Curtis.   II. Title.

JC181.F6 2012
320.1—dc22   2011014159

10 9 8 7 6 5 4 3 2 1

For my parents

Contents

Acknowledgments

Work on this translation was spread over many years, and it would be impossible to thank all the teachers, colleagues, and friends who contributed to its realization. Wilhelm Metz, in an extraordinary proseminar at the University of Freiburg, introduced me to the wonder of Fichte's thought. Peter Fenves encouraged me to take on this project while working on my dissertation at Northwestern University, and Sam Weber and Terry Pinkard offered crucial support along the way. Géza von Molnár, who died suddenly and tragically on July 27, 2001, spent several hours helping me figure out some of Fichte's more unusual idioms. Paul North read an early draft of the introduction and offered valuable criticism and invaluable encouragement, and Melissa Zinkin, Markus Hardtmann, Helen Lee, Chad Denton, Karin Schutjer, Michael Kim, Gabe Hudson, John Frankl, Kil-Pyo Hong, Paul Tonks, Aljoša Pužar, Mason Richey, Sarah Brett-Smith, Saein Park, Eric Fuchs, and Michael Weitz all offered advice, guidance, and assistance at various stages of the project. Yongkyung Chung and Jeehye Kim assisted with the preparation of the index. A very great debt of gratitude goes to Tom Rockmore, for helping find a home for this project, and also to Daniel Breazeale, Isaac Nakhimovsky, and Chris Pierson for the interest they have shown in it. Andrew Kenyon, of SUNY Press, has been extremely supportive of this project from the beginning, and has done a wonderful job shepherding me through the process of publication. I am also very grateful to the anonymous referee at SUNY for his or her extraordinarily insightful, helpful, and careful comments, and to Dennis J. Schmidt, the series editor.

I feel fortunate to have found an academic home at Yonsei University's Underwood International College. For these last six years, my students have become an integral part of my life, and their enthusiasm and curiosity, more than anything, has kept me going through the hard slog.

Finally, I would like to thank Hwa Young Seo, whose path, different from my own, is also my own.

Abbreviations and Editorial Apparatus

[ ] Insertion by the translator

[37] Pagination referring to the German text of *The Closed Commercial State* in the first division, seventh volume of the edition of Fichte's works published by the *Bayerische Akademie der Wissenschaften*.

{387} Pagination referring to the German text of *The Closed Commercial State* in the third volume of the edition of Fichte's works edited by I. H. Fichte.

1,2,3, . . . Notes by translator

i,ii,iii, . . . Notes by Fichte

SW Johann Gottlieb Fichte, *Sämmtliche Werke*, ed. Immanuel Hermann Fichte (Berlin: Veit und Comp., 1845–46; Berlin, Walter de Gruyter, 1971)

GA Johann Gottlieb Fichte, *Gesamtausgabe der Bayerischen Akademie der Wissenschaften* (Stuttgart-Bad Cannstatt: Friedrich Frommann Verlag: 1962–)

FIG J. G. *Fichte im Gespräch: Berichte der Zeitgenossen*, ed. Erich Fuchs in collaboration with Reinhard Lauth and Walter Schieche (Stuttgart-Bad Cannstatt: Friedrich Frommann Verlag, 1981)

EPW   Johann Gottlieb Fichte, *Early Philosophical Writings,* tr. and ed.
           Daniel Breazeale (Ithaca: Cornell University Press, 1988)

SOK   Johann Gottlieb Fichte, *Science of Knowledge,* tr. and ed. Peter
           Heath and John Lachs (Cambridge: Cambridge University Press,
           1982)

VOM   Johann Gottlieb Fichte, *Vocation of Man,* tr. and ed. Peter
           Preuss (Indianapolis: Hackett, 1987)

Translator's Introduction

The *Closed Commercial State* is not one of Fichte's most elusive or enigmatic writings. Yet it presents special difficulties to the translator. The most fundamental of these involve the tension between the different discursive levels and linguistic registers through which the text operates. This tension is already evident in the organization of the work as a whole: whereas the first book presents an abstract theory of ideal economic relations, the second book considers the "history of the present" and the third offers a concrete proposal for political action. Fichte, in a novel fashion, attempts to bring philosophy and material reality, the language of German idealism and the very worldly science of economics, into a commerce. The argument of the *Closed Commercial State* insists on closure and boundaries. Yet Fichte's rhetoric often seems to be doing the very opposite.

This presents a challenge to the translator, who must do justice to the very different expectations and conventions governing the translation of these different registers. Whereas English often forces us to choose between "earthy" Germanic words and a more abstract vocabulary of Latinate derivation, German, whose rich philosophical vocabulary is mostly cobbled together from rather ordinary root words, is extremely adept at moving between these different registers. Most modern readers would probably reject Fichte's own extravagant claims regarding German's "originality" and the superiority of "original languages" as media for philosophical thought.[1] Yet it is still worth noting that for Fichte, the linguistic difference between "original" and other languages suggests the difference between the open and the closed commercial state. The closed commercial state is not only a political construct, but the hermeneutic construction of a state in which the *meaning* of economic activity, rather than being imperiled by the hyperbolic inflation and deflation to which world currency gives rise, would be conserved by sealing off reference within a hermetically closed whole. Seen in this way, translating the *Closed Commercial State* into English is a somewhat paradoxical undertaking—like trying to realize the value of national currency in world currency.

xiii

Rigorous philosophical translations, especially of German, are with good reason expected to make at least a valiant attempt at preserving not only the apparent reference of a term, but its resonances and associations within both the source language as a whole and the dialects and idiolects represented by the text in question, the philosopher's other writings, and contemporaneous discourse. No one could be happy translating Heidegger's *Gestell* as "rack," though it is not unimportant to know that *Gestell* also has this very everyday sense. Economics, in contrast, was, or at least has become, a technocratic discipline with a vocabulary that claims precision in its reference. A philosopher might spend hours pondering the Latin roots of *interest*. For an economist considering the relation between unemployment and inflation, this is itself of little interest, and a translator who, translating a conventional economic text, felt the need to remind the reader that interest comes from a Latin word literally meaning "being-among," that a commodity was not only commodious but contained a due measure within itself, and that capital had itself inherited a rich metaphysical endowment, would probably be treated with a shrug. And if someone translated "interest" as "among-being," "commodity" as "the duly-measured" and "capital" as "head-part," he would be justly regarded as out of his mind. Fichte's *Closed Commercial State*, however, is neither fish nor fowl. Or rather, it is a fish whose scales are on the way to becoming wings—or a bird returning to the sea. Sometimes this does not create problems. Forgetting that *Anweisung* appeared in the title of another work by Fichte, where it roughly means "instruction," and also forgetting that it is related to a word meaning "to show" or "to point" and resonates with the German word for wisdom, we can happily translate it as "bill of exchange" in the sixth chapter of the third book.[2] The context in which it appears mutes these other senses and associations. But often things become more difficult. *Berechnung* must be translated as "calculation" to capture the ostensive meaning of the text, but it is also involved in an elaborate play of concepts, on which much of the meaning of the text depends. Not only is the closed commercial state one in which everyone can count on everyone else, and every activity counts on every other activity, but calculation, for Fichte, becomes the essence of "Right" (*Recht*). It might have been possible to capture this last association, and also the cognitive implications of *Berechnung* and *Rechnen*, by translating calculation as reckoning. Yet this sounds a bit antiquated and odd, and, moreover, has misleading theological resonances. So I stayed with "calculation," though the reader is advised to keep these other associations in mind.

Perhaps the greatest difficulties of translation, however, revolve around the three words in the title: *geschlossen*, *Handel*, and *Staat*. Each of these becomes the center of a network of associations that is very difficult to do justice to in English.

Geschlossen literally means "closed"; and yet the German word has implications that are not always obvious in English. Most striking, and relevant to the *Closed Commercial State,* are the political senses of the word. Just as in English, it can mean "closed to the outside." The *German Dictionary* of Wilhelm and Jacob Grimm cites Fichte's work to attest to this sense, erroneously characterizing the closed commercial state as a state that is closed off to the outside through protective tariffs.[3] The political senses of *geschlossen,* however, are much richer than this. To "stand closed" against the enemy is to stand united against him. Hence in Schiller's *Wallenstein:* "Do we not stand closed against the enemy; just as if glued and poured together."[4] And it can also mean "closed in number": a *geschlossene Zunft* is a trade guild in which the number of members is fixed—similar to the *numerus clausus* of the German university. A *geschlossene Gesellschaft* is an exclusive, elite society. And beyond these political meanings, generally more positive than in English, *geschlossen* also has aesthetic and moral implications. It can mean "full" or "complete," and even "well-rounded": as in a *geschlossenes Bild* (a full or complete picture) or a *geschlossene Persönlichkeit* (a well-rounded personality). And even in its more concrete application the nuances of *geschlossen* are rather different from the English *closed:* a closed woods is one in which the trees are thick together.[5]

I have decided to translate *geschlossen* consistently as "closed," even though some nuances are lost as a result, and sometimes the English sounds slightly unusual. To have done otherwise would have rendered the text incoherent, since so much depends on this one word appearing in different contexts. And in most cases, if we read with care, the context, and the slightly unusual sound of the English, point us toward these nuances. Precisely because "closed multitude" *does* sound a bit odd in English, it makes us think about what it must mean in order to make sense.

The word *geschlossen,* moreover, does not stand alone, but is implicated in a network of cognate words and expressions. These include *ausschließend* (exclusive) and *entschließen* (to resolve). The word *schließen* is used idiomatically, together with *Friede* (peace), *Krieg* (war), and *Bündnisse* (alliances), in the sense of "to conclude." Whenever possible, I tried to preserve these implications by choosing analogous expressions in English, using words such as "exclusive" and "conclude" that are related to the Latin *cludo* and *clausus.* To "conclude peace" and "conclude war," admittedly, sounds odd in English, but too much would have been sacrificed had I used more natural sounding yet less literal idioms. It is important for the argument of the *Closed Commercial State* that one of the most significant expressions of state sovereignty—the constitution of the relation of "friend" and "enemy"—implicitly involves an act of closure.

With *geschlossen* the Latin roots of the English graciously come to our assistance. Not so with *Handel.* Fichte's use of the latter reveals his great talent for philosophical prose, suggesting the ingenious manner in which he threads together the mundane sphere of the dismal science with transcendental philosophy. Yet it also calls attention to the difficulties that accompany translating a work that straddles two such different realms. Were one only concerned with capturing its reference, the word would prove relatively unproblematic: it can be adequately translated as "trade" or "commerce." There are other senses—the pluralizable noun can mean "quarrel"—but these are not very relevant to Fichte's text. I chose to translate it as "commercial" in the title to conform with existing usage, whereas elsewhere I opted for either "trade" or "commerce." In the case of *Handel*, however, the cognate words prove problematic. Fichte also uses *Handlung* in a similar sense to *Handel*—a usage that is now obsolete. Yet *Handlung* also, indeed principally, means "act" or "action." And indeed, the concepts of the *Handlung* and *Tathandlung* are absolutely central to his *Doctrine of Science*. This point is vital to understanding the *Closed Commercial State*, which attempts to return human economic activity to its roots in the active powers of the subject. The English language, however, provides few resources to capture this web of associations. Thus, I chose to forgo consistency in translation, and instead use different terms to establish an analogous set of associations, translating *Handlung* sometimes as "act," sometimes as "trade," and occasionally also as "to engage in commercial transactions." The last expression, ungainly as it may be, establishes the vital link between "trade" and "act."

The word *Staat* presents the opposite challenge. "State" is the appropriate translation for *Staat*. Yet Fichte also uses a number of words and idioms formed from the etymologically and semantically related word *Stand*. *Stand* is used, for example, to refer to the estates into which commercial society is to be divided. The word *Klasse* also appears occasionally in the same sense, and yet the connotation is rather different: whereas the estate is a class whose existence has become static and secure through the rightful ordering of things, Fichte's use of *Klasse* already suggests the spectral existence of the proletariat as the aggregate of those who have been given nothing, and hence can claim everything.[6] The connection between the state and the estates is clear: the rightfully ordered state is what allows for a class to become an estate—to have a secure existence—and the secure existence of the estates are the foundation for the state. Yet *Stand* also appears in other expressions where the relation to *Staat* is more subtle, but no less important. These include *Wohlstand*, which is not merely a chancy, adventitious good fortune, but a stable, enduring prosperity, and also *Zustand*. In both instances, I chose to preserve the coherence of the text by alternating between idioms that stress the sense of *Stand* and abridged forms of these idioms. Hence, *Wohlstand* is translated as either "prosperity" or "state of prosperity," and *Zustand* as "state of affairs," "state of existence," "present state," or simply "state," depending on context. This adds a certain metaphysical heaviness to the text, but this heaviness is a good corrective to the tendency to read the *Closed Commercial State* just as a work of political economy. It is, indeed, important to realize that for Fichte the arrangement of trade is a question of existential significance. No less than Plato, if perhaps less explicitly, Fichte regards the political and economic organization of the state as expressing fundamental possibilities of human existence. To exist in a truly human way is to stand on one's feet but look up toward the heavens, and this truly human stance is only possible on the foundation of secure economic relations. In translating *Stand* and its cognates in this way, I have multiplied the appearance of the word *state* in the text. I fear that, on occasion, this will lead to confusion: the state of prosperity is one thing, the prosperity of the state another. I had considered capitalizing "state" when used in the political sense, but I felt that this would give a misleading impression. I have, however, tried my best to avoid true ambiguity, and thus I almost always restrict the nonpolitical use of state to the subject position in genitive constructions. *Stehen* (standing) also appears in many idioms. Most of these seemed to be employed deliberately, and in every case I have tried as best I could to capture this connotation without torturing the English language.

There are many other words and semantic clusters that are also extremely important for the *Closed Commercial State*. Each of these presents its own dilemmas. It would be impossible to address all these terms and the problems attached to them, but I will try to discuss a few. *Recht*, which I mentioned before, must be carefully distinguished from *Gesetz* (law): *Recht* is grounded in pure reason, whereas the *Gesetz*, at least in the *Closed Commercial State*, is positive, and only comes about through an act of positing. With one exception—*römisches Recht* for "Roman law"—I have consistently translated *Recht* both standing alone, and in the many words derived from it, as "Right," and *Gesetz* as "law." Fichte uses *Berechtigung* for a right that is not original but has been granted by the state. I translated this as "title of right" in order to stress at once that it is grounded in Right and yet, involving the special privilege to engage in a certain kind of activity, is derivate and dependent on special agreements and acts of the state. The word *bestimmen* and its cognates also presented great difficulty. Like *Handlung*, *Bestimmung* is a keyword of Fichte's philosophy. Yet it takes on a range of meanings in the *Closed Commercial State* that cannot possibly be conveyed by a single English word. When possible, I have translated *bestimmt* with words derived from "determine," but it is also rendered as "set," "destined," and "specific." And in a few passages, *Bestimmung*, following an established convention, is translated as "vocation."

Fichte's use of more purely economic terminology differs somewhat from modern usage. *Produkt* does not refer generically to that which is brought forth through human labor, but rather first of all suggests raw materials and articles of immediate consumption as opposed to manufactured goods. Products or produce, in this sense, are what is won from the earth. Fichte consistently uses *Produkt*, and all the words derived from it, in this sense. Thus, he contrasts the *Produzent* and the *Fabrikant*, which I have translated respectively as the "producer" and the "manufacturer," with the *Gewinnung der Produkte* and similar expressions rendered as "the extraction of produce." *Verarbeitung* refers to the additional labor that is applied to raw materials in order to turn them into manufactured goods. I have sought to preserve the connection with labor when this seemed relevant to the context, yet I translate *Stoff zur Verarbeitung* simply as "raw material," since in this case the rather specific reference of the term seemed more important than its connotations. *Ware* (*Waare* in Fichte's spelling) is translated as "goods" in the plural, "ware" in the singular, and very occasionally as "commodity." The reader is alerted to the pun Fichte makes on *Ware* and *Wahre* (true). That the *Ware* is the true reality, that the truth is to be found in the ware and not its representation through money, is a point of the greatest significance for the argument of the *Closed Commercial State*.

The word *Mensch* presents special difficulties. The German term is more gender neutral than the English "man." While its grammatical gender is masculine, it is not also used to refer to the male gender in contrast to the female. For this reason, many choose to translate it consistently as "human" or "human being," and *Menschheit*, accordingly, as "humankind" or "humanity." In the case of Fichte's *Closed Commercial State*, however, I feel that insisting on this gender neutrality would be misleading. When *Mensch* is being used by Fichte to refer to the citizen as an economic agent, there is little reason to think he had both sexes in mind. Quite to the contrary: he never seems to consider the activities traditionally assigned to women, activities that certainly he could not have believed unimportant for the survival of the human race, as work in the economic sense. They fall completely outside of his purview. His concept of work is restricted to the extraction of raw material, the manufacture of finished goods, trade, the activities of state officials and civil servants, and the intellectual labors of the higher artists, scientists, and inventors. "Domestic labor" and the "service industries," which have often been treated with great mistrust by economists, are ignored, and, given his attempt to account in outline for the entire sphere of economic life, one can only imagine that these belong outside of it and can be left out of consideration. Likewise, when he describes the hypothetical natural condition that exists before the institution of property, it seems reasonable to suppose, even if it is never made explicit, that women and children, together with slaves, belong simply among the property that the solitary savages seize for themselves in exercising their natural rights. But this would imply, in turn, that women do not play a role in the constitutive treaties, and that the ideal state remains patriarchal. In one instance, indeed, he refers to the "family fathers."[7] Hence, I have decided to forgo consistency for nuance. When Fichte refers to *Mensch* in an economic and political sense, I translate it as "man," yet when he seems to intend *Mensch* in a more absolute sense, I translate it, when grammatically possible, as "human being."

Fichte's *Closed Commercial State* belongs within the tradition of "social contract" theories. The reader may be surprised that the word *contract* appears only once in this translation, though I use it more liberally in the interpretive essay. I have translated *Vertrag* as "treaty," using the word *contract* only in rendering *kontrahieren* ("enter into a contract"). I would argue, however, that the parties entering the *Verträge* establishing relations of property are, with respect to their economic existence, sovereign entities. Whereas "contract," at least to the modern ear and outside the context of political theory, suggests negotiation within an established framework, the *Verträge* of which Fichte speaks suspend a state of economic, and also political, warfare. Even though the first book of the *Closed Commercial State* involves a hypothetical construction, and thus the war of all against all he describes need not refer to a state of affairs that actually ever existed, the trade war of which Fichte speaks is constantly threatening to emerge, and in some cases already present, within the existing order. Those who are dispossessed, who have no property from which they can securely derive their livelihood, are in a state of war with everyone else. For this same reason, I translate *Menge* in the political sense as "multitude," thus stressing the fact that, before the juridical and economic closure of the state, one cannot speak of a unitary people, or even a group. It is only the process of closure that, by counting and fixing the number of members of the multitude and determining their relation to the outside, transforms the multitude into a people.

Eigentum is another concept that belongs both to the sphere of economics and philosophy, and moreover is rather sharply contrasted with *Besitz*. *Eigentum* is property in the full sense, and it is only established through intersubjective negotiations in which everyone voluntarily agrees to restrict his sphere of activity in such a way that each attains something that is truly his own. *Besitz*, in contrast, is a mere possession; something that, perhaps as a result of good fortune or superior power, one has seized for oneself. It is not surprising, given the metaphysical weight attached to the notion of property, that Fichte employs the various words derived from *eigen* very deliberately. Therefore, I have tried as much as possible to translate these with English words derived from *proper*. *Eigentlich* is, wherever possible, translated as "properly," while *wirklich* is translated as "actual(ly)."

The literary style of the *Closed Commercial State* also presents its challenges. At times Fichte is brutally logical. The method of early German idealism, with its insistence on deductions from principles, becomes a rhetorical devise: a philosophical hammer, bashing away at the stupid unthinking assumptions of the "mere empiricist" and the sort of politician who "awakens his predecessors from the grave one after the other, presents them again in his own age, and thus composes his political career from the very different pieces of very different men, without adding anything of himself."[8] At times we can feel, in his fiery language, the righteous indignation of one who has known poverty as few philosophers before him or after. Once or twice he gives us a glimpse of the desire that sustains his thought: the dream that human beings could one day all live a truly human existence, laboring in pleasure and joy, partaking of the good things of the earth, and having the leisure to raise their eyes to the heavens. I have tried to capture the moods and rhythms of Fichte's language, including his sometimes infuriating tendency to repeat words for emphasis. Often I rejected a more elegant-sounding translation simply because it would have no longer sounded like Fichte. Yet, in the end, I found that the more I brought my translation close to the original, the more it seemed to work as a whole. But this, if it is not the delusion of a translator as he finally prepares to let go of his work, is perhaps also not so surprising. The most difficult part of translation, after all, is being responsible for possibilities of the text that one cannot fully comprehend.

The spelling of all German words from Fichte's text, unless noted otherwise, has been modernized (e.g., *Ware* for *Waare*, *Ungefähr* for *Ohngefähr*, *Produkt* for *Product*, *Teil* for *Theil*, *Produzent* for *Producent*, *Sein* for *Seyn*).

Interpretive Essay

Fichte's Monetary History

§1. The Place of the *Closed Commercial State* in Fichte's Thought

Measured against the sublime architecture of Kant's three critiques, the vast and all-enveloping grandeur of Hegel's absolute spirit, or Schelling's prodigal succession of systems, Fichte—fated to be ranked fourth among philosophers who count by threes—never seemed to get his act together. Without ever abandoning either the title of the *Doctrine of Science (Wissenschaftslehre)*, or its vast systematic ambitions, his one system remains, from its first formulation in 1794 to his untimely death from cholera, in a state of ongoing flux and revision. However we may divide his lifework into different phases with different foci and emphases,[1] the boundaries between these remain porous, and indeed all the subsequent revisions of the *Doctrine of Science* refer back to the only version that Fichte himself published as a book, the *Foundation of the Entire Doctrine of Science* of 1794, and consequently cannot be understood apart from what they intend to replace.[2] Moreover, beyond the basic elements of his system—the doctrines of science, morality, and Right—we also find dispersed among these numerous other writings whose existence seems justified only loosely, if at all, by his systematic intention: a short treatise on language; popular works on politics, history, and religion; reflections on the French Revolution; remarks on Machiavelli; pedagogical writings; a theory of the state; and even a philosophical ascetic, not to mention the extensive notes that the new edition of his work have only recently made accessible.

While some of these are doubtless of limited importance, in the case of others, their topical, popular, and rhetorical character conceals a more probing philosophical inquiry, and one that even challenges crucial aspects of the *Doctrine of Science*. This is perhaps evident above all in the 1808

1

Addresses to the German Nation, itself the most topical and exoteric of his writings. By inquiring into the historical conditions of a truly philosophical language—a language capable of allowing a fluid commerce between ideals and praxis—Fichte, without rendering philosophical truth relative, nevertheless subjects the method of expressing philosophical truth, the generation of systems, to two conditions—language and history—neither of which finds immanent expression in the 1794 *Doctrine of Science.*[3]

If we take seriously these adjuncts to the system, we may be led to question, in more broad terms, the systematic nature of Fichte's thought.[4] While we can scarcely deny Fichte's overt allegiance to the ideal of the system, perhaps it is not only within the system itself and through a mode of interpretation centered around the *Doctrine of Science* that we find what is philosophically radical and penetrating in his thinking, but also in the veins that cross through, or even run against the grain of, its systematic core. Fichte had hoped to understand Kant better than Kant understood himself by endowing the spirit of the *Critiques* with a systematic form, allowing a deduction of the categories, and ultimately both the practical and theoretical functions of reason, from a single principle. In the following essay, I will take a different tact, emphasizing the importance of the margins, appendixes, adjuncts, and the exoteric, thus calling attention to aspects of the letter of Fichte's writing that resist reduction to the spirit.[5] In approaching Fichte this way, I do not wish to ignore or undermine the systematic aspect of his thought, but only to gain a greater appreciation for its originality and richness.

Even granting that one is justified in taking such an approach to Fichte—a project that has scarcely been broached by the scholarly literature[6]—the *Closed Commercial State* must seem, at first glance, like a rather unpromising point of departure. Within the labyrinth of Fichte's thought, with all its antechambers, byways, and dead ends, the *Closed Commercial State*, rather than standing off from or being at odds with the system, seems to occupy an unquestionably peripheral and derivative position. Unlike history or language, which condition the manner in which pure reason or spirit becomes manifest, economics, the worldly science par excellence, is concerned chiefly with the purely material conditions of human life, and thus must be, at first glance, farthest removed from the pure spirit that, wrested from the letter of Kant's philosophy, Fichte hoped to present as the foundation of all knowledge. Just as within the systematic divisions of Aristotle's philosophy—divisions that are still operative in Fichte's work—the *Oeconomica* is little more than a handbook of household management, and, in sharp contrast to the *Nicomachean Ethics* or the *Politics*, in no obvious way bears on the possibility of philosophy itself, the subtitle of the *Closed Commercial State* suggests a similarly ancillary position with respect to ethics,

Right, and the *proto philosophia* of the *Doctrine of Science*. It is "a philosophical sketch offered as an appendix to the *Doctrine of Right* and as a test of a politics to be delivered in the future."[7] Not popular in the strict sense, it belongs instead among the systematic and esoteric writings—the chain of deductions that develops out of the *Doctrine of Science*—yet it belongs to these only as an appendix. It hangs on to the system at its outer point, the *Doctrine of Right*, without touching it at its core. And moreover, far from laying claim to the certainty of a priori deduction, it exists only as a test (*Probe*), implying that, despite its affinity to systematic philosophy, it remains concerned with something irreducibly empirical and contingent.

Should we not then conclude that, as the peripheral work of a philosopher who, despite his extremely significant role in German idealism, has traditionally often been regarded as playing a merely transitional role in its development, the *Closed Commercial State* is of little more than antiquarian interest?[8] While the biographer can hardly ignore such a vivid illustration of both Fichte's political engagement and intellectual megalomania, and while the intellectual historian must grant at least a few passing words to a work that is not without influence in the development of socialist economic thought, it seems doubtful that those who approach Fichte with more fundamental philosophical concerns, regardless whether they seek to reconstruct the tendency and implications of his system or discover a thinking that runs against the system's grain, need pay it much attention.

Yet if the *Closed Commercial State* is merely an appendix to the system—merely a hanger-on to what, hanging together, constitutes a discrete whole—it must seem strange that Fichte, according to the testimony of his son, would speak of the *Closed Commercial State* as his "best, most thought-through work."[9] Nor was he alone in holding his work in such esteem. Just three years after its publication, Friedrich Schlegel, the great Romantic literary critic and philosopher, would describe the *Closed Commercial State* as "a model for how the philosopher can write for that public that interests itself, in the first place, for politics; indeed we seldom find writing of such clarity and at the same time such brevity. In no area of study, save the *Doctrine of Science*, does Fichte appear so much as an original thinker, and as regards the last-named writing in particular, as an observer of deep penetration."[10] In similarly hyperbolic terms, a reviewer from the *Literaturzeitung* of Salzburg claims that "the author himself has not yet delivered a work of this degree of perfection, and, in truth, there is hardly any other work in our literature that equals this work in consequent and complete derivation from a principle, precision of expression, and luminous representation."[11] Nor was it only its admirers who saw the consequence of Fichte's reasoning. Often it was the fiercest critics of the *Closed Commercial State* who recognized, if only ironically, the philosophical significance of Fichte's foray into economics. Thus, for

Gentz, the German translator of Edmund Burke's *Reflections on the Revolution in France*, the "speculative consequence" of the *Closed Commercial State*—a consequence that offers nothing more than a rather dubious compensation for the poverty and falsehood of its premises—is characteristic for a system that is "hostile to all true realism [*Realistik*]" and whose "consequent perversion has no limits."[12] It was, in other words, the most honest revelation of the true nature of the new Kantian philosophy; an unmistakable symptom of the speculative spirit that, blowing across Europe, threatened to ravage the existing order of things. While many questioned Fichte's competence as an economist and mocked the pretensions of the philosopher to address the mundane concerns of the practicing statesman, few doubted that, precisely in trying to subsume the most worldly of matters under a strictly a priori reasoning, the *Closed Commercial State* had revealed the inner tendency of a mode of thinking that no longer respected the traditionally enforced oppositions between theory and practice, esoteric and exoteric knowledge, or the affairs of spirit and the affairs of the world.

If it is still premature to place the *Closed Commercial State* at the crux of Fichte's thought, these testimonials suggest that, at the very least, there is more than meets the eye. Moreover, though, even a cursory look at Fichte's writings reveals that political economy is a vital concern throughout his life. In one of the earliest writings preserved in his literary estate, the 1788 *Accidental Thoughts of a Sleepless Night*, a young Fichte, not yet awakened to Kant's philosophy, rails against the vice and depravity of his age, proposing the need for a book that would at once expose the "complete corruption of our government and our morals" in a popular style suited to the tastes of a "frivolous age" and at the same time describe the foundations of a better government and better morals together with the means to obtain them.[13] Such vitriolic indignation was, in itself, nothing remarkable for an age captivated, as was Fichte, by Rousseau and other less subtle moralizers. Yet in these rather chaotically organized "accidental" thoughts, the problematic of political economy already appears as one of the principal factors influencing morality. While the chief cause for the "thorough moral corruption" of the age is the decline of the institution of marriage, the blame for this decline rests not only with the contempt that the people have for this institution, but in the culture of luxury, with its implicit economic inequalities, having made it more difficult to enter into a lawful union with the opposite sex. This results in the isolation of the individual and the suppression of the "more noble social sensations."[14] Licentious behavior (*Liederlichkeit*) and profligacy are, in this way, not the cause, but the result of poverty. Underlying Fichte's apparent moralizing crusade for "family values" is thus the burgeoning realization that the economic conditions of a society, without absolutely determining the nature of peoples' actions, influence the temporal horizon of human life. When people have little hope of directing their sensual desires toward a higher end such as procreation, they will end up living purely in the moment, with each trying "merely to enjoy a great deal during the days of his life, as much as he can lay hold of [*reißen*] for himself."[15] Economic injustice, this is to say, threatens to undermine the very possibility of future-directed action, and hence of politics itself.

These insomniac thoughts remain rather accidental in nature. Yet with the *Contribution to the Correction of the Judgments of the Public concerning the French Revolution*, a defense of political radicalism published anonymously in 1793, Fichte's thoughts on political economy assume a more rigorous and mature aspect. Even though the question that opens the main body of the text—namely, whether "a people [has] the right to change its constitution"?[16]—itself belongs squarely within the tradition of natural right and social contract theory, Fichte soon enters into a theoretical *terra incognita*, grounding his inquiry into rights in a specifically idealist concept of human nature while at the same time considering not just the nature of man's fundamental rights but the nature of property, to an extent even subordinating the former considerations to the latter.

Because this transformation is of such great importance for understanding the place of economics in the *Contribution* and throughout Fichte's thought as a whole, it would be useful to consider his argument in some detail. Whether a people has a right to change its constitution depends on whether this right can be alienated through a prior social contract.[17] Fichte, however, denies outright that a people could ever renounce its right to change its constitution, for renouncing this right not only contradicts the highest purpose of humanity, but also violates the very form of the contract, since if everyone *should* wish to change the constitution, the separate contracting parties would collapse into a single entity. A contract cannot oblige people not to do something that everyone agrees must be done, since the very structure of a contract implies diverging wills.[18] Hence, he need only consider if a people can collectively renounce the right to change the constitution without the permission of every single individual, or even more specifically—since forcing someone to accept a new constitution without their consent already violates the elemental rights of man—whether someone could relinquish the right to withdraw from the old constitution without the consent of all parties.[19]

Having refined and focused the leading question of the *Contribution* in this way, Fichte argues that every contract depends for its validity on the contracting parties honestly willing the fulfillment of its terms. As soon as either party changes his will in this regard, he is released from the contract, and hence, in the case of the founding treaties of a political community, released from the terms of the constitution, returning, in his relation to the state, to his natural condition.[20] In this purely formal sense, the right to constitutional change cannot be alienated. Even so, this merely formal right would be de facto of no consequence were we unable to "take any-thing with us" on our return to the state of nature; or if, in other words, the state, should we violate the social contract, were able to justly claim, as retribution, all our property, and thus deprive us of the essential means of sustenance. In this way, the very possibility of a just revolution in the pres-ent state of affairs comes to depend on the nature of property. To justify the French Revolution, against its conservative and moderate opponents, Fichte must prove that not only our inalienable human rights and our bodies, but also our external goods, exist prior to the state, and do not depend on the latter.[21] Needed, in other words, is a theory of property. The foundation of this theory of property is the claim that:

> originally we are ourselves *our* property. No one is, nor can anyone become, our master. We bear deep within our breast our own letter of emancipation, given to us under a divine seal. God himself has emancipated us and said: from now on be no one's slave. What being may then appropriate us for itself?
>
> *We* are *our* property: I say, and thereby assume something twofold in us: a proprietor and a property. The pure I in us, reason, is master of our sensual nature, of all our spiritual and physical forces [*Kräfte*]; it may use them as means to whatever end it wishes.
>
> Surrounding us are things that are not their own property; for they are not free: but originally they also are not ours; since they do not belong to our sensual I.
>
> We have the right to use our own sensual forces to whatever end we wish that is not forbidden by the law of reason. The law of reason does not forbid that, through our forces, we use those things that are not our property as means to our ends, nor that we make them fit to serve as such means. Thus we have the right to apply our forces to these things.[22]

As in Locke's 1690 *Second Treatise of Government*, our original rights are a function of natural activity, and our "own person" constitutes the original property from which every other form of earthly property is derived. Fichte likewise follows Locke in attaching central importance to labor in the acquisition of "secondary property."[23] Yet because Fichte conceives of this activity not as the action of the natural human body per se, but rather as the pure I—the spontaneity of pure reason—and likewise understands labor specifically in terms of the imposition of form on matter, the nature of this first property undergoes a subtle yet profound transformation. Whereas

Locke applies the term *property* ambiguously to both our own person and to property in the strict sense and yet retains a fundamental and unbridgeable difference between the two, for Fichte, the physical and spiritual forces of the individual are property specifically as the means or instrument through which pure reason realizes the ends that it wills for itself. In this way, our empirical, individual self—the totality of the forces through which we act directly upon the world—is property in precisely the same sense as external objects are property. Pure reason, itself identified by Fichte as a capacity for willing ends, creates further tools and means to its ends by transforming the world around it. The only difference is that in the latter case, property is acquired not by nature but by freedom, and no longer stands in an immediate relation to the original proprietor—pure reason. Because original property and secondary property are thus grounded in the same principle, there is no absolute boundary between them.

The far-reaching implications of this seemingly rather subtle and abstract shift in the nature of property appear, with particular clarity, in the polemic against Rehberg. In refuting the arguments of the conservative historian and political theorist, Fichte denies that we ever possess material qua material as property. Even land—the most obvious counterexample—only becomes our property when it is made arable through human labor or at least somehow demarcated through a physical boundary. Hence, to argue that a certain kind of property—e.g., landed property—, being material rather than formal in nature, is bestowed by the state rather than acquired through the individual's labor, issues in absurdity. For by the same token, everything would be a gift of the state, save the pure I itself, since no *thing* exists purely as form.[24]

The literature on Fichte for the most part conceives of the *Contribution* as belonging to a stage of Fichte's thinking that, despite certain socialistic tendencies, is still characterized by a commitment to the fundamentally bourgeois principles of political liberalism rejected in such later works as the *Closed Commercial State* or the *Addresses to the German Nation*.[25] In the *Contribution*, to be sure, Fichte strongly affirms the optimistic faith, given profound expression in Smith's *Wealth of Nations*, that granting to every individual the free disposal of his original property—his mental and physical powers—would lead both to greater equity and greater prosperity and ultimately allow whoever works to live without compromising his human dignity.[26] In later works, however, such as the *Closed Commercial State*, Fichte will abandon the notion that property could preexist the state. While the source of property remains the activity of the individual, property itself will come to be understood as intersubjective, never existing apart from reciprocal treaties and the recognition of the other.[27] In the *Closed Commercial State*, "the first and original property, the basis of all others" consists not in the activity of the will as such, but in *"an exclusive right to a determinate free activity."*[28] Nevertheless, the above reading of the *Contribution* also suggests that, already in this early stage of his political thought, Fichte conceives of the relation of property and rights in a way that forbids limiting the duty of the state to guaranteeing negative freedom. Rather, by extending property to the entirety of the sensible world and denying any essential opposition between primary and secondary property, he makes it impossible to conceive of political justice apart from economic justice. At the same time, we also see that, just as questions of politics and Right lead back to economics, economics leads back to philosophy. Already in the *Contribution*, itself written just before the theoretical breakthrough of the *Doctrine of Science*, Fichte is aware that the nature of property can only be grasped from the vantage point of critical philosophy; from a recognition of the distinction between the pure I—pure reason as the practical activity of willing—and the empirical I. Understanding the nature of property, this implies, can never just be a question of applying theoretical tenets to worldly affairs. Instead, property marks a point where the boundaries of the body and the world, the collective and the individual, and ultimately the theoretical and the practical, become fluid. If the human body is originally granted us by nature rather than produced through our freedom, thus justifying a distinction between natural and artificial property, nature is nevertheless not an unchanging absolute, but contingent and subject to the modifications of our will.

Fichte's final sustained confrontation with political economy appears in the 1812 *System of the Doctrine of Right*—twelve years after the publication of the *Closed Commercial State* and almost two decades removed from the *Contribution*.[29] In this late work, written only a few years before Fichte's death, the questions of political economy not only retain all the urgency that they have in the *Closed Commercial State*, but are themselves included within the system of Right itself, and indeed as its most central part. Not only does their discussion fill out one hundred of the one hundred and sixty pages of the *Doctrine of Right*, but they take precedence before questions of constitutionality and sovereignty. Moreover, while the 1812 *Doctrine of Right* retains the most fundamental tenets of the *Closed Commercial State*—the definition of property in terms of activity; the insistence that people have no rights if they are without property; and the demand for economic as well as juridical closure—there is also ample evidence that, in the intervening years, Fichte continued to reflect seriously on questions of political economy, taking pains to engage more with mainstream economic theory. Issues that he ignores altogether in the *Closed Commercial State*, such as the role of investment capital and wage-laborers, are treated in considerable detail, while at the same time, as if seeking some rapprochement with his critics, he moderates many of the more extreme proposals of the earlier work. Yet perhaps the most striking innovation of the 1812 *Doctrine of Right* is its unconditional defense of a right to leisure. Since Aristotle, the possession of leisure (*scholē*) has been regarded as a condition of philosophy and the *vita contemplativa*. By making leisure (*Muße*) essential to the definition of property—by conceiving of property in terms of the right to freely unfold one's rational nature—Fichte makes the fate of philosophy depend on economic conditions, while at the same time establishing the universal participation in the *vita contemplativa* as the highest aim of political economy.

This brief survey suggests that the problem of political economy, while apparently at the periphery of Fichte's system, is, perhaps precisely as this peripheral moment, of great significance for his thought. If economics is not concerned ultimately with the sustenance and quality of merely sensual human life, but rather with the production and distribution of the surplus as leisure, different economic regimes must themselves found different possibilities of philosophy—cultures of reason differing in both kind and degree.

There is yet another reason why we cannot neglect the *Closed Commercial State*, even if it seems quite peripheral to Fichte's system. Precisely as such a marginal, even transitional, text, it occupies a singular place among the writings of a philosopher whose life of extreme passages gave him to feel with peculiar intensity the mercurial nature of worldly goods and fortune.[30] Born the eldest son to a family of weavers, it is only by a strange turn of events that Fichte was rescued from the obscurity to which his humble roots had destined him, allowing him, through the support of a local lord, to study for the clerical vocation. Wrested from his family in the ninth year of his life, he was able to attend Schulpforte—the private ducal boarding school—and go on to university, yet the loss of the support of his patron forced him to abandon his studies and, destitute and with few prospects, begin a succession of often humiliating posts as a private tutor.[31] His dreams of a literary career and worldly influence might have remained unrealized, had not fortune once again intervened—and indeed fortune in the form of reason itself. Fichte discovered Kant's critical philosophy. Reborn through it—rescued from having to choose between deterministic reason and irrational faith—he wrote his first philosophical work in a Kantian vein: the *Attempt at a Critique of all Revelation*. Published anonymously, either by accident or at the whim of the publisher, it was mistakenly thought to be Kant's own promised fourth critique by several prominent reviewers. Till then an outsider and nobody, living on the fringes of the educated world, Fichte suddenly became one of the most famous men in Germany: the leading representative of the new philosophy, and indeed, in 1794, the successor to Reinhold in Jena. His fate, and his fame, seemed settled, and yet by the end of the decade he once again faced an uncertain future. Expelled from his position as a result of the Atheism controversy, he was forced to seek refuge in Berlin. No longer at the center of German philosophy,[32] he was soon overshadowed by Schelling and Hegel, and spent the rest of his career in relative obscurity until his untimely death from cholera.

Within the precarious life of a philosopher who, like Socrates, had been charged with impiety, the Closed Commercial State indeed itself marks numerous passages: from Jena to Berlin; from the first formulations of the Doctrine of Science to a more historically inclined phase of his system; from his political liberalism to socialism, statism, and nationalism. Published late in the year 1800, it stands not only at the halfway point of Fichte's literary career, but also at the cusp between the eighteenth and nineteenth centuries; between the Enlightenment and Romanticism; the French Revolution and the Napoleonic Empire. Moreover, though, the principal task of the Closed Commercial State is itself a task of transition: of tracing out, and even initiating, the passage from the ideal to the real—the realization of philosophy. This task, already implicit in Fichte's systematic philosophy with its focus on the practical nature of reason, dominates the bulk of Fichte's extrasystematic writings. Both the problem of language, as we see in the Addresses to the German Nation, and the problem of history concern nothing else. Yet this task is nowhere taken more seriously than in the Closed Commercial State. Here, as I will show, Fichte attempts nothing less than to spell out a specific, all-transforming, intervention into history. In other words, he addresses the practical nature of reason from the perspective of praxis. Fichte's economic treatise, in this way, is eminently the work of a philosopher in exile, and indeed of philosophy in exile from itself, or at least from the immediate realization of its ideal—from the self-sufficiency of purely theoretical contemplation—and forced to cross over into praxis.[33]

The aim of this interpretive essay is to show how the Closed Commercial State, precisely in its transitional and marginal character, is crucial to Fichte's thought as a whole, functioning as a passage and conduit leading between different dimensions of his work. In so doing, I also hope to introduce the Closed Commercial State to a general readership and provide a cohesive and original interpretation of a work that, up till very recently, has been largely neglected by scholarly literature.[34] While I aim ultimately to read his thought as a whole through this critical moment—thinking through the thought that is most thought through in the Closed Commercial State—this will not come at the expense of a "literal interpretation" of the work in question. Rather, it is by attending to textual details of the Closed Commercial State that its relation to the rest of Fichte's works will become most evident, even if sometimes the results of this more literal reading run against the grain of traditional interpretations of his thought. That I feel compelled, in what follows, to go beyond the relatively modest intentions of a scholarly introduction results from the special sort of challenge that the *Closed Commercial State* presents to its readers. Some works speak to the future through a rich and pregnant obscurity, some through the vigor of their central ideas, and yet others through the richness of empirical analysis. It is, however, the very lucidity of Fichte's economic theory that renders it mute to modern ears. So naive in its belief in the possibility of a planned economy, so lacking all appreciation for the subtlety of human nature, and yet presented with so much assurance and vigor, the *Closed Commercial State* appears strange, and even somewhat fatuous, when judged against the works of Smith, Ricardo, J. S. Mill, and Marx—indeed, as little more than a curiosity piece from the margins of a philosophy still too often regarded as a curious sideshow to the caravan of "great thoughts." Fichte insists, over and over again, that the greater part of his readers will not and cannot understand him; that a kind of vertigo will strike them as they try to find their way through a nexus of relations consisting not in facts but in concepts; not in what is given but what is possible. But for a modern reader, the arguments of the *Closed Commercial State*, despite their idealist framework, will probably seem too straightforward and simplistic, and ultimately misguided. For this reason, little is gained merely by clarifying Fichte's arguments—arguments that are, on the surface at least, already sufficiently clear. Rather, we must complicate and upset what seems simple. This means, first of all, seeing more in the *Closed Commercial State* than just a contribution to a positive understanding of economic relations that issues in specific, albeit radical, policy proposals.[35] Thus, I seek to show that the *Closed Commercial State* does not exhaust itself in revealing the nature of existing economic relations, or in deducing the relations that ideally should exist, or even in laying out in universal terms the path leading from the one to the other.

My strategy is twofold. On the one hand, I shall read the problem of economics over into the rest of his work, not only by exposing its persistence as an explicit theme in his writings but also by developing less obvious relations to his systematic philosophy. Economics shall, in this way, come to appear as the Ariadne's thread leading through the labyrinth of his thought. On the other hand, I shall read Fichte's more systematic discussions of history over into the *Closed Commercial State*. By attending to these crossings of economics and history, I shall show that, for Fichte, history is, above all, monetary in nature. The crux of history is money.

The medial nature of money, suggested in the literal meaning of commerce (*Verkehr*), is a major theme of the *Closed Commercial State*. Likewise, historical time for Fichte is not only the transition and passage from past to present, but involves the momentary, transitory convergence of different tendencies; different possible transitions. The transitional, transitory nature shared by economics and history, moreover, not only makes them analogous and complementary, but each complicates the other. Only by reading them in conjunction—discovering, as it were, their reciprocal intrigue—can we begin to discover the surprising complexity of Fichte's economic theory.

My own itinerary will, for the most part, follow the argument of the *Closed Commercial State* itself, which I will try to present in some detail. Since so much of the argument of the *Closed Commercial State* depends on these transitions, I do not rigidly distinguish between the exposition of the argument and its interpretation, but try instead to maintain a fluid relation between these two strands. This, however, makes it all the more necessary to orient the reader at the outset by outlining the trajectory of this interpretive essay.

In the second section (§2) of this essay, which immediately follows the present remarks, I address the dedication that opens the *Closed Commercial State*. Examining the opposition Fichte draws between the speculative and the practicing politician, I suggest that the peculiar character of this dedication, with its explicit engagement in philosophical argumentation, challenges conventional assumptions about the rhetorical function of the text as a whole. In the third section (§3), I turn to the introduction of the *Closed Commercial State*, where Fichte, by explaining the relation of the ideal to the real state, establishes the possibility of historical understanding and transformative historical action, both of which require a proper understanding of the relation between the empirical and speculative. Reading this discussion in the context of Fichte's critique of Rousseau's *Discourse on the Arts and Sciences* suggests both the difficulty of attaining such an understanding and the dangerous consequences of getting it wrong. To overcome the impasse of Rousseau, whose feeling and understanding were at odds with one another, leading him into absurd errors in his conception of history, nothing less is needed than a revolution in philosophy; the discovery of a mode of reflection prior to the split between rationalism and empiricism. The fourth section (§4) continues this discussion of Fichte's understanding of politics as a historical praxis and *technē*, placing special emphasis on the way in which he reconciles the historical and the technical, both in the *Closed Commercial State* and in later works. This reconciliation, I suggest, is brought about by reconceiving the relation of the real and the ideal and understanding art, the transition from the latter to the former, not principally as the act of an individual subject toward an objective reality but rather as the realization of infinite reason through a world—through a certain community of finite beings. Politics, as the most fundamental art, creates history as the continuum of time that connects the real with the ideal through an infinite series of mediating moments. In just this way, moreover, political, history-making praxis requires historical understanding: a grasp of the present time in which political action must intervene.

This sheds light on the division of the *Closed Commercial State* into three books. Each of these books establishes a necessary moment of political action as historical praxis: the first derives the just economic relations that are the end of political action, the second presents the historical tendency of the present moment through a history of the present (*Zeitgeschichte*), and the third describes the action that intervenes in the present in order to bring about the realization of the ideal.

The discussion of the first book encompasses sections five (§5) through seven (§7). For Fichte, I will argue, the first end of politics is neither life nor pleasure, but self-realization. Precisely for this reason, space and time play a crucial role in Fichte's rational construction of economic relations and the right to property. Property offers a mediation between the monadic time of the free individual and the monistic space in which the actions of free individuals come into collision with one another. Section six (§6) considers Fichte's attempt to reconcile the division of labor with an equality of property, and section seven (§7) examines Fichte's theory of value. Because Fichte is unable to represent the value of pleasure-producing luxury goods in terms of a purely utilitarian base commodity without presupposing the prior existence of anarchic market forces, his attempt at a rational construction of economic relations ultimately fails. This need not disqualify the entire project of the *Closed Commercial State*, yet it complicates our previous understanding of the nature of political praxis. The concept of the rational state, it becomes clear, is too weak even to exist as a regulatory ideal. Instead, it has merely a rhetorical function, presenting a glimpse of an ideal future that remains essentially unfathomable; a glimpse that inspires us to action without presenting a definite, rationally founded end to our actions.

In our reading of the *Closed Commercial State* up to this point, the question of history has come to assume ever greater significance and subtlety. Yet it is not until the second book that Fichte attacks the problem of history directly. The second book begins with an invocation of wonder, which, as I argue in section eight (§8), provides the transition to his account of the history of the present. Wonder, for Fichte, is the proper attitude toward the contingency of history; an attitude that is neither purely empirical nor purely speculative, but requires a receptivity for precisely that which, in a given state of affairs, is open to change. It involves descrying the conflicting tendencies that exist in a present moment. This helps (§9) us to see what is at stake in Fichte's explanation of the opposed tendencies of the ancient and the modern world. At the heart of his account of the tendency of the modern age, however, is the role of money. In section ten (§10), I argue that for Fichte money marks the point of contact between possible futures: a future of pure speculation, generated merely by an infinitely reflected opinion, and a future promising the true fulfillment of human need. The everyday present reality, the moment at which political action must intervene, exists between these two futures. Recapitulating the theory of history developed thus far in the *Closed Commercial State*, I claim (§11) that for Fichte, history is, of essence, neither materialist nor idealist, but monetary. It is money above all, itself both real and ideal, that announces at once the danger and the possibility of history.

Sections twelve (§12) through fourteen (§14) address the argument of the third book: the description of the money operation (the substitution of national for world currency) that will not only lead to the closure of the particular state in question, but will set off a chain reaction of national closures. For this operation to succeed, I argue (§13), the government must lay hold of and gain mastery over public opinion. Thus, Fichte's state, like Plato's, begins with a "first falsehood"; though in this case the lie disqualifies, rather than repeats, the valorization of gold. In section fourteen (§14), I again return to Fichte's account of history, reviewing the different aspects of history in the *Closed Commercial State* and also looking forward to Fichte's later writings, including both the *Fundamental Characteristics of the Present Age* and the 1813 *Doctrine of the State*. For Fichte, I will claim, money is the crux not only of historical understanding but also of historical action. The political act that inaugurates a history leading to a rational arrangement of commerce, and hence to the rational state as such, must not only grasp the present moment in the extremity of its opposing tendencies, but strike at its heart—at money itself. This, in turn, suggests the proximity of Fichte's economic and religious thought. The money operation aims at money as the crux of history: the death of the old money and its resurrection in a new form is the rebirth of the state, and it thus stands in a precise analogy to the Christology of his later period.

In the conclusion of this interpretive essay (§15), I will draw connections between Fichte's *Closed Commercial State* and more contemporary concerns, considering its contribution to economics and political philosophy and its relevance to the question of globalism.

§2. Philosophy and Politics

The three main books of the *Closed Commercial State* are preceded by a lengthy dedication, an introduction, and also a brief "preliminary explanation of the title." All three offer valuable clues for reading the work as a whole. Yet the dedicatory remarks, though not contributing directly to the systematic development of the argument of the *Closed Commercial State*, are especially important in this regard. Even the very existence of these remarks, directed to August von Struensee, the Prussian minister in charge of commerce and industry, is striking. Not only were Fichte's previous works published without even a cursory dedication, but Fichte, given his Jacobin leanings, must have regarded the dedication as a dangerous anachronism, rooted in an idea of patronage that reduced the thinker to a mere servant of the state. Especially given Fichte's strong appreciation for the art of rhetoric, evident above all in his popular writings and lectures, it must seem strange, and even to contradict the great value he would place on the *Öffentlichkeit* or *Publikum* (the public or δῆμος) and the art of public speaking, to have his work dedicated and even addressed not only to a single individual—even if nevertheless "in full view of the public"—but to a privy minister; a civil servant whose own official functions were shrouded in state-sanctioned secrecy.[36]

Stranger still, at the same time as he restores the convention of the dedication, with its implied relations of class and power, he also undermines the presuppositions on which it depends. Taking pains to justify himself through the precedent of past generations, he uses these remarks not merely to express, as is customary, his gratitude toward and veneration of his patron, but also to clarify the purpose of his work and its "probable result."[37] He gives his own patron, as it were, lessons in the art of reading, and instructs him on the very relations of authority that would seem to concern, above all else, his own relation to his client.

All this suggests that neither the goal of this work, nor its status as a work of writing, is self-evident. Instead, these require a special sort of explanation, and indeed precisely because, not merely a work of philosophy or scholarship, its purpose is no longer mere edification. Its goal passes beyond an enlightenment-seeking public and penetrates into the secret chambers of the absolutist government: into the locus of a mysterious and concealed power over history, and, above all, as we shall see, power over money.[38] It is not purely scholarly or philosophical but political. And this means, first of all, that it seeks nothing less than a passage from theory into practice.

It is perhaps because Fichte knew he was overstepping the bounds his own age imposed on the scholar, and thus subjecting himself to the danger of ridicule and even official censure, that these dedicatory remarks begin with an apologetic tone rare for a philosopher who, with the Atheism Controversy, had become notorious for his stubbornness and refusal to compromise.[39] Nevertheless, even this apology conceals, and only just barely, the demand posed to the world by the philosopher's awareness of the sovereign rights of reason. For at stake is not so much the right of philosophers to "offer their thoughts concerning the organization and governance of states"—a right that has, in fact, always been granted them—but rather the right to have their suggestions taken seriously by those in power. And while Fichte grants the reproach made against such suggestions, admitting that the purely speculative proposal of such "Platonic republics" and "their utopian constitutions" does not and cannot apply directly to the actual state of affairs in the world,[40] he nevertheless maintains that the philosopher, if he "holds his science to be not a mere game but something serious, will never either grant or presuppose that it is absolutely impossible to carry out his proposals."[41] The very dignity of philosophy itself, its seriousness, depends on the possibility of practical effect in the world. Several decades before Marx's *Theses on Feuerbach*, Fichte will emphatically claim that the task of philosophy is nothing else than to change the world.[42]

Thus, a contradiction seems to emerge between, on the one hand, the immediate unfeasibility of that which has been proposed at a purely theoretical level, and which, as a product of pure reason, is alone capable of representing the ideal organization of human affairs, and, on the other hand, the demand for feasibility that necessarily issues from philosophy. This contradiction is overcome by postulating a process of mediation between the ideal and the real. The purely theoretical suggestions, presented as they are in absolute generality, "*simply require further determination* if they are to fit an actually given state of affairs,"[43] with this further determination itself involving three separate stages. Beginning from a purely theoretical exposition of the ideal state, the political work applies these principles, themselves exclusively concerned with principles of Right, to a more limited state of affairs—for example, the common predicament of all the European states in a given epoch. Finally, it is the task of the practical politician to fit this to the particular case of a given state at a given moment of time.[44]

In the second half of the dedication, this more apologetic and moderate tone gives way to a fierce critique of a purely empiricist attitude toward politics. As long as a politics were rigorously and thoroughly developed according to the model Fichte proposes, beginning from solid principles of Right of state and a correct understanding of the present historical situation, it could "only seem useless to the mere empiricist, who trusts no concept or calculation, but only the confirmation of immediate experience."[45] Similar polemics against vulgar empiricism appear throughout his writings. While these are clearly aimed, in part, against the English philosophical tradition and in particular the Burkean conservatism represented in Germany by Gentz and Rehberg, Fichte regards the explicit and foundational claims of an empiricist epistemology as themselves rooted in the natural attitude of those who are incapable of freeing their minds from the contingency of sensual experience. Moreover, we must not confuse Fichte's critique of empiricism with a lack of historical sensibility. If, on the one hand, Fichte must reject the naturalistic collapse of the fact/value distinction and an identification of norms with historically and culturally contingent standards of behavior, he nevertheless attacks the empirical attitude to politics not only because it is mistaken about the truth of political relations, but because it makes impossible a genuinely *practical* attitude toward the present historical moment:

Let us merely ask such a politician: those who were the first to use the measures that he now approves and imitates—whom did they imitate? What did they rely on as they seized on these measures? Previous experience or calculation? Let us remind him that everything that is now old was once new, nor is it possible that the human race has fallen so far in latter times as to be left only with memory and the ability to imitate. We will show him that through the progress of the human race, which occurred without his doing and which he can do nothing to keep in check, a great deal has changed, making necessary entirely new measures—measures that previous ages could neither devise nor implement. It might be instructive, faced with such a politician, to conduct a historical investigation into the question whether more evil has arisen in the world through daring innovations or through a sluggish adherence to outdated measures that are either no longer able to be implemented, or are no longer sufficient.[46]

Having begun the dedication in a tone of defiance, Fichte ends in apparent resignation. Turning from more general considerations of the relation of the speculative and practicing politicians to the specific prospects of the *Closed Commercial State* itself, the "likelihood that it will achieve its intended aim," Fichte concedes that, because the balance of trade so favors Europe over the rest of the world, even the weakest European state benefits in some measure from "the common exploitation of the rest of the world" and will not give up hope of "improving the balance in its favor and thus gaining an even greater advantage."[47] Even if one were to counter such arguments by pointing out that the relations of colonialism, being neither just nor prudent, cannot endure, defenders of the status quo will nevertheless argue that one should "take advantage of this for as long as it continues, leaving it to the generations that are around when it finally comes to an end to figure out for themselves how they will cope."[48]

Fichte abruptly admits that he has no answer to this sort of reasoning. Yet perhaps we should not take this concession of defeat at face value. For in the end, as we shall see, Fichte does attempt to answer to even the most self-interested parties, and indeed by proposing a political intervention that appeals to a logic of self-interest in making a case for the need not only to act, but to act soon, by claiming that the first state that undertakes the measures he proposes will benefit the most.

His concession of defeat before the forces of history, and his resignation that his "sketch might also remain a mere school-exercise, without consequence in the real world—a link in the chain of his gradually developing system" might well prove, in the end, nothing more than a bluff.

§3. The Rational State and the Actual State: Fichte's Critique of Rousseau

The dedication, as we saw, considers the relation between the philosopher and the practicing politician. Having established that philosophy can and must be practical—that the ideals it posits demand realization in the world—Fichte explores in more detail how this realization is possible, clarifying the relation of the rational state to the actual state and of the pure doctrine of Right to politics. Because these relations are of such great importance for understanding the structure and argument of the *Closed Commercial State*, and above all its place in Fichte's thought as a whole, it will be useful to devote some time to understanding them in all their ramifications.

The kernel of Fichte's argument is, to be sure, quite simple: the rational state is an ideal that the pure doctrine of Right generates by considering human beings apart from all historical contingency and constructing the necessary relations between individuals in accordance with the concepts of Right. Since relations between human beings in the real world are for the most part products of "chance or providence" rather than "concepts and artifice,"[49] we can never expect to find people actually joined together into a rational state. Yet precisely because this argument seems prima facie self-evident, even for those who are skeptical of its epistemological foundations, we must, if we are to properly grasp its significance and implications, try to place it in the context of the contemporaneous discourses to which it answers.

The defense of the political relevance of norms and ideals, as we have already seen, attacks not only the purely empirical attitude of the practitioners of *Realpolitik*, but also a more philosophical commitment to dogmatic naturalism. That this ideal is a product of reason alone is, moreover, a rejection of a theological tradition of politics that admits the existence of norms with binding force and yet considers at least some of these to have been granted to man through a special, historical revelation that is beyond, if not necessarily in contradiction with, reason. Yet in offering such a definition of the rational state, Fichte also has a more specific target in mind: without naming Rousseau by name, this definition presents the fruit of a transformative critique of his political thought. First broached in the *Contribution*,[50] this critique is elaborated in depth in the fifth of the *Lectures on the Destiny of the Scholar* (1794). Through a sustained reading of the *Discourse on the Arts and Sciences*, Fichte argues that Rousseau's cultural pessimism—his belief that the advance of culture is the source of, rather than the cure for, society's ills—stems from his confusing the state of nature with the ideal state.[51] Properly conceived, the latter would not be the starting point but rather the destiny of human culture and history. This confusion, in turn, and all the contradictions to which it gives birth, is grounded in the peculiar nature of Rousseau's mind. Although he was possessed of an unerring sensibility (Gefühl), his feelings—the immediate source of all that is true in his thoughts—and his discursive reasoning conflicted with one another. Unable either to truly penetrate the former and unfold its content into conceptual lucidity or to renounce the claims of concepts altogether, Rousseau, in trying to give systematic articulation to his unerring feelings, ends up perverting them into falsehoods.[52] Only by acknowledging the error of Rousseau's reasoning without denying the divinity of his sensibility—understanding Rousseau better than he understood himself—would it be possible to realize the true relation between the real and rational state. Or, in other words, to realize that *"before* us thus lies what Rousseau, under the name of the golden age, places *behind* us."[53]

What is ultimately at stake for Fichte in his interpretation of Rousseau is the possibility of historical understanding and transformative action in history. The prefatory remarks to the *Closed Commercial State* already suggest two extreme threats to such theory and practice. Whereas the attitude of pure speculation sees only the future, and thus loses itself in a mere play of concepts, pure empiricism remains beholden to the past, creating only imitations of imitations. It is likewise clear that if, in contrast, we are truly to grasp the present as the point where contact between the ideal and the real is possible, we must conceive of it in its relation to both the past and the future. It is, however, Fichte's earlier treatment of Rousseau that suggests the true difficulty of this task of mediation, itself of such great significance for the project of the *Closed Commercial State*. For Fichte, as we saw, Rousseau's thought is neither purely speculative nor empirical but already represents a middle between these two opposed possibilities. Yet Rousseau fails to find a successful balance, and is consequently led toward the most dangerous contradictions. This failure, moreover, results not simply from mistaken premises, a lack of thoroughness, or even the peculiar nature of Rousseau's individuality. Rather, to achieve true integration and balance between empiricism and speculation would require nothing less than a fundamental revolution in philosophy; a new understanding of what it means to think, of how the conscious and explicit act of the philosopher relates to the immediate facts of consciousness and the unconscious processes of thought that constitute them. For as we learn from the *Doctrine of Science*, as long as the content and the form of thinking are believed to stand in a merely abstract relation to one another, philosophy is unable to explain either the theoretical or practical relation between subject and object—between the spontaneity of will and reason and the experiential givenness of the world.

When, in the fifth lecture, Fichte, describing Rousseau's failed attempt to explicate the content of his feeling, invokes an analytic epistemology in which discursive reason unfolds the originally given content of ideas, he at once describes Rousseau's error and diagnoses its cause. Likewise, by conceiving, in the introduction to the *Closed Commercial State*, of the ideal, the state of reason, no longer as what is first "felt" or intuited and then discursively elaborated, but rather as a *construct* of reason, Fichte presents, albeit in brief and unsystematic terms, the model for a mode of reflection that balances the empirical and the speculative attitude. This construction is a synthesis that begins not with the idea of the state, but merely of human nature and the concept of Right—both of which are given a more fundamental grounding in the *Doctrine of Science*. The capacity for synthetic a priori knowledge, as it were, is what allows for the rational construction of a political state; for the rational account of what is never simply given a priori, but comes into being, and thus, even while necessarily existing outside of the contingencies of real history, nevertheless has an essentially historical character.

We need only read a little between the lines to realize that, for Fichte, the great tragedy of Rousseau, considered not only as an individual but as a historical phenomenon, was that, while possessed of extraordinary rhetorical powers, a profound historical sensibility, and an acute sense for the practical efficacy of ideas, he was unable to think correctly about history. And since Fichte, throughout his philosophical career, identifies the French Revolution with Rousseau,[54] his critique of Rousseau develops into a critique of the revolution and a diagnosis of the causes of its failure. Thus, the problem of revolution, approached with such vigor and directness in 1793, is transformed, in his later works, into the question of history and a constellation of closely related problems.[55] While it is above all in the *Fundamental Characteristics of the Present Age* (1804) and the *Doctrine of the State* (1813) that Fichte will elaborate a theory of history, we already find its rudiments in the *Closed Commercial State*, and in particular in Fichte's account of the problem of the transition from the real to the ideal. Recalling a well-known passage from Schiller's *On the Aesthetic Education of Man*, itself a confrontation with Rousseau and the terror of the French Revolution,[56] Fichte warns that if the state were suddenly to destroy the constitution that binds people together in the real world, it would "disperse them and turn them into savages, thus nullifying its true purpose of building a rational state from them."[57] The task of politics, it follows, is not only to contemplate the ideal state of affairs— that which conforms to principles of Right—but to determine how much of this ideal can be realized under the given circumstances. Without ever forgoing its highest goals, it must try, as much as possible, to render change from the real to the ideal as smooth as possible.

§4. Politics and the Fiction of History

Politics, on this account, is not simply historical, but historical *praxis*.
Moreover, it is praxis of a very specific kind. For as Fichte explains in the
conclusion of his introduction:

> I need not defend the fact that I speak of a science and art that
> will gradually bring about the rational state. All the good things
> of which man should partake must be produced by his own art,
> guided by science. This is man's vocation [*Bestimmung*]. Nature
> gives him nothing in advance, save the possibility of applying
> art. In government as elsewhere, we must subsume everything
> under concepts that lets itself be subsumed under them, and stop
> abandoning anything that should be calculated to blind chance
> in the hope that blind chance will make it turn out well.[58]

Politics is an art—a *technē* guided by scientific knowledge or *epistēmē*. The
rational state is the form, an ideal brought about in the mind through purely
theoretical contemplation, and in turn applied by the practicing politician,
the political artisan, to a material—the actual conditions of reality. Yet
while Fichte's understanding of art reveals a deep debt to Aristotle, this
strong concept of politics as an art denies the foundational presupposition of
peripatetic political philosophy—the claim that man is an animal endowed
by nature with both a proclivity for political organization and a capacity for
rational speech.[59] Nature gives man nothing save the capacity for *technē*, just
as language itself, for the early Fichte, is created by reason as a tool for its
own realization.[60] In this way, not only the political state, but even man's
political nature, is ultimately a work of freedom. Nevertheless, since human
artifice rests ultimately on pure will, and hence pure reason, it escapes the
danger of naturalism. The art work of the state is never merely the expression
of the will to power of its creators, but instead realizes reason in the world.

There is, we observe, an implicit tension between the historical and
technical nature of politics. Whereas the paradigmatic form of artifice has
always been the creative act of the individual, in the latter part of the
eighteenth century, and in particular in the works of Herder, history comes
to be understood not merely as the body of knowledge to be gained by
the investigation of the past, but as a process of development prior to and
independent of the rational praxis of individuals.[61] Human institutions, thus
conceived as products of history, are organic rather than artificial: products
of nature rather of men. The political implications of this are clearest in
Burke's arguments against the French Revolution. A revolutionary praxis

that imposes an abstract ideal of Right and freedom, blind to the organic, historical nature of human institutions, must issue in tyranny.[62]

It would be wrong to think, however, that this tension represents an inconsistency or weakness in Fichte's understanding of politics. Instead, we find that Fichte, throughout his philosophical career, struggled to reconcile these two facets of political action, fully aware of the danger of privileging one before the other. This point is of special significance if we consider Fichte's relation to later manifestations of German idealism. To appreciate the singularity of Fichte's thought, it is important to recognize that, even when, in works from his middle period such as the *Fundamental Characteristics of the Present Age*, he introduces a more strongly teleological concept of history, he never discounts either the transforming power of praxis or the role played in history by visionary individuals. Particularly revealing, in this regard, is the last phase of his thought. While still offering a vision of historical providence, he now stresses the foundational political significance of the division of society into two classes: the people and the scholars. Whereas the former only act toward the immediate present, the latter possess the ability to see farther (*Weitersicht*) and to act on their foresight. They are, indeed, "the free artists of the future and its history, the thoughtful master-builders of the world" from out of a material unendowed with consciousness.[63]

As I hope to show in what follows, the germ of Fichte's final and most subtle understanding of history already appears in his confrontation with the problem of economics and money. The *Closed Commercial State*, one could even say, contains insights into history that Fichte struggles to reach again in his more explicit formulations. For now, let us return to the text at hand, considering how Fichte balances the historical and technical nature of political praxis in the *Closed Commercial State*. He achieves this balance, I will now suggest, above all through the opposition between the rational and real state developed in the introduction.

We observe first of all that art, conceived by Fichte not simply as a way in which humans, as finite rational beings, relate to the world, but rather as the realization of pure reason, is in an essential way constitutive of human nature. Human beings are not simply given as one class of beings among others, but rather create themselves in their ever particular way of being through a radical assertion of freedom; an act of freedom that is not grounded in the knowledge of human essence. This point is to some degree obscured by the popular, rather than precise language of the introduction to the *Closed Commercial State*, with its passing, theologically noncommittal, invocation of providence. It is asserted unambiguously, however, in the *Vocation of Man*, also published in 1800, where, already anticipating the last versions of the *Doctrine of Science*, the privileging of praxis and faith before knowledge leads not to a radical subjectivism, but rather to an idealist inversion of Spinoza's pantheism, in which the radical self-positing of individuals through free will is itself an expression of the infinite, putting the individual being in its place in the world and drawing the limits of its personality.[64] Because, in this way, individual beings do not exist prior to the act of self-constitution, there is no reason to limit art to individual actions. Even if we restrict art to conscious acts, excluding the preconscious autonomous assertions of reason from which consciousness itself arises, we may still suppose that the realization of reason takes the form of free acts that occur through the mediation of individual agents, and yet neither originate nor end with man in his individuation. Indeed, in the *Fundamental Characteristics of the Present Age*, Fichte will speak not only of history itself as the life of mankind as such and not just of an aggregate of individuals, but of actions that originate with, and act toward, the species (*Gattung*). Accordingly, freedom is not restricted to individual praxis, but "should appear in the total consciousness of the species, and enter as its own freedom, as true actual deed and as the product of the species in its life, and as emanating from its life."[65]

Keeping in mind at least the negative possibility of a free human art that is not principally the art of individuals, let us now approach the question of the reconciliation of the historical and technical from the opposite direction, which is to say, from the side of history. In a sense, I have already answered this by suggesting that, for Fichte, the aim of politics is to make the transition from the real to the ideal as smooth as possible. This smoothness itself, I would now suggest, is the free product of political action. Politics seeks nothing less than to create time as a continuum, free of all gaps, between the given and the ideal.[66] In a word: it makes history. This suggests the deeper implications of Fichte's characterization of the scientific elite as the "free artists of the future and its history."[67] Yet because this continuity can only be grasped over a duration of time, historical praxis in turn requires historical understanding; a sense for the continuous trajectory of history as expressed in the present moment of time, its "fundamental tendencies." The historico-political praxis and *technē*, this is to say, requires its own *epistēmē*. The latter consists not only in knowledge of the ideal of the rational state, the form that is to be realized in the world, nor even of both the form and matter in isolation, but of their integration into the tendency of history manifesting itself in the past and continuing into the future.

This way of conceiving of political praxis, implied in the terse arguments of the introduction, is the key to the *Closed Commercial State* as a whole. This is already clear from its division into three books, the first of which deals purely with the doctrine of Right, the third with politics in the strict sense, and the second with the history of the present. If a specifically historical understanding is needed to mediate between the doctrine of Right and politics, it is above all because human artifice is now conceived in historical terms. Were the political art essentially ahistorical—involving merely the imposition of a form on the matter at hand—there would be no need to consider the material of politics in its historicity; in its inner tendency toward formation. The matter would have no life, no formative principle, of its own, but at most certain qualities of resistance or malleability.[68] At best one could differentiate between a young and old people; between a people open to new laws or hardened in its ways. But precisely because politics is concerned with nothing else than history—because, indeed, it creates history precisely by forming the future in continuity with the past—the *more geometrico* introduced with such naiveté in the dedication breaks down. It could no longer be possible to use the angles of a land surveyor (save perhaps the one from Kafka's *The Castle*) to illustrate the relation of politics to philosophy, since the particular is not subsumed under the universal, but rather both the ideal and the real are produced synthetically from out of their mediation. It is not, as it were, a *more geometrico* but a *more synthetico* or *integrale*; a differential and integral calculus of the political.

§5. The Space and Time of Politics:
Fichte's Rational Construction of the State

The first book of the *Closed Commercial State*, as already mentioned, considers the question of political economy purely from the a priori perspective of the doctrine of Right, seeking to deduce "what is Right with respect to commerce in the rational state."[69] In the first chapter, Fichte introduces the principles for answering this question, juxtaposing the paternalism of the past with the liberal ideal of the present. Whereas the former regards the state as the "unlimited guardian of humanity" in all its temporal and spiritual affairs, the latter limits the state to preserving and protecting the property and rights of the individual citizen.[70] The opposition is not simply between economic regimes, but rather between two fundamentally different concepts of the nature and scope of state power, each of which, moreover, is grounded in an opposed concept of property. Whereas a paternalistic absolutism cannot recognize any truly individual ownership, but regards even the individual's soul as its property and concern, the latter regards the property of the individual as existing wholly independent of and prior to the state.

The true concept of politics, Fichte insists, lies midway between these extreme ways of conceiving of state power. We should not understand this, however, merely as an insipid insistence on the "golden mean" or a formal, abstract application of dialectic. Since these opposed concepts of state power are founded on equally contrary concepts of property, their mediation cannot be achieved simply by mixing their traits and balancing their vices. Needed, instead, is a more fundamental concept of property, prior to the abstract and formal opposition between its individual and social qualities. Thus, in the first numbered section of the first chapter of the first book of the *Closed Commercial State*, Fichte, through his construction of commercial relations in a rational state, also provides a rational construction of the true concept of property as such.

This construction of rational commercial relations begins by imagining an aggregate—Fichte refers to this as a multitude (*Menge*) or even as a heap or crowd (*Haufe*)—of people who live within a common territory and yet only recognize and act on their own needs and desires. Because he excludes from consideration all questions of individual morality, Fichte can conceive of the state as a purely juridical institution, in which individuals are driven to mutual recognition and negotiation not by moral duty but solely to preserve their own freedom of activity.[71] This suggests a parallel with Hobbes, who discovers the origins of the state in the fear of violent death.[72] Yet for Fichte, the grounds of the political are not purely negative. It is not merely a question of fear, but self-consciousness.[73] This point is of the greatest significance, since it means that, insofar as the contracting individuals need and desire more than mere life, the ultimate aim of the state cannot be physical security or even prosperity. Rather, as Fichte argues in the *Foundations of Natural Right*, the state is willed into being as the condition for the self—the will—to become conscious of itself in its willing. And since the will ultimately wills nothing else than its own autonomy, the will for freedom and rationality is in fact the ultimate, if not the proximate, foundation of political union. The state, to be sure, is not a moral institution—it is not concerned with people's will or conscience, but only with their actions in the world, and only insofar as these affect others. Yet it is also not merely the servant of worldly, sensual ends.

The significance of self-consciousness and self-realization for Fichte's construction of rightful commercial relations is particularly evident in a subtle yet persistent emphasis on the spatiality and temporality of politics.[74] The essential characteristic of the hypothetically constructed prejuridical and preethical condition—Fichte's equivalent of the state of nature—is that, although people are completely isolated in their *ideal* nature qua will, they are already *really* completely united, sharing a common circle or sphere of efficacy. The material world that is the object of their activity—the means of self-realization—is not originally individuated, but is common to all, allowing their individual actions, and even their bodies, to come into collision. These collisions, in turn, result in the degradation of the temporal conditions of purposeful action, and hence the negation of freedom. Indeed, in the original natural condition "no one is free, since all are free without limitation. No one can carry out anything purposeful and count for a moment on its lasting."[75] Just as Aristotle would conceive of happiness as something that can be truly realized only over the course of an entire life, Fichte's individuated wills posit time itself, qua duration, as the condition of the possibility of realizing goals in the world, and thus ultimately of realizing their own nature as free beings.[76] Yet this original positing of time, which emanates from each individual will as if in monadic isolation, is undermined through its confrontation with a spatially extended material world that, shared by all, is constantly being given contradictory determinations. Property in turn comes into being through a process of negotiating treaties, whereby the different parties agree to renounce those activities that harm others in return for others renouncing the activities that harm them. They reciprocally limit their own activity, and in such a way that each comes to have a sphere toward which their activity is directed that is limited in relation to the others in such a way that it is possible for the will of each one to realize itself without negating the will of the others. Only then does "each have something that is *proper* to him, that is his own, belonging to him alone, and in no way to anyone else; a right, and an exclusive right."[77] Recapitulating his argument, and clarifying the principle alluded to in the title of the first chapter, Fichte further characterizes the nature of property: "Property, rights to determinate things, prior rights, and exclusive rights arise solely from the treaty that was described. Originally all have the same right to everything, which means that no one's right takes precedence over the right of anyone else. Something only becomes my property when, in accordance with my desire to keep it for myself, everyone else renounces their claim to it. This act of renunciation by the others, and this alone, is the basis of my right."[78]

Keeping in mind the importance of time and space—the aesthetic in the sense of which Kant speaks in the *Critique of Pure Reason*—to this original construction, we are able to recognize both the power and the subtlety, but also the difficulty, of Fichte's understanding of property. What is at stake in property relations is, as it were, nothing less than the mediation, within the realm of praxis, between monadic time and monistic space. Since each, conceived in its purity, negates the other, and yet human beings necessarily exist both in space and time, property cannot simply be regarded as the right of the individual. Rather, it is constitutive of *realized* individuality. And hence it is also the basis of all other political relations, and even of treaty negotiation itself. Yet at the same time, property, in the full sense, only comes into being through the treaties negotiated by the state, which is necessary precisely because the state alone can unite "an indeterminate multitude of men into a *closed whole*, a *totality*," posing "questions to everyone whom it receives into its alliance."[79] Property thus appears as both the condition and the result of political union, implying a circularity that ultimately threatens the validity of Fichte's entire argument.

This vicious circle results from the fact that the *Closed Commercial State*, unlike the *Contribution*, conceives of property as fundamentally inter-subjective. We might try to avoid such difficulties by distinguishing between the human body as a pre-intersubjective first property, and the secondary properties established through reciprocal treaties. Yet this would make the derivation of rightful relations of property depend on ethics—precisely what, as Fichte explains in no uncertain terms in the introduction to the *Foundations of Natural Right*, he seeks to avoid.[80] Rather, while he overcomes the circularity by positing the body between will and world, it is not the body in the strictly ethical sense that takes on this mediating function, but the "juridical" body deduced in the *Foundations*. Whereas the body in the ethical sense is the immediate instrument for the realization of the intentions of the will in the sensible world, the body in the juridical sense involves intersubjective mediation. Because this deduction, moreover, is of such importance for the *Closed Commercial State*, it will be useful to follow out Fichte's argument in some detail.[81]

The deduction of Right, to begin, does not merely involve the applica-tion of the *Doctrine of Science* to a practical sphere. Rather, as the deduction sets out to show, the concept of Right is itself an action of the I necessary for self-consciousness, and thus we cannot understand the process through which self-consciousness constitutes itself—the self-positing of the I—apart from the Doctrine of Right. In this sense, the *Foundations of Natural Right* are integral to Fichte's system: the ultimate justification of the concept of Right, and all the deductions that follow from it, rests in the fact that a rational being cannot posit "itself as such with self-consciousness without positing itself as an *individual*, as One among a number of rational beings, which it assumes [to exist] outside of itself, just as it assumes itself [to exist]."[82]

In the first of the three main divisions of the *Foundations*, Fichte deduces the concept of Right as a formal reciprocal relation between free beings that share a single sensible sphere. This relation between free beings is purely symmetrical and hence entails a seemingly vicious circle, since the existence of any individual presupposes the existence of a community of individuals. In the third division, in turn, Fichte embarks on a concrete deduction of rightful political relations following this principle of mutual recognition. Here too, the starting point is a perfectly symmetrical reciprocity: "[E]very free being [must] make it a law for itself to limit its freedom through the concept of the freedom of others."[83] It is only in the second division, where Fichte deduces the applicability of the abstract concept of Right, that he is able to account for the actual genesis of these symmetrical and reciprocal relations of mutual recognition, without involving himself in an infinite regress of conditions. This is possible precisely by presenting a dialectic of intersubjectivity that begins asymmetrically. And it is here, moreover, that he deduces the existence of the body (Leib). The human body, this suggests, is what allows for a nonsymmetrical relation between rational beings, and, in just this way, it alone allows, if not for the genesis of rationality itself, nevertheless for the process of its realization in the world, and hence for the coming-into-being of the conditions of political relationships.

Fichte's deduction of the juridical body—the instrument of will that is necessarily involved in reciprocal relations with other instruments of will—takes its departure from two claims. On the one hand, the rational being must posit "an exclusive sphere for its freedom"[84] in the form of a closed (geschlossen), articulate whole, immediately responsive to the directives of its will.[85] On the other hand, it cannot posit itself as consciousness without supposing that it is affected from without in such a way that at once cancels and does not cancel its free activity, since indeed the exterior cause must affect it as something foreign to its will yet without completely negating its freedom.[86] These seemingly contradictory conditions can only be reconciled by assuming that the influence itself issues from a rational being: a being capable of limiting its own freedom and power consequent on its recognition of the other's rationality.[87] Yet, in this case, whether we are made into *free* beings—whether we become *really* and not merely *potentially* rational—depends entirely on the free will of others: whether they choose to act toward us as rational beings. And hence, my own personality would not exist as something independent, but would become merely an accident of the other, leading to an infinite regress.[88] Hence, I must somehow be able to compel the other to act toward me as a rational being, even before I am able to act—before I am realized in my rationality—and indeed before I am an I.[89] Needed is a paradoxical effect without effect (Wirken ohne Wirken): an effect that issues from the body as mere capacity (Vermögen).[90] Hence, the body must act not as a moving instrument of will, but through its sheer resting shape (Gestalt). In a remarkable passage, Fichte explains that indeed the human body acts in this way. The articulation of the human body doesn't indicate, as with animals, "a determinate radius of arbitrary movement . . . but everything that can be thought ad infinitum." Present in the body is not "formation [Bildung], but formability [Bildsamkeit]."

> In short, animals are complete and finished, man is only indicated [angedeutet] and sketched out [entworfen]. The rational observer cannot unite the parts [of the human body] apart from the concept of his equal, in the concept of freedom given him through his self-consciousness. He must attribute the concept of himself [to it], since no concept is given; according to that

concept, however, he is able to explain everything. Every animal
is what it is: man alone is originally nothing at all. What he
should be, he must become: and since he should be a being for
himself, [he must] become [this] through himself.[91]

The mere shape of the human body, the body as a completely unrealized
capacity, acts upon others, even before it is capable of conscious action, by
announcing its unlimited potential. In exhibiting the complete absence of
a finite concept, it summons the other to treat it as free, as an end rather
than a means, and limit its own actions upon it accordingly. Grounding
the possibility of political relations, relations founded on the free activity
of rational beings, are infections of potentiality.[92] And at the same time,
the end of politics itself is not given, first of all, through rational deductions, but rather is sketched out in human shape; descried at the sight of
the other. Politics, in this sense, is the project of answering to this original
projection, though not by *filling it out* and giving it content, but by creating
real institutions that do not efface the original sketchiness of humankind.

Because the *Closed Commercial State* presupposes the conditions of
the possibility for entering into political relations, there is no need for
it to repeat the deduction of the body or even treat the problem of the
body in depth. Nevertheless, if we keep in mind the place of corporality
in Fichte's philosophy of Right, we see that political economy, despite its
ancillary place in the system, is perhaps more fundamental, or at least of
more critical importance, than the juridico-political relations accounted for
in the third division of the *Foundations*. Whereas these relations concern the
protection of the body and its right to activity, the economic doctrine of
the *Closed Commercial State*, precisely in guaranteeing each body a discrete
sphere of activity—giving each person what is theirs by Right—secures for
the body the autonomy that is the condition of political negotiation. For
indeed, if the body lacks a sphere of activity allowing for its sustenance, its
very existence as a body—and ultimately as an instrument of free will—is
compromised. And precisely because, as we will see, commercial anarchy
tends to generate gross inequalities of wealth, ultimately reducing people
into commodities, one may even argue that the economic doctrine of the
Closed Commercial State addresses itself, first of all, to the degradation of the
community of bodies—a community that is the necessary condition of a just
state. If the sight of the baby, born naked and helpless into the world, will
always remind us of our endless human potential, it is nevertheless possible
that, in most domains of everyday life, the other will appear to us not in
the infinite openness of his humanity, but only as the realization of a limited
function. Indeed, the very fact that the human body is a free creation—that,
for example, we *will* to walk on two feet rather than four, or to have our

spirit concentrated in our hands—suggests that, in positing ourselves as a community of bodies through which reason is realized, we also posit reason's almost absolute vulnerability: the possibility of the near complete extinction of those infectious communications of potentiality through which the life of the state, the free community of rational beings, renews itself.

These points will become clearer in what follows. For now, it would be useful to address an even more general criticism that may be made of Fichte's concepts of politics and property. In a recent article, Jay Lampert, comparing the concepts of property developed by Locke, Fichte, and Hegel, argues that while Locke lays too much stress on the individual basis and nature of property rights, Fichte falls to the other extreme, making property solely a function of social recognition. It is left to Hegel to reconcile these extremes.[93] Although Lampert refers principally to the 1796 *Foundations of Natural Right*, the *Closed Commercial State*, with its comprehensive regulation of commerce, would only seem to confirm his thesis, leaving us in turn to conclude that Fichte, despite his best intentions, failed in his attempt to reconcile liberalism and paternalism. The picture that Lampert gives us of Fichte's political thought is, to be sure, altogether frightful: Fichte's text degenerates into "a nightmarish parody of recognition, where intersubjectivity has been replaced by mutual surveillance" and where "the need for recognition by other people has become a moment-by-moment phobia of not being seen and has as a corollary the phobia of a silent intruder sneaking into one's house."[94] There is, without doubt, no small truth in Lampert's thesis, itself already anticipated in Hegel's 1801 *Difference between Fichte's and Schelling's Systems of Philosophy*.[95] Property, in the more narrow sense that it has in the *Closed Commercial State*, does come into being only through mutual treaties of recognition. Yet applying Fichte's own conceptual distinction, we can say that this applies only to the *form* of property, the constitution of a given x as property. The *content* of property, in contrast, has its roots in human beings as wills that will their own realization in the world. It is clear, even if never stated explicitly, that whereas property qua form can be established merely through a constitution that protects the rights to property in an abstract sense, property qua content requires that the state concern itself not only with the *that*, but also the *what* and *how much*, of property. This, moreover, must lead to conclusions that directly contradict the conventional assumptions of a liberal-bourgeois politics. For in this way, the rational state constitutes itself not just as a juridical system of mutual recognition enforced through a single highest power representing the alienated force of all its members, but rather as a shared time and space. Property not only articulates and divides the physical world through signs that allow recognition of boundaries and limits, but constitutes the duration of time in which it is possible to engage in purposeful action.

Having thus established that property arises through a treaty dividing the sphere of free activities among individuals, Fichte goes on to develop a calculus allowing for this division to be made rationally. Since every human being, qua human being, demands and has a right both to live and to live pleasantly, the division must be made in such a way as to first enable everyone to live, and indeed to live as pleasantly as possible. Hence, simply by dividing the total pleasantness issuing from the sphere of efficacy—a gross national product of sorts—with the total number of human beings inhabiting the said sphere, it would be possible to ascertain "what each should receive under the given circumstances."[96]

§6. The Division of Labor

Thus far, Fichte has considered human beings as at once both consumers and producers,[97] without drawing a distinction between these two aspects of free activity. Yet in a society that has reached even the least stage of development, production and consumption no longer coincide: people produce things they do not consume, and consume things they do not produce. This suggests the principal challenge that Fichte faces in applying a general principle of economic equality—of an equal right to life-sustaining and pleasure-producing free activity—to public commerce. What he must show, first and foremost, is that economic equality can be preserved even given a high degree of the division of labor. He must prove that a group of people, led by reason in their negotiation of treaties, can divide themselves into different classes bound by reciprocal obligations in a way that allows them to enjoy a high total level of consumption—of life and pleasure—without sacrificing the rights of any individual to an equal, or rather, as Fichte will explain, relatively equal, share of the whole.

Fichte undertakes this rational construction of the division of labor in the third chapter of the first book. Significantly, he begins not by considering the relations between individuals, but rather between *Stände* (classes or estates), each of which is defined according to the particular mode of its activity. Likewise, the treaties that provide the basis for all commercial relations within the state are between estates and not between individuals. Since the most fundamental division in the mode of activity is between the producers, who bring forth the vegetable and animal (and possibly mineral) "fruit" of the earth, and the manufacturers, who modify these raw materials toward some human purpose, Fichte begins with the treaties that must bind these two estates in their reciprocal relations to one another.[98] In addition to a merely negative treaty, excluding each from the activity of the other, a positive treaty is necessary. The producers must be obliged to provide the manufacturers with a quantity of raw materials sufficient to allow them to live and work while enjoying the degree of pleasure that is possible under the given circumstances, and, likewise, the manufacturers must do the same with their finished goods. In addition to the producers and manufacturers, Fichte then also introduces a third estate—the tradesmen—binding it to the others with an analogous system of positive and negative treaties. In the second section of the second chapter, he divides each of these estates into sub-estates, and these sub-estates, in turn, into individuals, making it clear that each stage of division requires a new set of treaties.

Having considered the three principal estates and the treaties between them, Fichte in turn asks what the government must do to ensure that these treaties are observed.[99] This transition may seem a bit confusing, since Fichte, at this point, has yet to consider the officials of the government as a separate estate, or explain the nature of the relation of the government to the state and to the treaties that compose the latter. The crucial point—that the state is endowed through the consent of all the citizens with the power to enforce the treaties governing their relations by reciprocally limiting their freedom—is not itself developed in the Closed Commercial State, but instead is borrowed from the Foundations of Natural Right.[100] It is, nevertheless, in answering this question that Fichte first suggests the significance of commercial closure. If indeed the government is to guarantee the reciprocal fulfillment of the treaties between the estates, it must limit the number that is permitted to enter each estate according to a calculation of the prosperity of the nation, making sure that there are enough producers to sustain the other estates, and that the manufacture of necessary goods does not suffer for the sake of luxuries. In this way, Fichte proposes a planned economy, in which the government periodically readjusts the relation between the estates in order to preserve the just relations between them while nevertheless making allowances for any increase in property.[101] In place of market forces, Fichte envisions a system where supply and demand, calculated in advance, will always harmonize.

Nevertheless, Fichte, concerned throughout with maximizing efficiency, goes to great lengths to avoid a bloated regulatory bureaucracy. Rather than investing an army of government agents with the task of enforcing the positive treaties, he proposes an almost completely decentralized system of regulation, in which the burden of oversight, though not enforcement, rests entirely with those who are directly affected by the violation of the treaties. At the crux of this ingenious, if somewhat naive, system are the tradesmen, who are at once required by law to buy and sell certain quantities of goods, and yet at the same time, having provided the government with a list of the sources from which they seek to obtain their goods, may lay claim to this supply, backed up, if need be, by the authorities.[102] Even so, Fichte is not able, in every case, to avoid the need for more bureaucracy. To ensure that manufactured goods are of the highest degree of quality possible in the country, a board of examiners is necessary, exclusively endowed with the right to admit people into a certain trade.[103]

It may seem that Fichte, by emphasizing the opposition between the producers and the manufacturers, follows the physiocrats in drawing a rather specious distinction between "productive" and "unproductive" labor.[104] Yet while he admits that agriculture and other forms of production (in the narrow sense) have a certain priority over the other estates, if only because manufacture and trade cannot do without the raw materials that they provide, this natural inequality, rather than justifying a privileged status for producers, only makes it all the more necessary, through the inclusion of positive treaties, to guarantee equality between the estates.[105] All activity, to the extent that it really constitutes a portion of the total free activity of a nation, is useful—generating something tangible or intangible that is recognized as good by the society. To the extent that the size of the estates is properly calculated by the government, the farmer, artisan, and tradesman all contribute equally to the life and pleasure enjoyed by all. Even luxury goods are not less useful in this sense, as long as the prosperity of a state permits their manufacture. Likewise, Fichte grants no special privilege to landed property. The right of a farmer to use a specific plot of land and the right of a manufacturer or tradesman to exclusively pursue a certain trade are both property in the same sense. The only difference is that the first, unlike the second, involves an essential relation to the object toward which it is directed. And, what is more, they are only property insofar as they grant their proprietor his just share of life and pleasure.

The division of the total quantity of free activity into estates represents one of the chief applications of the concept of closure to commercial relations. Each estate, Fichte argues, must be regulated and limited through a *numerus clausus* of sorts. The deeper meaning of the closure of the commercial state, however, only emerges in the sixth section of the second chapter. Here we find the pivotal claim that, if the state is to fulfill its obligations toward its citizens, it must prevent all foreign influences on trade, since foreign entities, not standing within the reach of its juridical power, cannot be regulated, and thus, if allowed to interact with the citizens, will expose the latter to contingencies that may ultimately jeopardize their fundamental right to an equal share of the nation's goods.[106] The state, consequently, must close off not only the individual subdivisions of activity, but the total activity of the nation as a whole. A closed juridical state that is not, at the same time, a closed commercial state is in its very nature inconsistent, being ultimately incapable of securing its citizens what is theirs by Right.

The third through sixth chapters of the first book address a number of possible objections to Fichte's construction of commercial relations, dealing with such questions as the uncertainty of agriculture; the nature of taxes; and the implications of the introduction of currency and increasing prosperity for the balance of trade. Since Fichte's answers to these problems, while displaying considerable ingenuity, are of little consequence for the larger argument of the *Closed Commercial State*, and since his arguments, in any case, speak for themselves, I will pass over these points. In the seventh and final chapter of the first book, after recapitulating the main results of his theory, Fichte presents what he considers to be a much more fundamental cause for resistance to his argument:

> In my opinion the fundamental error of the opposed theory of property—the first source from which all false assertions about property derive; the true reason for the obscurity and oversubtlety of many doctrines; and what is, properly understood, the cause of their one-sidedness and incompleteness when applied to actual life—is this: that one posits the first, original property in the exclusive possession of a thing. . . . In opposition to this theory, our theory posits the first and original property, the basis of all others, in an exclusive right to a determinate free activity. . . . In our theory there is no property of land [*Boden*], or at least not until those who assume that there is such a thing can make us understand how such a right to property might be practiced in actual life—if indeed these truly understand what they are saying, and really mean, as these words declare, a property of land, and not, as in our interpretation, a right that is exclusively one's own to a certain use of the land.[107]

This point is of great importance for Fichte's construction of rightful economic relations. It is only by imagining property as a right to determinate activity rather than to a thing that Fichte is able to conceive of every estate within the state, including civil servants, as ideally having an equal property, and thus an equal, or at least relatively equal, share of the prosperity of the whole. Whether it consists solely in a right to a determinate activity (as with the manufacturer, tradesman, or civil servant), or in a right to a determinate activity toward a determinate object, property is essentially the same, and there is no reason to privilege one form of ownership over another, or regard one as proper and the other as improper. The principal target of this critique are the physiocrats, and all those who give precedence to landed property. By suggesting that *things* are an accident rather than the essence of property, Fichte is able not only to deny landed property any privilege over other forms of ownership, but even to deny that there could ever be any such thing as landed property. The ownership of land is really just a figural expression for the ownership of a right to a certain use of the land; and hence to claim to own land as such, while demanding rent from others in return for the right to cultivate it, is not only an injustice against man but a sacrilege against God; an usurpation of his rights. For indeed: "The earth is the Lord's; to man belongs only the capacity to cultivate and use it for his purposes."[108] Fichte, hounded out of Jena for his supposed atheism, while fully aware that the real blame lay with his republican sympathies, provides his most damning answer to those defenders of the established order who uphold religion as the bulwark of the state: the god that defends landed property and that landed property defends is not the one and true God, but the landed proprietors' own self-deification.

§7. Fichte's Theory of Value

Fichte's definition of property, already prefigured in the *Contribution*, represents at once his most original and valuable contribution to the science of economics, and the point where the deeper influence of his philosophical project on his economic theory is most evident. What Fichte proposes, indeed, is nothing less than a Copernican revolution of sorts: a turn from dogmatism to idealism realized in the realm of economic theory and with profound worldly consequences. The conventional account of property deduces actions from things. Relations of property, involving a purely abstract, juridical right of ownership independent of economic, pleasure- and life-producing activity, entail determinate intersubjective relations between individuals, concretely delimiting their separate spheres of activity. For Fichte, in contrast, relations between things, including the entire system of divisions of land in the sensible world, should follow from relations of activity.

I will return, at a later point, to consider these connections between the *Closed Commercial State* and Fichte's thought as a whole. Before concluding my discussion of the first book, however, I would like to consider an aspect of its argument that I have neglected up till now: the question of price and value. Although this is addressed right in the middle of the first book, it suggests more severe difficulties in the argument of the *Closed Commercial State* than I have yet considered, and in this way also offers a natural transition to the second book and its "history of the present."

Fichte introduces the problem of price and value through the claim that, if the established treaties between and within the different estates are to guarantee everyone what is theirs by Right, they must regulate not only the quantities of goods that come into circulation, but also the price of these goods.[109] To explain how such regulation would be possible, Fichte addresses the problem of fixed prices in detail, devoting particular attention to the problem of value. Developing an account of value independent of the concept of money, which indeed does not yet play a role in the argument of the *Closed Commercial State*, Fichte conceives of the sustenance of life as the fundamental criterion by which value is measured: "The measure of the value of things relative to one another would be the time during which we could live from them."[110] In order to quantify the relative value of goods, it becomes necessary to single out a single commodity, such as grain, that "*in the general assumption of the nation, everyone should and must have in order to live,*"[111] and that is therefore regarded first and foremost as a means of sustenance, with no special degree of pleasure associated with it beyond that which belongs to nourishment itself. This commodity, in turn, is used as the basis for all other calculations of value. Thus, the intrinsic value of a good is inversely proportional to the quantity needed to nourish someone for a set amount of time. If half as much meat is needed to nourish someone as bread, the intrinsic value of a given quantity of meat will be twice as much as the same quantity of bread.[112] With manufactured goods, value is calculated not directly according to their "use value," but rather according to the quantity of the base commodity needed to sustain the manufacturer during the time of production, with this latter duration factoring in the time needed for his training.[113] "Produce intended as raw material," on the other hand, "are worth as much grain as could be produced from the field where they were grown with the effort expended in their cultivation."[114]

It is the valuation of pleasure, however, that presents a particular difficulty for Fichte. Since the goal of free activity is not merely existence but pleasant existence, Fichte must be able to account for pleasure itself in the rational construction of rightful commercial relations. He must provide an objective and universally valid measure of that which is, in principle, purely subjective, having reference only to a private inner experience of the subject. In extending the calculus of value to pleasure, nothing less is at stake than the very possibility of rationally ordering the relations between humans qua sensual beings without doing violence to precisely that which is most human in their sensibility—the fullness and range of their desire.

It is precisely by acknowledging, in this way, the legitimacy of the human desire for pleasure that Fichte is able to preserve *self-realization*—specifically, human life—rather than mere survival, mere life, as the highest goal of politics. Yet given the significance and scope of this problem, Fichte's solution seems rather unsatisfactory. Assuming both that the base commodity is the form of nutrition most easily produced by a given nation and that the nation nevertheless expends its resources on other commodities, Fichte concludes that this extra expenditure of forces relative to a given quantity of intrinsic nutritional value is the value of the pleasure that it provides. Such a foodstuff is "worth not only its intrinsic value, but, because of its pleasantness, also that quantity of the primary means of nourishment that could be grown through the application of the same force, time, and soil were the extraction of the former not to occur."[115]

This argument presents several difficulties. By making the calculation of the pleasantness of a commodity depend on how much resources the nation expends on its production, Fichte sneaks in market forces through the back door. It is these alone, after all, that would determine demand in a state whose commerce has not yet been submitted to rational calculation. One might respond that it is the mere existence of demand, and not its degree, that plays a role in the calculation of pleasantness; that its value is determined not by the extent of demand, but rather by the same principle of substitution used to calculate the value of raw goods. Yet for this to hold, we must assume that the effort expended in the production of a given quantity of a given commodity is independent of the total quantity produced, since otherwise the demand of market forces will continue to determine, indirectly if not directly, the value of its pleasantness. Yet this assumption, which Ricardo explicitly rejects in his celebrated theory of rents, is manifestly absurd: not all land is equal in natural productivity, and thus it is quite possible that an increase in the production of a given ware would require utilizing land with higher production costs. And even if we allow that the value of a pleasant commodity may be derived exclusively from a calculation of the quantity of the base commodity that can be produced through an equal expenditure of labor and capital, it is unlikely that this principle of substitution could provide a foundation for equating the value of heterogeneous forms of activity. If classical economics makes the mistake of allowing a merely abstract exchange value to eclipse use value, Fichte, in trying to ensure that the prices of things signify their true objective value, is forced to suppose a real commensurability between the real factors of production or manufacture. He must assume that all pieces of land *could* produce grain, even when his very definition of production encompasses quite different sorts of activity, and, moreover, that all three factors of production—force, time, and soil—can be measured against one another.

These considerations suggest that a purely rational construction of rightful commercial relations is impossible. Because the entire system of commodity values in a rational state depends on private desire expressing itself as demand through the free operation of market forces, and because, in particular, the objective criterion for the value of pleasantness assumes its prior objectification through the market, the rational arrangement of economic relations must necessarily follow on nature's anarchy. Not only did the rational arrangement of commercial relations never actually exist, since their very purity would undermine their foundations, but commercial relations are necessarily natural, since they refer, at their base, to functions of desire that can only be brought to the surface through the natural, unregulated interactions of human beings.

One might simply argue that Fichte lacked the empirical sensitivity, and talent for economic investigation, to recognize problems such as these. Yet perhaps Fichte's ultimate concern is not with the rationality of economic relations, but with their rationalization; with a process of transformation that, beginning with an anarchic present, fixes prices and brings public commerce under control. Too weak even to serve as a regulatory ideal, the construction of the closed commercial state in the first book functions first and foremost rhetorically: as inspiration toward a world-transforming political action, and as a vision of the form that just economic relations might take.

What this means shall become clearer when I turn to the second and third books of the *Closed Commercial State*. For now, however, it would be useful to leap ahead and consider an aspect of Fichte's larger argument that reveals, with particular lucidity, the difficulties of his attempt at a rational account of the value of pleasantness, suggesting indeed that he might have been aware of the difficulties in his account of value. When, in the final book, he describes the process of closure itself—the political intervention in the present reality—Fichte makes clear that while the citizens of the state retain a certain right to continue to enjoy the pleasures to which they have become accustomed, the government, while allowing them these pleasures—if only through some substitute ware—must nevertheless try to gradually wean them from luxuries that cannot be supported by the present circumstances of the nation. Here Fichte introduces a distinction between real and merely opined needs that seems to contradict his theory of value:

> Yet both with regard to transplanting foreign industries into the country and to gradually weaning the nation from those plea-sures that, in the future, will no longer be satisfied, a distinction must be made between those needs that can actually contribute something to well-being and those that only take opinion into account. We can quite well suppose that it would be hard for someone to suddenly do without Chinese tea, or have no fur coat in the winter and no light dress in the summer. Yet it is hardly clear why the coat must be of sable or the dress of silk, when the country produces neither sable nor silk. And it is even less clear why it would be so terrible if one day our clothing suddenly lacked all that embroidery through which it is made neither warmer nor more durable.[116]

Whereas before Fichte had supposed that the nation's needs, realized in production, could provide the basis for an objective and universal determi-

nation of the value of pleasantness, he now implies that a further distinction is possible between goods that can "actually contribute something to
well-being and those that only take opinion into account"—or, in other
words, between a pleasure whose objective validity is a function merely of
opinion as expressed through the market forces of an anarchic economic
order, and a well-being that reflects rational insight into human nature. If
such a criterion—a measure of pleasure that is not dependent on market
forces—exists, we may wonder why Fichte did not simply introduce it in
the first book. By integrating the life-sustaining and pleasurable function of
free activity into a single term—well-being—it would have been possible
to measure every commodity according to its intrinsic use value without
either differentiating between different forms of activity or presupposing their
ultimate commensurability. I will return to this question in my discussion
of the third book, since, as we will see, it is crucial to an understanding
of the process of closure and hence of politics as a whole. For now, I will
only suggest that, for Fichte, this calculation of *intrinsic* well-being cannot
simply be the work of reason.

§8. Wonder and Historical Inquiry

The task of the second book, as mentioned, is to give a history of the present time (*Zeitgeschichte*). Real history, in this phase of Fichte's thought, does
not unfold of necessity toward the realization of rationality as its *telos*, but
rather possesses an essential contingency that can only be overcome through
free praxis. The ideal state, the end point of history, is the free creation
of mankind, representing the complete domination of nature (sensibility
and contingency) by reason.[117] Yet if the movement of history cannot be
derived from reason, neither is history itself purely empirical in character.
For indeed, as I suggested earlier, the history of the present provides the
necessary mediation between the purely philosophical principles of the doctrine of Right and political action. Assimilating an unchanging and absolute
ideal into the maelstrom and flux of empirical reality, it must itself exist as
their fluid integration.
     The peculiar epistemological status of historical understanding, and the
nature of the stance proper to the historian, appear with the greatest force
and clarity in the invocation of wonder that opens the first, preambulatory
chapter of the second book. While wonder may rob "us of our composure"
and disturb "our calm reflection," the "ability to wonder about something"
also contains "the predisposition to wisdom, thinking for oneself, and freely
producing concepts."[118] As in Aristotle's *Metaphysics,* wonder (in Greek,
θαυμάζειν) is the speculative attitude par excellence.[119] Yet for Fichte, this

speculative attitude not only lies at the origins of a purely philosophical investigation into first principles, but is also the beginning of true historical understanding.[120] Because the nonthinker, the pure and naive empiricist possessing only sense perception and memory, suffers the "incurable illness" of "regarding the *accidental as necessary*," he is incapable of conceiving a state of affairs different from that to which he is accustomed.[121] In contrast, the true thinker, whose thoughts are no longer bound to the mimetic reproduction of the given but "freely create within himself what is possible," and who is thus able to imagine possibilities different from those that are given, not only recognizes the contingency of the given state of affairs, but finds it *wunderlich*—wondrously strange—and is, in turn, led to ask how things have come to be the way they are, given all the other ways in which things could have turned out.[122] This question, which seeks a rational explanation of the genesis of the contingent without deducing its necessity and rationality, is the basis of every historical investigation. Since true history is thus always in part speculative, it is not enough for the historian merely to catalogue facts or even investigate the causal connections between them. Instead, he must reveal the inner tendency of history as it manifests itself in the present moment of time. In just this way, Fichte's own investigation into the genesis of the commercial relations of the present passes fluidly from the description of the past to the projection of the future. Past and future indeed exist not in abstract isolation as points of time, but only through their interrelation, mediated through the present. Moreover, since the very contingency of history implies that it is born both of necessity and freedom, we cannot deduce this tendency merely from the facts. Their interpretation already requires the insight that man's only vocation and determination is to freely create his destiny. Yet it must also be stressed that this tendency is itself only contingent, and does not represent the necessary movement of history toward its *telos*. It is not deduced from reason per se, but merely represents insight into the curve of history and the tangent of this curve at the given present moment.

§9. The Historical Tendencies of the Modern and Ancient Worlds

In the second chapter, Fichte begins the historical investigation proper. He starts by characterizing the fundamental distinction between the ancient and modern world. Whereas the ancient world was rigidly divided into distinct peoples, each of which considered the others as enemies or barbarians, the people of modern Christian Europe can be thought of as a single nation, bound together from the outset by a common descent and customs as well as also later "by a single common religion and the same submissiveness to its visible head."[123] The difference between the modern world and the ancient is thus ultimately a difference in tendency. Whereas the latter developed from particularity to universality, culminating in the Roman Empire, the former exhibits precisely the opposite movement. Beginning as a single nation that was only loosely bound by political relations and for the most part existed in a state of natural anarchy, it only gradually acquired "proper political concepts and institutions."[124] When modern states finally came into being, they arose not from the "collection and unification of unattached individuals under the unity of the law,"[125] but instead were haphazardly torn off from the whole.

This fact is of the greatest consequence for understanding the nature of commercial relations in the present. In the beginning of its history, Christian Europe constituted a single commercial nation, in which "every part of the great whole—every individual—cultivated and manufactured and acquired by trade from other parts of the world whatever was most expedient given its natural situation, and brought its goods unhindered to market through all the parts of the great whole, with the prices of things arising of their own accord."[126] While Europe later divided itself off into distinct states, these states continue to be united by trade and commerce. In adopting properly political concepts, the nation-states of Europe have closed themselves off juridically and yet not commercially, and thus they have only half realized the aim of the political art. Instead of fashioning themselves into true states, whose governments would be able to guarantee their citizens what is theirs by Right, they present a bizarre mixture of contradictory principles.

Recapitulating his argument while preparing the transition from the past to the future and from theory to praxis, Fichte writes:

> We have now arrived at the source of the greatest part of the still-existing abuses. For a long time there were no states at all in modern Europe. At present, one is still attempting to form them. Moreover, one has up till now only one-sidedly, only half comprehended the task of the state, conceiving of it as an institution that, through the law, should preserve the citizen in whatever state of possession it finds him in. Yet one failed to see that the profounder duty of the state is to put each in possession of what is his due. Yet the latter is only possible by eliminating the anarchy of trade, just as one gradually is eliminating political anarchy. The state must close itself off as a commercial state, just as it has already been closed off in its legislative apparatus and judiciary.[127]

It would be bad enough were the modern European nations only able, as a result of their hybrid nature, to fulfill half of their obligations to their citizens. In truth, though, the consequences of the half-closure of the state are more dire, not only undermining all legitimate goals of the state, but even leading to its destruction. Because Fichte regards economic rights as the real condition of political rights, this could not be otherwise: ultimately, there can be no true juridical closure without commercial closure, since the deeper legal obligation of the state is to guarantee each citizen his share of the total economic activity of the nation. Yet the account that Fichte provides in the second book of the self-annihilation of the half-closed nation depends not on the general nature of the relation between the commercial and juridical functions of the state, but rather on a more concrete account of the catastrophic inner tendency of the history that unfolds out of open commercial relations.

§10. Money and Temporality: The Allegory of Money

To understand Fichte's account of the fate that befalls nations under anarchic conditions of trade, we must begin by observing that he never denies that free commerce is, in and of itself, anything but a boon to the general prosperity. If free trade involved nothing more than the fair distribution over the largest possible region of those goods that can be produced with the least effort in each of its localities, it would maximize the common good—the sustenance of life and the pleasure enjoyed by each individual. The problem, though, is that while money, understood as an abstract sign for value—an indication of a certain share of activity—is needed for the efficient distribution of goods, it also gives rise to a completely different system of relations between individuals, in which the gain of one individual implies another's loss.

To better grasp this point, it will be useful to consider Fichte's account of money. While money functions as a sign rather than a thing, this signifying function in no way contradicts its existence as a commodity. Money is not a non-commodity, but rather a special limit case of the commodity present to a certain degree in every ware prior to being completely consumed. The specific nature of this money function becomes clearest when Fichte explains how gold and silver came to be privileged as world currency. Whereas previously, he had insisted that the value of *pleasurable* goods could be determined from the extra effort expended in their production, now he argues, contra Smith, that the worth of these metals rests on a completely different principle:

> I must, however, explicitly recall that the value of these metals rests merely in the general agreement about their value. Each

person accepts these at a certain ratio to his goods since he is certain that everyone with whom he can engage in commerce will accept them in turn from him at this same ratio. The true intrinsic value of these metals, their usefulness as raw materials, is far from equal to their extrinsic value, which rests merely on opinion. The goods manufactured from them obtain their value only in consideration of the fact that one can, or at least should have been able to, again make money out of them. The money material that they contain must also be paid for.[128]

This implies that the signifying function of a given commodity stands in a direct relation to its extrinsic value, or at least a certain form thereof: a value based not on life or pleasure but on opinion. This sort of extrinsic value, moreover, is different in kind from the pleasantness of opinion that Fichte mentions in the third book. In the case of the former, there no longer remains any necessary connection with pleasure. It is no longer a question of believing that something would provide pleasure, and thus falsely esteeming its intrinsic worth, but rather of opining a value entirely independent of pleasure. This opinion, moreover, is constituted through a sort of original intersubjectivity. It is an opinion regarding the opinion of others, since indeed it matters not so much what we think the value of gold and silver to be as what we think others think this to be. We must believe that others will continue to value it and accept it in exchange for their goods, and thus that these will in turn believe the same of others, and so forth. In this way, indeed, money involves a structure of infinite reflection; an order where value is constituted through an ultimately groundless infinite regress and refraction of opinion. At the same time, money also has a specifically temporal character—a point that is perhaps most clear if we consider how the signifying function of money depends on an opinion that is not merely intersubjective and infinitely reflective, but necessarily future-directed. What we believe, in valuing gold and silver or anything else as money, is that people will continue to value money, and hence that they will continue to believe in the continuing belief of others *ad infinitum*. The opinion about money, as it were, conjures forth the future as the continuing spectacle of infinitely reflected opinion.

Previously I claimed that in the rational state property emerges as the synthetic mediation between the monistic space of the world considered as the real and shared basis of economic activity and the monadic subjectivity of free will, dispersed among different individuals. This mediation gives birth to the space-time of the political state as a sphere of efficacious activity, articulated into individuals, within which it becomes possible to take time in the realization of goals. The individual, so conceived, exists first of all as a sort of fullness of time. Pleasant life, in this sense, is a duration of time filled out with the realization of goals. Fichte, we note in passing, also allows for the possibility of a life that is lived for more than pleasure; for the political, artistic, philosophical, and religious lives. In the case of these, their goals reach beyond the limit of individual life, and into a political, no longer individual, time. Historical time is itself the highest creation of the state, and indeed, as Fichte will argue in his 1813 *Doctrine of the State*, the ultimate form of historical time—and hence the absolutely greatest work of the state—is eschatological: its own elimination through the passage into a purely moral existence.[129]

It must now become clear, however, that through money—through a sign of value based solely on opinion—a new order of temporality, and a new sort of future, comes into being. Besides the future of politics, there is also a future of opinion, based on signs and pure speculation—a future that exists only as an infinite multiplication and refraction of hope, divested not only from life and pleasure, but also from truth, beauty, and goodness. These two temporal orders—the one involving an Aristotelian logic of teleological fulfillment (though with pleasure, rather than happiness, the proximate goal), the other pure allegory—collide in the money sign, and precisely because—as the medium of exchange, interceding between production and consumption—it allows the individual to pass fluidly between the political order, defined by real goods, real pleasures, and real needs, and the allegorical order, with its strictly allegorical pleasures, of infinitely reflected opinion.[130]

The nature of this movement between intrinsic and extrinsic value—politics and allegory—as well as the dangers that it poses, is vividly illustrated when Fichte describes the relations between individuals in a single "great commercial state." Since the entire sum of money signifies the entire sum of goods available,[131] one individual is proportionately richer or poorer than another depending on whether he has a larger or smaller share of money. Or, more precisely, he is richer "if he periodically earns a quantity of goods whose value in money exceeds what he would receive through an equal division of all goods, and then knows how to convert these goods into money and the money obtained thereby into goods that he had not himself earned."[132] Because the total money, at any given point, refers to a fixed quantity of goods, there arises a zero-sum game in which each individual tries to amass as much money as possible so that he can claim as much as possible of the services of others while denying others the claim that this same money would give on his own services. In other words, in mediating between production and consumption, money, as an abstract signifier of real goods, allows relations of gross inequality to emerge despite the relative equality of real activity. Moreover, this results specifically from money's capacity to conjure up a future based solely on opinion. Since real goods, considered qua goods, are always perishable to some degree or another, producing pleasure and life only through an act of usage that places demands on possession and possessor alike, there is little point to either their temporary or permanent hoarding. Unless directed toward a concrete future goal—such as a feast or banquet, a military action, or to provide security against famine—hoarding could only amount to wastefulness. In contrast, money, by signifying a continuing future claim, promises that through its accumulation one could gain even more control over the goods and services of others, and thus it leads to an internecine war of all against all, in which each party, by sacrificing present consumption, connives to gain a greater share of future goods.

We already begin to see clearly what is at stake in the collision of these two futures. If the political future is, first of all, the promise of self-realization through the equal (or at least relatively equal) division into individual property of the activity that is common to all and to which all have a right, the future of money involves bettering one's lot through scheming intrigue at the expense of others. Not a commons, but its tragedy; or, rather, its mourning-play. Through these reciprocal intrigues, true action—action directed toward a purpose in the rational expectation of its realization—becomes impossible. Recapitulating his description of the relations between individuals in the great commercial state, Fichte writes: "In short, no one will be provided with the slightest guarantee that, if he continues to work, he will continue to enjoy his present state of existence. For men wish to be completely free that they may destroy one another."[133] Even the most basic work—the work that brings nothing more than life and pleasure—becomes impossible.

Up till this point, Fichte has only considered individuals insofar as they relate to one another through their engagement in commercial activities. The fourth chapter extends his analysis to the relations of states to one another in the "great commercial republic." It is here that he explores the disastrous consequences of the partial attempts by juridically closed states to also close off commerce. The particular dynamic in question emerges only when governments begin to collect taxes directly from their citizens. Whereas previously the government of the state could be regarded simply as one individual among others in the great commercial republic, direct taxation brings the government into an entirely new relation to its subjects. From now on it regards all the subjects under its jurisdiction as united into a single body, a common wealth. The affluence of its citizens now becomes its most vital concern.[134]

It might seem that this new interest that governments take in their subjects' welfare could check the internecine trade war between individuals. Instead, a new zero-sum game, and a new tragedy of the commons, emerges. Like individuals, national economies may be either rich or poor in relation to one another. In the case of nations, however, the role of money in allowing relations of inequality to emerge is even more evident than before. Relative wealth or poverty depends on the relation of the intrinsic value of the goods that it imports and exports. The nature of this calculus, though, seems at first sight rather counterintuitive. A nation is relatively rich if the intrinsic value of its exports exceeds the intrinsic value of its imports, or, in other words, if it produces more life and pleasure for others than others produce for it: if it serves the other nations more than these serve it. What explains this seemingly perverse claim is the mediating function of money, which, by first of all signifying extrinsic rather than intrinsic value, gives an inverted image of the intrinsic relations. In return for exporting more intrinsic value than it imports, the nation imports more money, more extrinsic value, than it exports. And whereas intrinsic value, being realizable only in consumption, belongs only to the political sphere of self-realization—it exists, this is to say, either in the present of immediate enjoyment or the future of a purposeful work—the extrinsic value of the money sign allows for the accumulation of the promise of a future power over other economic agents. Through the government's intrigues, the nation is forced from the sphere of real activity—of the lower, merely sensual goals of life and pleasure as well as the higher goals of politics, art, philosophy, and religion—into an allegorical mode of being. Instead of realizing itself now and later, it hoards gold and silver: signs of an opinion about opinion infinitely reflected into the future.

It is not possible, though, to live forever in this future, outside of politics and history. Precisely because the extrinsic value of money depends on opinion, it has no value but through distribution. It must circulate and "help determine the price of goods in all regions." If, in contrast, it were concentrated in one nation, only entering into relations with that nation's goods, its value, being determined only in relation to these, would fall in proportion to the ratio between the intrinsic value of the goods of that nation and of the great commercial state as a whole.[135] Hence, a relatively rich nation must spend the surplus of money that it periodically accumulates abroad, thereby restoring the equilibrium in the expenditures of the nations. Yet this very equilibrium is gained only by inverting the original relation of the intrinsic utility of exported and imported goods. Whereas previously the relatively wealthy nation had worked for the life and pleasure of other nations, now "the rich nation receives goods that it could do without in exchange for this surplus, and compels the foreigner, who can scarcely provide himself with the bare essentials, to work for its pleasure."[136]

In the next pages, Fichte vividly describes what must happen to those nations who are at the losing end of this relation. If we do not actually witness their complete impoverishment, it is only because its "obvious spectacle" is concealed "by an ever worse national economy, where everything possible is offered for sale and transformed into a commodity, and where the capital, the nation itself, is consumed once the interests on this capital, the work of the nation, no longer suffice."[137] The people will emigrate, or the government will sell them into slavery, transforming them into a commodity; raw produce will be sold abroad rather than utilized in manufacture; farms will be abandoned and their lands will become the object of foreign speculation; and finally the state will sell "itself, its very independence," depending permanently on "subsidies, thereby turning itself into the province of another state and the means to whatever end this other state pleases."[138]

Up till now, we observe, Fichte has considered the interaction of nations whose governments, while grasping that the realization of their political aims, whether legitimate or illegitimate, depends on the prosperity of the nation, have not begun to take economic measures or countermeasures to increase their prosperity or restore equilibrium. They are aware of their dependence on national wealth, without yet acting on this awareness. Even the recirculation of accumulated wealth is, in this way, not a conscious action, but a reflex belonging to the economy as a sort of political subconscious. The inner tendency of money is to circulate, and the government does nothing more than allow it to do so. Just as completely free commerce is the natural condition of modern Europe—the origin of its history—a policy of laissez-faire defines the original relations between European states. For Fichte, in sharp contrast to Adam Smith, such a state of affairs is already fundamentally unstable, necessarily undermining the autonomy of states and degrading their inhabitants to a barely human existence. Likewise, the half-measures that governments take against the effects of this original anarchy do not result simply from an erroneous grasp of economics—a failure to recognize the benefits of free markets—but rather constitute the first dim awareness of the danger that completely free commerce poses to their political goals.

Behind all these measures is the attempt to control the natural impulse of money. Because its extrinsic value ultimately refers to the intrinsic value of the totality of circulating goods, it depends on and tends toward circulation. A nomad and eternal wanderer, it resists the will of nation-states, mocking their boundaries and evading their jurisdiction. Hence, just as the government realizes its dependence on national wealth, it also finds itself confronted with an element that, in sharpest contrast to the infinite malleability of the citizen in the Machiavellian state, defies every assertion of national sovereignty. The intrigues of gold, the most malleable of metals, strike into the very heart of the princely court, subjecting even the sovereign to its mercurial dictates while at the same time offering the possibility of gaining power over its subjects by directly controlling the element that itself mediates their interactions. The mercantilist and protectionist policies that the government undertakes in response represent a crude attempt to subordinate money to its will and power. They try to control money by hoarding, drawing the foreigner's money into the country, and holding on to the money already there. To this end, they engage in three different strategies. They encourage agriculture and promote its export while at the same time preventing the export of whatever could serve as raw material for manufacture; they hinder or burden the import of foreign manufactured goods; and they encourage their citizens to act as proxy traders for other nations.[139]

To understand the implications of Fichte's critique of mercantilism, we must first of all consider in more depth the relation between the conscious policies of the states and the unconscious and essentially anarchic tendencies of money. Since unlimited hoarding must undermine the value of money, no government could ever pursue these policies exclusively: cooped up within the nation, money must necessarily grow in strength in relation to the foreign goods in proportion as it loses value in relation to the goods within the nation, until finally its foreign value so much exceeds its domestic value that it is drawn, as if by irresistible gravitational attraction, back into circulation. Hence, the mercantilist policies do not belong to a time outside of the catastrophic history that would unfold were governments simply to grant economic forces free rein. Rather, they are seamlessly interwoven into this history. The government, as it were, does not control money or counter its nomadic nature, but merely intensifies the moments when, constantly mediating between production and consumption, money crystallizes into temporary accumulations before passing back into circulation. Rather than conquering the intrigues of money by intriguing with it, trying to take advantage of its circulation, their very attempts to directly resist its nature or use it as a means to assert their own sovereignty transform them into its most submissive agents. Even if they may gain in prosperity as a result, they will become more and more subject to a power alien to their juridical control.

It is already clear that these half-measures cannot promote the highest end of politics, the submission of nature to human reason. If Fichte does not stress this point, it is because, in his critique of mercantilism, he aims his arguments against the more proximate goals that governments, themselves barely cognizant of the true notion of politics, aim at in using them. Showing that, even judged by the standard of these proximate goals, these measures must fail, he opposes the assertion that the reciprocal machinations of nations would give rise to a balance of power, counteracting the destabilizing effect of the anarchy of money. Against this, Fichte claims that the means that nations use against one another to advance their interests will undermine rather than strengthen their productive capacities, ultimately leading to secret intrigues and even actual wars, together with the most dangerous political concepts. Moreover, when weaker nations do succeed to some degree in restoring equilibrium, this will provoke a catastrophic collapse of the stronger nations, which, having become dependent on a large military, are incapable of absorbing a loss in their national prosperity. A stable equilibrium, in this way, cannot result from these measures. He further suggests that they cannot serve the true (if not the highest) goal that governments must organize their commerce toward, which is "to secure for their subjects the living conditions to which they are accustomed."[140] This goal, demanded no less by prudence than by justice, is necessarily compromised by the continuing presence of foreign influence on the economy. Finally, the half-measures not only preserve the disadvantages of open commerce, but add a whole new set of problems. In imposing tariffs and bans on goods, blocking or limiting access to these, the government becomes hateful in the eyes of its subjects, provoking them to covert or open revolt. Committed to the impossible task of regulating what cannot be regulated, the government will collapse under the weight of its own bureaucracy.

§11. Monetary History

Having now reached the end of the second book, let us consider, in more general terms, the place of history in the Closed Commercial State. History, it is now clear, does not and cannot have a single meaning: it is neither the realm of chance nor providence, and least of all is it the all-encompassing dialectical process of absolute spirit, unfolding toward its inner telos, preserving particularity in generality and freedom in necessity, and allowing nothing to exist outside its limits. Rather, if we can still speak of history in the singular, it is only as a name for the different tendencies that converge in a single point of time, opening up radically different possibilities for the future. Here it is not a question of the contingency and arbitrary choice worshiped and marveled at by a culture that, having outsourced its own humanity, can only recognize freedom in the uncertainty and chaos of an external reality, but of a fundamental decision that opens up in every present moment between three essentially different kinds of history. On one side: the history of politics, which posits the true state as its proximate, and the elimination of the state as its final, goal. This history enables purposive action, and in this sense it is teleological in character. Yet the possibility of having a telos is not given by this history to human individuals, but rather history is itself created as the possibility of acting on ever more far-reaching goals. History is, in this sense, and as we already suggested, the political work par excellence. On the other side: the future conjured forth by an infinitely reflected opinion that, if untethered from reference to real utility, becomes subject to a law of hyperbolic increase, a continual and unchecked hyping and trumping up of the future. These two paths, the two fundamental tendencies of history, run parallel to each other, and yet intersect at each present moment. Finally, between the two extremes—of truth and of opinion; of limited self-actualization and infinite passivity—is ordinary life: the continuum formed of these intersections from the synthesis of present moments. This is the time in which, for the most part, we live; the grayish realm of half-truths and half-measures and of a mole-like groping after the truth. The point where these twains meet, and thus the means and medium of everyday life, is money. Passing to and fro between the intrinsic value of pleasant life and the extrinsic value of mere opinion, money is always at once the invisible hand that weaves the grey strands of real life but also the opening toward the extremes; the point where one could choose between real politics and its spectral opposite; between creating history as the realization of the radical freedom of human nature, and sacrificing history to the dreamy revelry of infinitude. Money, in other words, presents humankind with the choice between, on the one hand, radically affirming the possibility of human freedom by subjecting money itself to an arbitrary determination derived from rational calculation and thus ultimately bringing money, and with it all human existence, under the sphere of rational control, and, on the other hand, continuing to allow human purposes to be foiled by the seemingly uncontrollable sway of opinion.

History is thus neither idealist nor materialist, but monetary. The *Moneta*, the coin—the mother of the muses and the goddess of recollection (derived from *moneo* and ultimately from the root *MAN / MEN*)[141]—warns, reminds, instructs, and teaches. Above all, it keeps us mindful of our nature as human beings. We could compare its monition with Schiller's discussion of the function of art in the *Letters on the Aesthetic Education of Man*. The ninth letter begins at an impasse that would seem to render the art of politics impossible. If theoretical culture conditions practical culture and vice versa, then it is through the prior realization of the political ideal that human character would assume a form allowing for this ideal to be realized. The beautiful work of art, however, offers a way out of this vicious circle: released from all human convention (in Greek, νόμος), it is a source for political renewal that preserves itself intact through even the most degenerate periods. It is, indeed, a pattern *(Muster)* of harmonious relations, stamped with the form of the beautiful. Warning *(moneo)* and demonstrating these to the future, it is even something monstrous: a *monstrum* or divine omen.[142] Yet for Fichte there can be no such faith in the political function of art. Indeed, in the *Fundamental Characteristics of the Present Age*, he not only argues that beautiful art, conceived precisely as an art that is submitted to the higher spiritual needs of human beings, depends for its emergence on the political and economic conditions of human life, but even suggests that only true eternal peace could give birth to the arts; and thus that the arts, in their true form, do not yet exist.[143] In turn, the warning that points the way to politics does not owe its origin to a place outside the history of convention and contingency. For money, whose very worth derives purely from opinion, is, above all, the coin of convention and custom: a νόμος and νοῦμμος.

It would be wrong, moreover, to think that the possibilities that money reveals appear, at every given moment of time, in perfect clarity. While history can only be created through free and conscious action, the possibilities that open up to us in the present are always clothed in grey. They are given to us not through the lucidity of reason, but through dim or dark feelings. Thus, against the objection that states would never recognize the welfare of the worker as their duty, he counters:

> Yet in states enjoying civil order [poliziert], manufacturers whose workshops were forced to come to a sudden standstill for lack of sales or raw materials, or a people in danger of doing without its primary means of nourishment, or compelled to pay for it at a rate out of all proportion to past prices, have always turned to the government with an obscure feeling of their right. And their governments never dismissed these complaints as if they did not pertain to them, but offered council to the best of their abilities, with an obscure feeling of their duty and a clear view of the dangers posed by the uprising of mobs of people whom direst need has left with nothing to lose.[144]

Likewise, when the state deprives its citizens of goods to which they are accustomed, "this injustice—it is indeed unavoidable, and protects against manifold other injustices, but it nevertheless remains, strictly speaking, an injustice—is dimly felt by the nation, even if it perhaps cannot yet clearly explicate it in rational terms [aus Gründen entwickeln]."[145] And when the territory of a state does not encompass its natural boundaries:

> The governments will dimly feel that they are missing something even if perhaps they don't clearly see what this, properly understood, is. They will speak of the necessity of arrondissement. They will protest that for the sake of the rest of their lands they cannot do without this fertile province or these mineral and salt mines—always aiming obscurely at the acquisition of their natural borders. All will be driven by the thirst for conquest—be it blind and indefinite, or indeed clear in vision and very definite in its aims.[146]

The ultimate task of the philosophical inquiry into history—an inquiry that, like philosophy itself, begins with wonder—is not to construct the process of its unfolding from rational principles, or even give rational interpretation to contingent events, but rather to unfold the meaning of the dim feelings given us in the present. The dictates of reason, the summonses of freedom, must themselves be developed from these feelings, yet without submitting to the passivity of feeling. We recall that, for Fichte, Rousseau failed to understand history in part because he could not properly mediate between his feelings and his understanding. Fichte's account of "dim feelings" in the *Closed Commercial State* may thus be seen to overcome the Rousseauian impasse.

It is perhaps in the *Closed Commercial State* that Fichte gets closest to the heart of the feeling he has been given by history to feel and understand—and namely by interpreting the monition of history as the *moneta*, the monetary. If it is Fichte's most "thought-through" work, it is because it begins with what is farthest, rather than nearest to thought, and thus has to pass through the longest way. Only in a strange element, the element where reason is least at home, would it be possible to feel money as the heart of the present and the opening to the future. This is not the feeling or the work of the well-placed academic, but of the one in exile, the asylum seeker.

§12. Dark Feelings of History: The Claims of Habit and the Task of Closure

The third book of the *Closed Commercial State* addresses politics: the passage, brought about through decisive and conscious action, from the real to the ideal.[147] It will not surprise us that this political action, the "proper point of transition" from the present systems of commerce to the "system that . . . is alone true and that reason itself requires," consists in the state closing itself off to all foreign trade and forming a "closed commercial body."[148] More telling, perhaps, is that the groping half-measured attempts by governments to control the commercial destiny of their nation do not represent, in and of themselves, progress toward this closure. This reveals above all else the nature of the relation between politics and the history of the present, and in turn is of great significance to Fichte's argument as a whole. The present moment in which politics intervenes is determined only by the combination of juridical closure with commercial openness; only by the peculiar constellation of conflicting tendencies—above all, the collision of a true political future with the future of pure opinion—and not by the everyday reality that gels into being between these extremes. The truly political act must grasp the present moment at its extremities and in its epochal character.

There is nevertheless a weaker sense in which the politician still cannot ignore ordinary reality. Since individuals and the state as a whole are not without prior relations, "but have instead emerged, respectively, as free citizens of a great commercial republic and as a part torn off by chance from the great whole," they have acquired "special rightful claims."[149] While these claims are born of habit rather than reason, and indeed a habit acquired under political conditions that are themselves almost thoroughly unjust, Fichte does not deny their legitimacy. Through both his own contribution to the general flourishing of commerce, and the silent consent of the state, the citizen has earned the right to count on continuing in his present condition. With this notion of habitually acquired rights, Fichte acknowledges that there is at least some validity to Burke's organic view of the state and his ethical naturalism. And indeed, it is precisely these traditional claims that make necessary a gradualist, rather than revolutionary politics. If the government were simply to have the state closed off to the outside without further ado, it would violate its citizens' rights and thus contradict its own aim. Rather, political action is not so much the act of closure as the process of closure, and it is precisely these acquired habits, and the rightful claims issuing from them, that offer resistance to this process, and require that it take time, determining the goals that the state must realize before it can close itself off completely. Moreover, though, this is not one political activity among many. Rather, the politics demanded by the present time exhausts itself with the establishment of commercial closure. "Once this closure has been brought about," Fichte thus explains, "everything else will follow quite easily, and the measures that should be pursued from this point on no longer lie within the domain of politics but rather of the pure doctrine of Right, and have already been set forth by us in the first book."[150]

What the citizen claims, first and foremost, is the right to continue to enjoy the goods that, as a citizen of the great commercial republic, he had previously been able to procure for himself. The government, in closing the state off, may overcome this resistance in one of two ways. On the one hand, it must try, as much as possible, to cultivate and manufacture actual or substitute forms of these goods within its territory. Even when this is entirely impossible, it must not ban these goods all at once, but instead gradually wean its citizens from them.[151] It is here, as I mentioned earlier, that Fichte introduces the distinction between needs that truly contribute to well-being and those that depend solely on opinion. It is "hardly clear," he maintains, that the sudden deprivation of the latter would do any real harm. This distinction has the potential to vastly simplify the task of closure by excluding a whole class of goods and needs from consideration. If Fichte nevertheless presents this point rather cautiously, and only following other considerations, it is because the boundary between the two classes of needs, obvious in some extreme cases, is for the most part endlessly blurred in the history that itself unfolds between truth and opinion. For it is clear, at the very least, that the people who feel these needs will not immediately recognize their emptiness, and will not themselves be capable of drawing a distinction between legitimate and illegitimate habit that even Fichte's own argument does not really support. Hence, only the process of time, and not the fiat of government, can disentangle the two strands from which ordinary life is woven.

Yet something more is at stake than just the accustomed rights of the citizens. Human nature, in discovering and satisfying its merely sensual needs, also unearths its deeper spiritual nature. Fichte's denial, contra Schiller, that the artist can create beauty independent of the conditions that surround him is anticipated in a passage from the first book of the *Closed Commercial State*. Here, Fichte explains how the surplus forces that arise through a nation's economic development must be distributed in "a relatively equal fashion" allowing all to "live equally pleasant lives." "By 'relatively,'" he means, clarifying his rather odd turn of phrase:

> in such a way that each one will maintain the kind of force and well-being he needs for his specific occupation. Thus, for example, a man who occupies himself with deep thought, and whose imagination should soar up toward invention, would lack even the bare necessities were he to feed himself like the farmer, who engages from day to day in a mechanical labor that only strains his physical forces. It won't hurt the farmer to still his hunger during his workdays with a mass of vegetable foodstuff—a nourishment that he will without doubt gain by his labor out in the open air. In any case fine and clean clothing would soon be ruined with his sort of occupation. By comparison, someone who works with his hands while sitting inside a room needs nourishment that satisfies in smaller quantities. And the one who, be it in higher forms of art or in science, must invent, requires a more varied and revitalizing nourishment, and an environment in which the cleanliness [*Reinlichkeit*] and nobility that should rule him within is constantly placed before his eyes in the outside world. Yet even the farmer, however, on his day of rest, when he enters into a thoroughly human existence, deserves to enjoy together with the others the better things that the soil of his land grants, and wear clothing worthy of a free man.[152]

This argument not only asserts that spiritual labors require a more refined standard of living, but also implies that, outside of these material and environmental conditions, man's higher spiritual endeavors could either never come into being at all, or at least never flourish, arising only in the most haphazard fashion without ever gaining a foothold in the life of the nation. This suggests, in turn, that these deeper spiritual needs emerge in conjunction with, and can never be completely sundered from, their merely sensual counterparts. Indeed, one could never know whether the ornaments of life—"that embroidery through which it is made neither warmer nor more durable"—do not also allow the fine artists or scientists to glimpse in the outside world the very "cleanliness and nobility" that should rule within them.[153] Perhaps, by purging life of its trifles and leaving only "real" needs, one would jeopardize the attainment of the higher purposes of mankind.

We are now finally in a position to answer the question posed at the end of our discussion of the first book. There I asked why Fichte did not simply make use of the distinction between real and opined need to determine the value of *pleasant* commodities, instead of relying on a somewhat tortured if not altogether circular principle of substitution. The reason, I propose, is that the precise lines of this distinction necessarily fall outside rational calculation. At the present moment, human nature does not yet understand itself; we do not recognize the truth of our own nature or our real needs, but only the idols—to use the language of Bacon or Plato—generated by the chattering commerce of opinion. Even if the philosopher is able to unbind himself from the cave and glimpse the true vocation of humankind, he can but slowly bring others along with him. If the multitude are to be swayed from their proximate desires, this must happen through themselves and not through others. The philosopher and the government must lead them, but rather than doing violence to their accustomed needs, it must allow the social imagination to do its work at its own pace, undermining the tyranny of opinion and slowly gaining insight into what it truly means to be human. At the very heart of the process of closure and thus of politics itself, we discover the dialectics of taste, of its gradual cultivation in history through strife—one of the most important themes of Kant's third *Critique*.[154]

This, in turn, suggests the deeper meaning of the words that follow Fichte's invocation of imaginary needs: "[T]he closing off of the commercial state, of which we are speaking, would not involve renouncing what we once enjoyed and modestly restricting ourselves to the narrow circle of produce previously cultivated in our country, but rather appropriating vigorously, so far as we are able, our share of all that is good and beautiful upon the entire face of the earth. This share is due us, since our nation, through its work and its artistic sense, has without doubt also contributed for centuries to this common possession of humanity."[155] It is not that we would get more stuff, but rather that we would live for, and appropriate as our property—as our own proper nature—the ideal.

Fichte, however, speaks not only of the claims of the individual citizens, but of the state itself, and principally its right to take possession of all the territory within its natural boundaries. Nature indicates these boundaries both through certain visible marks—bodies of water and impassable mountain ranges—but also through the fact that the productive capacities of the differ-ent tracts of land within these boundaries compensate for one another and balance one another out, providing at least the potential for its inhabitants to enjoy a relatively high standard of living.[156] Nevertheless, these "signs" are only "hints": nature's providence does not reveal itself immediately to human reason, but only through interpretation.[157] Furthermore, precisely because the natural boundaries depend on man's sense of his needs and understanding of his nature, and yet these only come to light through history and cannot be derived through rational deduction, it would not be possible to bring this hermeneutics of nature under rules and systematize it into a scientific method. Rather, the interpretation of nature's limits is the work of history, and, like the interpretation of the limits and possibilities of human nature, happens through dim feelings. Or indeed, the politico-military history of mankind—the history of the ceaseless clashes of ruling families driven by the "thirst after conquest"—is nothing else than this labor of interpretation in which individual states, dimly feeling that "they are missing something even if they don't clearly see what this actually is," will try to take posses-sion of natural borders that they only dimly sense, endowing nature's hints with a manifest political meaning.[158]

The state that is closing itself off must hence assume its natural boundaries through either military or diplomatic means before its complete closure, since otherwise it will not only not be able to satisfy the rightful claims of its citizens, but it will also remain beholden to its own dim feelings and thus incapable of freely willing its own destiny.[159] That Fichte, in this way, not only recognizes the inevitability of war under the present histori-cal conditions, but also justifies the need, under certain circumstances, for waging a war of conquest unprovoked by the enemy, must seem like a rather disturbing anticipation of the National Socialist concept of *Lebensraum*. In his defense, however, we observe that he hopes, in articulating the above principle, not to justify war as such, and least of all as a good in itself, but rather to bring to light the rational kernel of the forces impelling states toward seemingly irrational conflict, and thus allow them to pursue war with a view to rational and manifest ends, ultimately reaching the point where they could leave this history of strife behind them. Once a state has assumed its natural borders and closed itself off, it will renounce all further military actions and eliminate the large and onerous standing army that had once been necessary.[160] Indeed, its own commercial closure is a necessary guarantee of this renunciation, since it demonstrates to other states that it no longer has any need to engage in military aggression.[161] If the *Closed Commercial State* represents the beginnings of nationalism, it is nevertheless a nationalism that is not only rooted solely in the economic and juridical closure of the nation and not in shared history, racial identity, ethnicity, or religion, but that indeed stands in sharpest opposition to imperialism and colonial exploitation and that, Fichte will argue, itself provides the necessary conditions for a true community of nations.[162]

§13. The Dialectics of Opinion

For Fichte, we saw, the government of a state must achieve two tasks before the state could be closed off completely. These two tasks are the central aim of politics, understood as the transitional activity preceding the full closure of the state. After first appropriating its natural boundaries, the state must then render its domestic economy adequate to the needs of its citizens, both by gradually modifying their needs and by steering the development of production and manufacture, while at the same time extracting itself from commercial relations with other states. Although this closure is itself a gradual process, it begins with a single, absolutely decisive act: the world currency "that is found in the hands of the citizens, viz. all gold and all silver, must be brought out of circulation and converted into a new national currency, a currency—that is to say—that would be valid only in the country, and would be the only currency valid there."[163] The government must compel its citizens to exchange their old currency for the new, while granting the new currency validity by accepting payments only in this form and assuring that it will not arbitrarily increase the supply of money for its own gain.[164]

With this act, the state in effect divides itself into two completely separate commercial entities bound together only by the sovereign power of the government. It is at once a closed relation between citizens, and a state existing in relation to other states. These functions remain completely discrete, and indeed a boundary is erected between them that no one and nothing can pass through without the express and special permission of the government. Moreover, with this doubling of the commercial state, the national wealth also doubles itself into two forms—national and world currency—and thus acquires nearly double its original value. While the new money given to the citizens has almost the same value as the old with respect to the goods available within the state, the government gains a mass of gold and silver that, directed abroad, can be used to command the forces of other states. This allows it to become a "considerable and dominant monetary power toward these." Yet the government can and must avail itself of this newly gained power quickly in order to assume its natural boundaries and develop its domestic economy, and thus "accomplish the goal set forth above and vigorously appropriate for the nation its share of all that is good and beautiful upon the entire face of the great commercial republic."[165]

Just as none of the half-measures described in the second book bring the state closer to closure, with this first act, the state enters into a fundamentally different mode of history: no longer a history caught eternally in the middle between truth and opinion, but a political history defined by a directional, progressive tendency toward a rational order. The first act of closing the state off, in other words, does not merely begin its closure in time, but produces the time of closure; a time that can be closed and fulfilled. It is the radical grounding of politics as the possibility of a history that drives toward the realization of rationally posited aims; of the possibility of action itself qua self-realization. It is the act in which history first gets its act together, opening up as the domain of true praxis. Moreover, though, it is not really a *Handlung* or act at all. Rather, Fichte refers to it explicitly as an operation (*Operation*), with the word *Operation* being used only in reference to the specific interventions that initiate and enable the closure of the state—principally the money operation (*Geldoperation*) and the occupation of the state's natural borders. This suggests a violent, if nevertheless precisely targeted, surgical intervention into the body of the state. Indeed, the etymology of the word *operation* leads us to *opus* (work or labor), and ultimately the root OP/AP, a specialization of AP meaning to lay or hold.[166] Through the money operation, the government lays hold of the nation as the site for the realization of the activity of reason. It appropriates the nation, through the closure of the state, as the first property, from which all other property is derived; the property of reason itself—the sphere in which its realization would be possible.

The Latin *opinio* derives from this same root, suggesting "mentally laying hold of, supposing."[167] It is, in this sense, the first and natural *laying hold* of the world; its first interpretation or *Auslegung*. Significantly, the money operation takes place in and through opinion (*Meinung*).[168] If indeed the government is able to substitute the one national currency for the world currency and do this without violence, it is precisely because the value of all money rests not on what people know with certainty, but what they believe: what they think they know.[169] In turn, to make its citizens accept the new currency, the government must produce the opinion among its citizens that the new currency is worth the same as the old. This new opinion will, however, be of an essentially different nature than the old. Whereas the old opinion was handed down from generation to generation and individual to individual, disseminating itself in a more or less natural and organic fashion, without submitting itself either to reason, tradition, or the will of men, and thus existing in precisely the same way as gold and silver money itself (both, one could say in English, exist as *currency*: they hasten and run about, traversing to and fro)—the new opinion is a product of the will of the government. In willing there to be a different opinion, the government does not merely pass on what it has heard from elsewhere and takes to be the truth, but it starts an opinion, while fully aware that, precisely because this opinion is an opinion about the opinion of others, it cannot be true at first, but can only become true in time, when experience has confirmed that the new currency does have the value that the government claims it to have, and precisely because everyone thinks it does and acts toward others as though it did. The government, in other words, lies, and yet with a lie that grounds its own truth, becoming true in the new time to which it gives rise.

If this will to lie can fulfill itself, realizing itself as truth, the government must be able not merely to ignite rumor, but master and control opinion itself. Above all, this will be necessary at the beginning, before this opinion has yet become a habit confirmed by the experience of others. The original dissemination of a new opinion, in other words, requires nothing less than a mastery of propaganda; the explicit manipulation of the belief of the subjects. For just this reason, a certain obscurity is attached to the manufacture of the material of the new currency, which must be something completely unfamiliar to the population, while at the same time "commending itself to the imagination even more than the old," sparkling and shimmering.[170] It is, as it were, a luminescence brought forth from within the inner chambers of the court, transfixing the new population, capturing its imagination, and thus making it pliant to the will of the state.

Thus, Fichte's state, like Plato's, begins with a noble lie—a γενναῖόν ψεῦδος—and, indeed, a lie that must not be told, but instituted as a new belief.[171] Yet while Plato wrests gold and silver from the hands of the city's guardians,[172] he preserves their potency in the very myth that founds the ideal city, grounding human worth itself, and the differences in dignity between human beings—the class divisions within the state—in the precious metals.[173] He merely passes on the first falsehood of economics and world history—namely, that value is a property of things and not of free activity itself. Fichte's lie, in contrast, deprives gold and silver of their value, freeing human dignity from their insidious influence. Whereas Plato had grounded the possibility of the *Republic* itself in a sort of original hoarding of gold—a coinage within the soul that, never allowed to circulate among the multitude, retains its purity,[174] Fichte counters by refusing to return gold and silver themselves, the most harmful of all possessions, to the tradition that handed them over to him—to philosophy and politics. For both philosophy and politics have become, through the possession of gold and silver, mad, and their practitioners madmen.

Fichte's lie is, in this way, not just propaganda but counterpropaganda. It replaces the familiar properties of the precious metals with a new sort of luminescence, born of darkness, almost as if this were itself the visual manifestation of free activity, or indeed as if the first work of the state, and the first beautiful work of art, is not a new sort of form, but an absolutely new material, which, known only to the government, is incapable of imitation.[175] The first work of the state, once its will toward its own creation (its own fiction) is in place, is to create—and this is perhaps the first beautiful work in all human history—a new material, without precedent. True art, as it were, is not mimetic but synthetic; even chemical—an artificially produced luminosity.

§14. The Closure of the State as the Overcoming of the Allegory of Opinion

Through the institution of the national currency this original lie becomes truth: through the dissemination of the opinion of the worth of the new material among the population, this opinion is itself validated as having a truth that it did not at first possess, since the opinion to which it refers through an infinite regress now actually exists. This suggests that there is a structural relation between money and opinion, or, in other words, that money has an epistemic valence.[176] It would be useful, in turn, to consider in more fundamental terms how this relation changes with the new currency. How does propaganda and counterpropaganda change the very nature of value itself? And how can this transformation, despite its origins, serve the true agenda of politics—the realization of freedom. It is clear that, in both cases, the value of money exists only through the infinite reflection and regress of opinion into itself. Yet there is this difference: in the case of world currency, the process of infinite reflection—the allegory of opinion—is indeterminate, vague, and diffuse with respect to both its past and future. Having arisen only through being handed down, it reaches back into the obscurity of lore and myth, and perhaps even into the dark past of a "golden age." And at the same time, since the dissemination of opinion does not halt at the limits of the state, it always extends into an equally ambiguous future, open to all the contingencies that arise through the unregulated and anarchic future activity of the foreigner. In contrast, the national currency originates with the *original lie* of its value and the unprecedented manufacture of the money material. And at the same time, rather than reaching out into the future and into contingency, the infinite reflection of opinion is reflected back into itself through the limits of the state; its activity, through a second reflection, is turned back in on itself, and consequently assumes a

closed form, indeed becomes a pure circulation, rather than a mere eddy-
ing within the river of time. Or in short: whereas with world currency the
structure of opinion, considered independent of the fixed quantity of life and
pleasure that it represents, is purely allegorical, with the national currency,
even within the purely semantic sphere (the sign considered independent
of the real that it signifies), allegory is subordinated to, or rather captured
within, the closure of the state. This closure, moreover, grants it a new
temporal character: the temporality of pure allegory is subordinated to a
time structured through the possibility of accomplished action; a time with
a beginning, middle, and end, or, in other words, a *dramatic* time, defined
precisely by the unity, rather than the infinite diffusion, of action. With
the onset of the closure of the state, the mourning-play of history brought
about through the intrigues of money is cast aside. What takes its place,
or perhaps what returns, is tragedy. Or rather its inversion. For the tragic
structure of beginning, middle, and end remains, and yet its directionality
has been reversed. Rather than leading from the security of knowledge (the
solution of the Sphinx's riddle) into wandering and error, it moves from the
errancy of opinion to the absolute firmness of truth.

Here we may recall that at the beginning of his history of the present
time, Fichte implies that with the passage from the ancient world to the
modern, the very direction of history changes. Whereas the ancient world
began with division and moved toward synthesis, the modern world starts
with unity and only gradually develops into closed nation-states. The deeper
ramifications for the *Closed Commercial State* and for Fichte's thought as a
whole, however, only emerge in light of Fichte's later and more elaborated
account of world history. Fichte's first comprehensive account of world history appears in the first eight lectures of the *Fundamental Characteristics of
the Present Age*.[177] Here he divides history into five ages that, taken together,
present the transition from a natural paradisiac condition to the free creation
of a rational state. In the first half of history (the first and second ages),
the human race exists without freedom: reason orders society, yet without
being consciously willed by the multitude, existing first as a universally
distributed natural instinct and then becoming concentrated into the com-
manding authority of a ruling elite. In the second half of history the human
race develops freedom, with reason realizing itself as a free deed that orders
human relations not unconsciously or through force, but as something consciously willed. This, in turn, happens through two stages: in the fourth age
the science of reason emerges, and in the fifth age this science is realized in
the world through human artifice. In this way, it is clear, the second half of
history presents an inversion of the tragic tendency of the first, while the
third age, the middle period, presents the moment of transition between
these two halves. During this third age, which Fichte identified with his

own, external authority has been destroyed, and thus reason itself, which had previously been present in the world only in this alienated form, ceases to play any role in human affairs. Mankind thus enters a period of complete sinfulness. Human beings act only from naked individualism, seeking merely their physical survival and well-being, with the idea of the human race surviving only as an abstraction.

The third age, in the *Fundamental Characteristics of the Present Age,* is a moment of the deepest ambiguity, and it is precisely this ambiguity that allows it to serve as the turning point of history. During this epoch, freedom emerges, but only in a completely abstract form; as an absolute, absolved from every relation to concrete reality. This freedom opens up the possibility of the freedom to be free—to truly appropriate freedom through the rational ordering of human relations—but it also allows its opposite: the complete occlusion of man's deeper freedom through the unfettered empire of his merely sensual nature. It poses the choice, in other words, between mere choice, the endlessly varied satisfaction of man's endlessly variegated sensual nature, and a sacrifice of this to the imperative of reason.

His second major account of the problem of history involves a binary division between the new and the old world, with the appearance of Christ separating the former from the latter. This conception of history appears already in the ninth through sixteenth lectures of the *Fundamental Charac-teristics,* but is developed in greater depth in the 1813 *Doctrine of the State,* where Fichte altogether abandons the fivefold division and the impression that it gives of a continuity, emphasizing instead the opposition of tendencies and the ambiguity that is the crux of history; the crisis at its heart. Here there is no longer one history, but two histories, the one ancient and pagan, the other modern and Christian. These do not join up to each other in a single moment that marks the passage from one to another, but rather, the end of the first and the beginning of the second overlap without the period of overlapping appearing as its own age with its own autonomous epochal character. There is no transition between the two ages that would belong to a single overarching historical continuum, but only a radical transformation—a sudden and groundless leap—from one to the other.

This transformation happens with Christ. Through his teaching and his life, he announces to mankind the possibility that, at any moment, one could penetrate from death—from the tragic order of this world—into life, raising oneself above death by changing one's "essential fundamental property," becoming no longer the means to worldly ends, but the tool of the eternal will of God.[178]

Recalling Fichte's changing conceptions of history, we see that in many ways the *Closed Commercial State* stands closer to the *Doctrine of the State* than to the first chapters of the *Fundamental Characteristics of the*

Present Age. This suggests, in turn, that a principal source of Fichte's reflections on the problem of history is the *Closed Commercial State*, and that
the more strongly teleological language of the *Fundamental Characteristics*,
with its implications of a continuous path of transformation, is something
of an anomaly in his thought. It betrays a temporary influence of Schelling
and Schiller that later on, above all by restoring the central place of Christ
in history, he moves away from. While he continues to affirm the idea
that history has a certain *telos*, and while, in the beginning of the *Closed
Commercial State*, he claims that politics describes "the continuous path"
through which the given state will be transformed into the rational state,
nevertheless this "continuous path" begins with a decisive action taken at a
critical moment. The continuous movement toward the end of history is no
longer a natural law of its development. Rather, the continuity of progress is
constructed and imposed through an act of radical freedom that announces
itself in a moment of discontinuity.

Should we then suppose that a Christian eschatology takes the place
of economics, and that, in this way, the *Closed Commercial State* plays only a
transitional role in Fichte's thought? Two things argue against such a verdict.
First of all, as we already suggested, the problem of the political returns, with
full force, in the late period of his thought, not only in the 1812 *System of
the Doctrine of Right*, but also in the *Doctrine of the State* itself. Secondly, it
is not difficult to place the fragmentary discussions of history in the *Closed
Commercial State* within a wider eschatological context. That, at the very
least, the *Closed Commercial State* aims at more than merely a strong and
secure national state is evident in its closing words:

> The only thing that entirely eliminates all differences between
> peoples and their circumstances and that belongs merely and solely
> to the human being as such and not to the citizen, is science.
> Through science, and through this alone, men will and should
> continue to be connected to one another once their separation
> into peoples is, in every other respect, complete. This alone
> will remain their common possession when they have divided
> up everything else among themselves. No closed state will
> eliminate this connection. Instead it will encourage it, since the
> enrichment of science through the unified force of the human
> race will even advance the state's own isolated earthly ends.
> Academies financed by the state will introduce the treasures of
> foreign literature into the country, with the treasures of domestic
> literature offered in exchange.
>
> Once this system has become universal and eternal peace
> is established among the different peoples, there is not a single

state on the face of the earth that will have the slightest interest in keeping its discoveries from any other, since each will
only use these for its own needs inside its boundaries, and not
to oppress other states and provide itself with superiority over
them. Nothing, it follows, will prevent the scholars and artists
of all nations from entering into the freest communication with
one another. The public papers will no longer contain stories of
wars and battles, peace treaties or alliances, for all these things
will have vanished from the world. They will only contain news
of the progress of science, of new discoveries, of progress in
legislation and the police, and each state will hasten to make
itself home to the inventions of others.[179]

The complete closure of the national states, far from blocking historical
progress toward an eternal peace and cosmopolitan order, alone makes these
possible. Since it is only through science, conceived in a broad sense, that
human beings have commerce with one another purely as human beings, a
truly universal republic can only be built on the foundation of man's lesser
needs, and must not try to encompass these within it. This is the realm of
true history, which only becomes possible when the state has accomplished
its goals; when its political agenda is fulfilled. True history is, in this sense,
purely a history of the culture of reason: the perfection of the command of
reason over sensual nature, and thus ultimately, as becomes clear in Fichte's
later concepts of history, the sublimation of politics through morality. Economics, far from being replaced by Christian eschatology, is the site of its
realization.

It is now possible to bring together the different aspects of Fichte's
understanding of history in the *Closed Commercial State*. To begin with, we
find, at the center of all history, the time of the present. The present time
exists not as a simple unity, but only by way of its two contrary tendencies: the purely allegorical function of money qua sign, and the real needs
and desires of human life. For the most part, this present is experienced
through the ordinary, mediocre life that emerges in the middle between
these two tendencies. This life, which combines opinion and need, truth
and falsehood, in a grey blur, is woven through the intrigue of money as
it shuttles back and forth between extrinsic and intrinsic value, mediating
between the two through an endless series of exchanges. This ordinary
life includes not only the economic sphere of everyday life (where our life
and pleasure are obtained through the mediation of world currency), but
also all the half-measures of the state, and indeed the whole of political,
or rather pre-political, history born of these half-measures. This half-time
and half-life, moreover, is unbounded: it has no true origin in the past or

destination in the future, but, at most, gains a certain internal contour and texture through the half-measures of a politics unenlightened by reason—the intrigues and counterintrigues of half-closed states—and, going back even farther, the introduction of political and religious concepts from the outside. Even the catastrophe that Fichte describes in the second book of the *Closed Commercial State*, the return of human beings to a state of anarchy, entirely lacks an eschatological dimension. The dispersion of human populations, destroying the very conditions for any sort of historical movement, does not bring time to a close but merely precludes the time of history.

Here we must also recall, once again, that the history of the present time for Fichte has a specific ethnic character. It begins with, and is born of, the Germanic tribes. These originally have neither genuine political nor religious concepts: they only have freedom. Defined only by their lack of determination, lacking all individual qualities, they express, in completely unrealized form, the highest potentiality of mankind. Everything that gives a specific contour to their lives, allowing them to approximate a historical existence, comes from the outside, and indeed the internal history of the Germanic peoples begins only when another history, completely external to their own, collides with them.

This other history is, specifically, the tragic history of the ancient world—a history that begins with individual political states and ends with the fall of the Roman empire; the inner exhaustion of its political form. If the history of the ancient world is necessarily tragic in its structure, it is above all because it lacks the only thing that the Germans can call their own: freedom. As Fichte explains in the 1813 *Doctrine of the State*, the ancient state failed precisely because theoretical understanding was unable to become practical. What the ancient world, and the Romans in particular, lacked was the practical drive, the art drive (*Kunsttrieb*), the desire to form for the sake of forming.[180] Lacking freedom, even the apparent progress of the ancient world, culminating in the Roman empire, only made it ripe for its destruction.

The collision of the ancient world with the Germanic tribes brought political concepts to these, and also, through Christianity, true religion—an explicit and theoretical notion of freedom and of the unity of mankind.[181] In this way, it first allowed there to be a genuinely political history; a history that, beginning with the process of commercial closure, is itself closed and positively teleological, accomplishing itself in the creation of the rational state. This closure and accomplishment is itself, however, not the end of history, but its real beginning: the onset of a no longer political, but cultural history, which takes place through the formation of human nature itself—the self-formation of man in his species being. Indeed, this marks the transition from the political life to the life of contemplation.

Money is thus the crux of the history of the present—the point where its different tendencies (its different histories) cross. Through the transformation of money, its transubstantiation from gold to a yet unknown substance issuing forth from the secret chambers of the government, born not of nature but of human ingenuity, a new history is born; a history that is neither tragic, nor allegorical, but eschatological. The death and resurrection of value, its recreation in an entirely new substance, is, as it were, the political corollary of Christ's advent.[182] The philosophical politician could only follow Christ, doing as Jesus would do, by abolishing world currency. It is through this act that secular history becomes open to the possibility of the future announced through the life and death of the Messiah.

Moreover, money, as the crux of history, originates from within the state and its government, be it through the merely formal act of stamping, the exclusive privilege of the royal mint, or through the creation of a wholly new material. Thus, it marks the point where history crosses with sovereign power, and hence where the extreme possibilities of politics emerge: where the sovereign can either gain power over history, or become the servant of alien forces. Recalling our discussion of the dedication of the *Closed Commercial State* to Struensee, the Prussian minister of commerce and industry, we now see why, in sharp tension with Fichte's prior republican leanings, his rhetoric is aimed not so much at the public as at the secret chambers of the court. It is here alone, where the intrigues of history, money, the sovereign, and his ministers collide, that true political action—the creation of history—would be possible. And thus this alone is the proper target of those intrigues that the philosopher himself undertakes on behalf of truth.

The new money is indeed nothing less than the rebirth of the state: its passage from death into life. The existence of world currency, and the at once exploitative and chaotic relations that follow from this, brings history to a point of crisis. While this crisis imperils the realization of the true goals of mankind, it opens up a possibility. The money operation, which transforms money from world currency to national currency, destroying it as the one but bringing it back to life as the other, is at the same time the death and resurrection of the state. In Fichte's words:

> It is clear that in a nation that has been closed off in this way, with its members living only among themselves and as little as possible with strangers, obtaining their particular way of life, institutions, and morals from these measures and faithfully loving their fatherland and everything patriotic, there will soon arise a high degree of national honor and a sharply determined national character. It will become another, entirely new nation. The introduction of national currency is its true creation.[183]

Yet it is not just the death and resurrection of the state, but of human history. The money operation redeems history from allegory and creates a time that could be full and fulfilled. It is only with the money operation that a true history of rational, linear progress toward the realization of the highest ends of humanity could begin.

§15. Conclusions and Transitions

In the previous sections, I have traced out the argument of the *Closed Commercial State*, placing it within both the broader expanse of Fichte's writings and the Western tradition of political philosophy. In this way, I have tried to demonstrate the importance of this peripheral moment for his thought as a whole. The *Closed Commercial State*, I have argued, represents not merely, and indeed not principally, a positive contribution to economic theory, but rather the transition from the first phase of his systematic thought, dominated chiefly by the transcendental concerns of the *Doctrine of Science*, to the more deeply historical thinking of the second and third phases. It is indeed the *Closed Commercial State* that first opens onto not only the secularly historical, but the eschatological dimension of Fichte's thought, with both of these remaining, up to the end of his career, rooted in the problems of political economy. Money, precisely as the messenger between the ideal and real, is at the crux of history. It not only allows a subtle theorization of the latter, mediating between necessity and freedom, teleological closure and voluntaristic openness, but it also presents a moment of vulnerability, in which a radically transformative intervention in history is possible. Rather than reason demanding human freedom for the accomplishment of its teleological process, humans, through a completely unprecedented exertion of will, call forth a new history—a history in which closure, and the dominion of reason over nature, is possible. This act or operation, moreover, is not exhaustively justified through rational grounds. Instead, it responds to obscure feelings, and acts toward a vision of the future that is not the secure possession of reason, but only the dark descrying of a reality and a new manner of truth that can become possible through a new manner of political action. Even the *Doctrine of Science*, the center and starting point of Fichte's system, may, with its many revisions and conceptual fluidity, be conceived as an attempt not so much to give a final form to philosophy, but rather to envision and affirm the possibility of free praxis; of actions that escape the ring of determinism. Thinking itself belongs within a *praxis* that attempts to lay the foundation, in the present, for the future advent of a new mode of being that is not given to reason with certainty, but only glimpsed through an attitude of wonder amid the nexus of becoming.

While I have tried throughout to show that the *Closed Commercial State* should not be read simply as an economic treatise, it would not be useless to attempt a cursory comparison of the *Closed Commercial State* with classical and Marxist economic thought. With regard to the former, we may say, to begin with, that despite the many weaknesses in Fichte's account of economic relations, his definition of property as free action represents a decisive theoretical advance over the physiocrats and Adam Smith. For while the latter assign labor a role in the construction of value and contest the gold and silver fetish of mercantilism, they do not try to develop their economic notions consistently from an anthropology of man as an active being. Even if we may question the idealist presuppositions of Fichte's account, it seems no more possible to return to the simple identification of property with a thing than to wholeheartedly embrace a dogmatic empiricism. That the dominant tradition of economic thought has nevertheless failed to make this theoretical leap suggests its philosophical groundlessness. It provides a theory of the production and distribution of value without referring this back to a consistent account of the nature of property itself. Rather, it simply assumes that property (the appropriation of value) exists. I would even suggest, somewhat more speculatively, that the *Closed Commercial State* anticipates the attempts of Hannah Arendt, Michel Foucault, and Giorgio Agamben to critique the conceptual foundations of political economy. Fichte recognizes the critical importance of the economy, and yet he seeks to order economic relations in a way that supports a fully human form of life rather than mere survival, merely biological existence. Man is a *homo laborans*, but not only this, and it is above all Fichte's subtle anthropology, based on the primacy of human activity, that keeps human life from collapsing into merely bare life. The *Closed Commercial State*, in this way, is a sort of proleptic response to the rise of biopolitics.

Nevertheless, Fichte's rigorous way of conceiving of property in the *Closed Commercial State* is bought at the price of even the most rudimentary understanding of the function of fixed capital. In order to maintain the liberal notion of a right to property (of property as a right) without validating the right to past possessions, Fichte identifies property not only with human activity but with *present*, actually *realized* activity. While this allows him to deny the general legitimacy of past and inherited possessions, it also makes it impossible for him either to recognize the existence of fixed capital as a concrete, determinate accumulation of past activity, or acknowledge its role in production. Thus, his critique of trade anarchy is one-sided, only addressing mercantilist policies of hoarding, without taking account of either the economic growth or instability that results from capitalist accumulation. Significantly, in Fichte's later economic writings, he tries to integrate both investment capital and the employment of unattached laborers into his theory. The somewhat unsatisfactory result is the integration of capitalism into centralized economic planning, with the utilization of surplus capital and labor a function of government rather than private individuals.

This suggests a natural transition from Fichte to Marx. If the latter's account of the alienation of labor and the commodity fetish, despite all lack of concrete influence, echoes Fichte's critique of the traditional concept of property, Marx nevertheless attempts, through his theory of surplus value and economic crisis, to integrate the productive function of capital into his critique of political economy. Whereas for Fichte, the crux of history is the tension between immediate activity, its simple representation in money, and the hyperbolic, speculative order of pure opinion, Marx, in conceiving the class struggle of the proletariat and the bourgeoisie, stresses the conflict between actual labor and its alienation and layered accumulation.

There is perhaps another way, though, that we may conceive of Fichte's project—not in relation to political economy but to the broader tradition of political philosophy. What Fichte sought, first of all, was to restore the Platonic and Aristotelian ideal of the self-sufficiency of the state. While, in one sense, this project is clearly reactionary, opposed to the tendency of his times, Fichte nevertheless hoped not to turn back time, but rather to rescue what he saw as the true meaning and value of the modern age: human freedom. Only the juridical and commercial closure of the state could guarantee the possibility of a truly free and human existence, since only this could fulfill the liberalistic need to protect the individual from the incursions into his freedom by wills not under his power.

This in turn suggests the complexity of the relation of the *Closed Commercial State* to the question of globalism.[184] It is perhaps wrong to regard Fichte's economic theory as the advance guard of the defense of a narrow regionalism and nationalism. On the one hand, the question of globalism is, for Fichte, entirely subordinate to the question of the rationality of commercial relations. Since the juridical closure of the state is impossible apart from economic closure, the sphere of economic relations must coincide with the sphere of juridical relations. He does not reject a global economy under any conditions, but only in the present state of affairs. Nor is it even clear that the actual tendency of history is not in fact toward more, rather than less, national control of the economy. At the very least, history seems ambiguous in this regard. If, on the one hand, recent years have seen the increasing importance of transnational entities and globalization of capital flow, from a broader perspective this looks slightly different. Not only has national currency been universally implemented in the years after the publication of the *Closed Commercial State*, but the first half of the twentieth century indeed saw the worldwide abolition of the gold standard (the pegging of paper money) and the widespread utilization of so-called fiat money: money produced at the will of the state.[185] Similarly, there is probably far more, rather than less state involvement in capitalism throughout the industrialized world than before, and even the most liberalistically inclined democracies seldom act without considering the implications for the economic welfare of their citizens, or at least invoking these considerations in their rhetoric. Moreover, if it was perhaps once possible to suggest, as did Toni Negri and Michael Hardt in *Empire*, that political power was no longer centered around national sovereignty, the events following the millennial turn have proved this claim to be premature.

On the other hand, there are also many factors operative in the modern world that would force one, applying the very reasoning of the *Closed Commercial State*, to reject national sovereignty in both juridical and economic matters. Global environmental and health problems, in particular, involve a threat to the rights of individuals that can no longer be controlled by national entities acting alone in the interests of themselves and their citizens. One may even argue that many of the cases where national sovereignty is compromised in favor of transnational, nongovernmental organizations fall within these categories, and thus confirm, rather than contradict, Fichte's understanding of history.

Furthermore, there is a sense in which, for Fichte, globalism could never be a valid name for the anarchic conditions of trade with which, in his view, modern history begins. The simplest geometric characteristic of the globe, after all, is its closure; the fact that a straight line described on its surface runs back on itself. Anarchic trade, in contrast, is not global but infinite and essentially linear, if errant, in its movement: money, a perpetual nomad, is always opening out onto new frontiers. Even if the space of the earth is itself exhaustively bound together with networks of trade, the future remains as the frontier of speculation. True globalism, in turn, could only be achieved through closure; the actions of individuals, rather than opening out into the frontier and limit of what is known, must be reflected back into themselves. All must form a single sphere of activity, divided up among individuals through the law, with each recognizing the individual sphere of all the others. If Fichte rejects apparently global relations of trade and commerce, and even foreign travel for the sake of mere tourism, it is only because he sees this rejection as necessary to advance the cosmopolitan ideal of a community of states. The true community of states, and the truly global commerce of individuals, can only occur in the sphere of science and fine art, where there is no possibility of self-gain or exploitation.

Yet even if we cannot credence reading Fichte's economic and political theory as a proto-nationalist attempt to check the forces of globalization, there remains a sense in which the *Closed Commercial State* remains limited in its horizon. Not only does the insistence on the Greek ideal of self-sufficiency preclude a political relation to radical alterity, but politics itself is conceived of as the dominance of nature by human will. In this way, it stands in sharp contrast to the understanding of politics that Hölderlin would develop in response to Fichte in the latter half of the last decade of the eighteenth century. Here reason is not the lord of nature, but its offspring. The aim of politics—or, better, the politics proper to the modern age—is not to dominate and subdue nature, but comply with its gesture: the movement between the becoming and passing away of historical forms of life. For Hölderlin no less than for Fichte, political action choreographs an openness to a certain kind of truth. Yet whereas for the latter, this truth is the unity of reason—a truth that must express itself in the organization of the sensible world—for the former, in contrast, it is a process of natural becoming that originates in, and retains a relation to, chaos. Nature, as it were, offers a horizon of truth beyond rationality. Although in the later stages of his thought Fichte comes closer to Hölderlin by affirming leisure, boredom, and wonder as the aim of economic life, he situates the experience of wonder, and of the insecurity of life, not within, but beyond, economic relations themselves.

The Closed Commercial State

A philosophical sketch offered as an appendix
to the Doctrine of Right and as a test
of a politics to be delivered in the future

Table of Contents

Preliminary clarification of the title

A closed multitude of men, standing under the same laws and the same supreme power of coercion, forms the juridical state. This multitude of men should now be restricted to reciprocal trade and industry with and for one another, and everyone who does not stand under the same legislation and power of coercion should be excluded from participating in this commerce. The multitude would then form a *commercial state*, and indeed a *closed* commercial state, just as it now forms a closed juridical state.

{389} [39]

To his Excellency the Royal Prussian Acting Privy-Minister
of State and Knight of the Order of the Red Eagle Herr von Struensee.[1]

from the author

Dedicatory Remarks

[41] Your excellency,

Please allow me, following the custom especially of the dedication writers of past ages, to lay down before *you* my thoughts concerning the purpose and probable result of a writing that I hereby dedicate [*zueignen*] to *you* publicly as a memorial of my free veneration. In the beginning of his edition of Polybius, *Casaubon* talks quite uninhibitedly with *Henry IV* about the study of the ancients and the usual prejudices regarding this study.[2] May *your Excellency* permit me to talk just as uninhibitedly with you, in front of the public, about the nature of the relation of the speculative to the practicing politician.

The latter have at all times granted to the former the right to present their thoughts concerning the institution and administration of states, and yet they have not otherwise paid much attention to these thoughts, never taking serious notice of such Platonic republics and their utopian constitutions. One may even grant the reproach that has always been made to the speculative politicians' prescriptions, namely that it is impossible to {390} *immediately* carry them out. Even this reproach need not dishonor the originators of these prescriptions, as long as they remain with their proposals in an ideal world, either confessing this explicitly or proving it through their deeds. As certain as there is order, consequence, and determinateness in the thoughts of the speculative politicians, it is equally certain that these prescriptions, in the form set forth, apply only to the state of affairs presupposed and contrived by their authors, who hope to present the universal rule through this as if through a mathematical problem. It is not this presupposed state of affairs that the practicing politician finds before himself, but a wholly different state of affairs. It is no wonder that a prescription will not suit a state of affairs that, in the form set forth, it did not take into account. [42]

Nevertheless, the philosopher, so long as he holds his science to be not a mere game but something serious, will never either grant or presuppose that it is *absolutely* impossible to carry out his proposals. For in this case, he would without doubt employ his time toward something more useful than what is, by his own account, a mere play of concepts. He will assert that his prescriptions, if set forth at a *purely theoretical level*, are indeed incapable of being immediately carried out, and for the very reason that, in their highest generality, they suit *everything* and thus *nothing determinate*. Yet he will maintain that they *simply require further determination* if they are to fit an actually given state of affairs. In just the same way: through our knowledge of the universal ratios of the sides and angles of a triangle to one another we do not yet know any single actual side or angle within a field. We must always still actually apply a standard measure and protractor to some piece of land and measure it with these. Yet having done this, we will be put in a position to figure out the rest by *mere calculation* using our knowledge of the universal ratios, without actually having to apply the standard measure.

The further determination of the universal rule set forth by pure Right of state occurs, in my opinion, in the science, whose concept I will determine in what follows, {391} that I call *politics*, holding it also to be the business of the speculative philosopher *as such* (for it follows automatically that the practicing politician could at the same time be a speculative philosopher, and perhaps even the reverse relation can take place). If a writing is advertised as political, then the reproach and the proof that its proposals are impossible to carry out would be a greater cause for dishonor than if the work were merely concerned with Right of state. In my opinion, indeed, even politics, so certain as it is a science and not however itself praxis, does not take its departure from a state that actually exists and is thoroughly determined in its every aspect—since then there would not be a universal politics, but only a particular politics for, say, England or France or Prussia, or indeed for one of these states in the year 1800, indeed in the autumn of the year 1800, and so forth. Rather, politics takes its departure from the state of affairs that is, say, common to all the states of the great European republic during the age when it is set forth. The practicing politician must still always apply to the particular case a rule that still remains in a certain regard universal, and that must be applied a bit differently to *each* particular case. Yet this universal rule nevertheless lies far closer to its application.

If a politics were carefully worked out according to this idea, and, informed by a correct knowledge of the present situation and starting out from solid principles of the Right of state, correctly drew the consequences [43] from these, this politics could, in my opinion, only seem useless to the mere empiricist, who trusts no concept or calculation, but only the confirmation of immediate experience. He would reproach it for not containing facts, but only concepts and calculations of facts, or, in a word, for not being history. Such a politician keeps stowed away in his memory a number of individual cases and the successful measures that others before him took. Whatever confronts him, he will think of one of these cases and proceed like one of the politicians before him, whom he awakens from the grave one after the other, presents again in his own age, {392} and thus composes his political career from the very different pieces of very different men, without adding anything of himself. Let us merely ask such a politician: those who were the first to use the measures that he now approves and imitates—whom did they imitate? What did they rely on as they seized on these measures? Previous experience or calculation? Let us remind him that everything that is now old was once new, nor is it possible that the human race has fallen so far in latter times as to be left only with memory and the ability to imitate. We will show him that through the progress of the human race, which occurred without his doing and which he can do nothing to keep in check, a great deal has changed, making necessary entirely new measures—measures that previous ages could neither devise nor implement. It might be instructive, faced with such a politician, to conduct a historical investigation into the question whether more evil has arisen in the world through daring innovations or through a sluggish adherence to outdated measures that are either no longer able to be implemented, or are no longer adequate.

Does the present writing meet the aforementioned requirements for a thorough treatment of politics? On this point the author dare not speak. With regard to its actual proposal to close the commercial state along with the juridical state, and the decisive means it proposes to this end—the abolition of *world currency* and the introduction of a *national currency*—the author certainly foresees that no state would *want to* accept this proposal unless it *must,* even though in the latter case it will not benefit from the promised advantages of these measures. Thus he also realizes that it would not be possible to firmly resolve to do what has been proposed. Since, moreover, an action that one cannot resolve on doing won't be carried out, it will therefore be deemed *impossible to carry out.* [44] The reason for this unwillingness, be it thought through clearly or be it not, is that Europe has a great advantage in trade over the remaining parts of the world, whose forces and products {393} it takes for its own use without giving anywhere near a sufficient return payment. Every single European state, however unfavorable its own trade balance stands in relation to the others, still draws some advantage from this common exploitation of the rest of the world, nor will it ever abandon the hope of improving the trade balance in its favor and thus drawing an even greater advantage. With its departure from the greater European commercial society it would have to renounce all this. If we are to remove the reason for this unwillingness, we must show that a relation like that which Europe has to the rest of the world—a relation grounded neither in Right nor in fairness—cannot possibly continue. The proof of this lies beyond the limits of my present intention. But even if this were proved, one could still always say to me: "This relation at least continues up till now: the colonies remain submissive to the motherlands, and there is still a slave trade. Nor will we live to see the day when all this shall cease. Let us then take advantage of this for as long as it continues, leaving it to the generations that are around when it finally comes to an end to figure out for themselves how they will cope. They can investigate, if need be, whether they can take something useful from your thoughts. We, who can't even wish for the same end as you, scarcely need instruction on the means to bring it about."—I confess I have no answer to this.

The author is content that this sketch might also remain a mere school-exercise, without result in the actual world—a link in the chain of his system, a system that is to be gradually realized [ausführen].[3] And he will be satisfied if, by making it known to others, he should do nothing more than induce them to reflect more deeply about these matters and perhaps strike upon one or another invention that will be both useful in and applicable to a sphere from which, as things stand, one will not wish to leave. And so the author limits himself explicitly and with careful consideration to these ends.

{394} May your Excellency be so gracious as to accept my assurance of the veneration I owe you both as one of the principal state officials of the monarchy where I found a refuge when I could not hope for refuge in the remaining parts of my German fatherland, [45] and as that man whose personal qualities it was granted me to observe and to venerate.

Berlin, the 31ˢᵗ of October, 1800

Introduction

On the relation of the rational state to the actual state, and of pure Right of state to politics

Pure Right of state lets the rational state arise under its eyes according to the concepts of Right, by presupposing men to be without any of the relations that, resembling rightful relations, had previously existed.

Yet we never find men in this state of existence. In every quarter they are already living together under constitutions that, for the most part, arose not according to concepts and through art, but rather through chance or providence.[4]

The actual state finds them in this latter state of existence. It cannot suddenly destroy this constitution without dispersing the men and turning them into savages, thus nullifying its true purpose of building a rational state from them. It can do no more than gradually approximate itself to the rational state. It follows that we may represent the actual state as in the process of gradually instituting the rational state.

With the actual state, the question is not merely, as with a rational state, what is *right*, but: how much of what is right *can be carried out* under the given conditions? If we give the name of *politics* to the science of government of the actual {398} state according to the maxim just indicated, this politics would then lie halfway between the given state and the rational state: it would describe the continuous path [*Linie*] through which the former changes into the latter, and will itself terminate in pure Right of state.

Whoever undertakes to show the particular laws under which to bring the public commerce in the state would thus first have to investigate what is right in a rational state with regard to commerce. Then he must indicate the custom of the existing actual state in this regard. And finally he must show the path by which the state can pass over from the latter state of existence to the former.

I need not defend the fact that I speak of a science and art that will gradually bring about the rational state. All the good things of which man should partake must be produced by his own art, guided by science. This is man's vocation [*Bestimmung*]. Nature gives him nothing in advance, save the possibility of applying art. In government as elsewhere, we must subsume everything under concepts that lets itself be subsumed under them, and stop abandoning anything that should be calculated to blind chance in the hope that blind chance will make it turn out well. [52]

FIRST BOOK

Philosophy—what is Right with respect to commerce in the rational state

First Chapter

Principles for answering this question

A false proposition is usually suppressed by a contrary proposition that is equally false. It is not until quite late that one discovers the truth lying in the middle. This is the fate of science.

The opinion that the state is the absolute [*unumschränkt*] guardian of humanity in all its affairs, making it happy, rich, healthy, orthodox, virtuous, and, if God so wills, even eternally blessed, has been sufficiently refuted in our day. Yet it seems to me that in turn, coming from the opposite side, one has too narrowly limited the duties and rights of the state. It is indeed not exactly incorrect, and could be given some good sense, were one to say that the state has to do no more than preserve and protect each in his personal rights and his property—as long as one did not often seem to silently presuppose that property could take place independently of the state; that the state only has a view to the state of possession in which it first finds its citizens, without having to inquire into the rightful basis of acquisition. In opposition to this opinion, I would say: it is the vocation of the state to first *give* each what is his, to first *put* each *in possession* of his property, and only then to *protect* him in this. I will make myself clearer by returning to first principles. {400}

1.

A crowd of men live together within the same circle of efficacy.[5] Each one stirs and moves about within this circle, freely pursuing his nourishment and pleasure. One of them crosses the path of the other, tears down [54] what the other had built, and either destroys or uses for himself what the other was counting on. The other, from his side, does the same; and so each acts

91

toward each. One should not speak here of morality, fairness, and the like, since we are standing in the domain of the doctrine of Right. Nor however does the concept of Right let itself be applied in the circumstances we have just described. Obviously, the soil that has been trod upon, the tree that was robbed of its fruit, will not enter into a conflict over rights with the man who did these deeds. But even if another man were to do so, what reason could he offer why everyone else should not tread on the same soil, or take fruit from the same tree, as he himself?

In this state of existence, no one is free, since all are free without limitation. No one can carry out anything in a purposeful fashion and count for a moment on it lasting. The only remedy for this conflict of free forces is for the individuals to *negotiate treaties* among themselves. One of them must say to the other: it harms me when you do this. And the other must answer him: it harms me, on the other hand, when you do this. The first must declare: then I'll desist from the things that are harmful to *you* on the condition that you desist from the things that are harmful to me. And the second, from his side, must make the same declaration, and from now on both must keep their word. For the very first time now each has something that is *proper* to him, that is his *own*, belonging to him alone, and in no way to anyone else; a right, and an exclusive right.

Property, rights to determinate things, prior rights, and exclusive rights arise solely from the treaty that was described. Originally all have the same right to everything, which means that no one's right takes precedence {401} over the right of anyone else. Something only becomes my property when, in accordance with my desire to keep it for myself, everyone else renounces their claim to it. This act of renunciation by the others, and this alone, is the basis of my right.

It is the state alone that unites an indeterminate multitude of men into a *closed whole*, a *totality*; only the state can go around asking questions to everyone whom it receives into its alliance, and thus only through the state would it be possible to provide a basis for a rightfully existing property. As the state becomes acquainted with the rest of the men occupying the earth's surface, it will negotiate treaties with these, as a state, in the name of all its citizens. Outside of a state, I will certainly preserve, through my treaty with my closest neighbor, a property right *against him*, just as he would likewise have a property right *against me*. But if some third person were to come along, he would not be bound by our negotiations. He would keep just as much right as before to all that which we, *between ourselves*, call ours. Just as much right, that is to say, as we have.

I have described the right to property as an exclusive right to [55] *acts*, not to *things*. So it is. So long as all remain quiet in their neighbors' midst, they will not come into conflict; it is only when they first bestir themselves

and move about and create that they collide against one another. Free activity is the seat of the conflict of forces. Hence, it is free activity that is the
true object [Gegenstand] concerning which the conflicting parties negotiate
treaties. In no way are things the object of the treaty. The ownership of the
object of a free act first issues and is derived from the exclusive right to a
free act. I will not weary myself pondering how I could maintain the *ideal
possession* of this tree if no one who approaches lays his hand on it and it
stands to me alone to pick its fruit at whatever time pleases me. For then
without doubt it will be me, and me alone, who picks its fruit and enjoys
them, and this is all I care about.

Treating the task in this way saves us from {402} a multitude of useless
subtleties, and we are sure to exhaustively cover all forms of property under
a thoroughly comprehensive concept.

2.

The sphere of free acts, therefore, will be divided up among the individuals
through a treaty of all with all, and this division will give rise to property.

Yet how must this division be made if it is to accord with the law of
Right? Or is it enough simply to divide things up, however this division
may turn out? We shall see.

The purpose of all human activity is to be able to live. All those
whom nature has put to life have the same rightful claim to this possibility of life. Therefore, the division must first of all allow everyone to exist.
Live and let live!

Everyone wishes to live as pleasantly as is possible. Since everyone
demands this as a human being, and no one is more or less human than
anyone else, everyone has an equal right in [making] this demand. In
accordance with this equality of their rights, the division must be made
in such a way that one and all can live as pleasantly as is possible when
so many men as they are exist next to one another in the given sphere
of efficacy. Each, in other words, must be able to live about as pleasantly
as the other. I say: be able to, and not have to. Should someone live less
pleasantly than he is able, the reason for this must lie with him alone and
not with anyone else. [56]

Let one posit, as the first of two magnitudes, a determinate sum of
potential activity within a certain sphere of efficacy. The value of this magnitude is the pleasantness of life resulting from this activity. Let one posit,
as the second magnitude, a determinate number of individuals. If you divide
the value of the first magnitude in equal parts among the individuals, you
will discover what each should receive *under the given circumstances*. Were

the first sum larger or the second {403} smaller, each would of course receive a greater part. Yet you are able to change neither the one nor the other; your sole concern is that *what is available* be divided equally among all.

The part that comes to each is *his* by Right. He should receive it even if it has perhaps not yet been granted to him. In the rational state, he will receive it. Yet in the division made by chance and violence [*Gewalt*], before the awakening and dominion of reason, not everyone received it, as indeed some took more than their part. The aim of the actual state approximating itself to reason through art must be to gradually help each to what is *his* in the sense just indicated. This is what was meant when I previously said: it is the vocation of the state to give each what is *his*.

Second Chapter

General application to public commerce of the principles set forth

1.

There are two chief branches of activity through which man preserves his life and makes it pleasant: extracting the products of nature, and then further laboring on these with a view to the final purpose that one posits for oneself with them. The chief division of free activity would therefore involve the division into these two main occupations. A certain number of men who have become an *estate* through their separation from others would receive the exclusive right to extract the products of nature, and a second estate will gain the exclusive right to perform further labor on this produce with a view toward recognized human purposes.

The treaty between these two chief estates would be as follows. The latter [57] estate promises not to undertake any act that aims at extracting raw produce, and also, as {404} follows from this, to refrain from any act directed toward an object exclusively devoted to extracting produce. The former, in return, promises to refrain entirely from performing any further labor on this produce once nature has brought its work to a close.

Yet in this treaty the estate of the *producers* clearly has the advantage over the *artisans* (for the sake of brevity, I shall refer in this treatise to the two chief estates by these general names). Whoever is in exclusive possession of the products of nature can at least live in a tolerable manner without the help of others. He can hardly be forbidden the slight labors that this produce still needs in order to provide nourishment and meager shelter, since it would hardly be possible to supervise him in this regard. The artisan, in contrast, cannot do without this produce, needing it partly for his nourishment and partly as raw material for the further labors that have been granted exclusively to him to perform. The artisan's ultimate purpose, moreover, is not merely to work but to be able to *live* from his work, and if he has not been assured the latter by means of the former, he has in fact been assured nothing. It clearly follows then that if our intended division is to be in accordance with Right, we must supplement this merely negative treaty, which only promises the avoidance of every disruption [of the other's labor], with a positive treaty—a treaty promising the reciprocal provision of services. Its content is as follows:

The producers oblige themselves [sich verbinden] to extract enough produce to feed not only themselves but also all the artisans who are known to exist within their state federation [Staatsbund], and enough, moreover, that the latter have raw material to work on. In addition, they oblige themselves to leave this produce with the artisans in exchange for the goods the artisans have manufactured, following the standard that the artisans should be able to live just as pleasantly while manufacturing the goods as the producers were able to live while extracting the produce.

The artisans oblige themselves, in return, to deliver to the produc-ers as many manufactured goods as they are accustomed {405} to having, following the indicated standard [for the determination] of the price, and of the degree of quality [Güte] that is possible within the given sphere of efficacy of this state.

Thus, an exchange—first of produce for manufactured goods and of manufactured goods for produce—is negotiated, and indeed an obligatory exchange. It is not merely that one *may* exchange and deliver these goods, but that one *must*.

Lest the producers and artisans be disturbed in their labors by trav-eling about and searching around for [58] the goods that they now need, negotiating the conditions of exchange and other such matters, thus giving rise to a loss of both time and force, it would serve our purposes to have a third estate intercede between these two, taking care of the bartering on their behalf. This is the estate of *merchants*, with which the first two estates will conclude the following treaties. The first is negative: the producers and artisans agree to renounce all direct trade between themselves, and in return the merchant, like the artisan, agrees to renounce directly extracting produce, and, like the producer, directly laboring on it.

Then a positive treaty: both estates promise to deliver to the mer-chant whatever produce and manufactured goods are superfluous for their own needs, and to take from him in return what they require, following the standard rule that, beyond the basic price that we determined above, the merchant will be left with enough produce and manufactured goods to allow him to live as pleasantly as the producer and artisan while he is taking care of the trade. The merchant, in return, promises both to supply at all times the customary needs of the people, determined by the standard rule we just discussed, and obliges himself to accept at all times all the customary articles of exchange at the basic price that was previously determined.

The three estates we have presented are the fundamental constituent parts of the nation. Here I am only concerned with the reciprocal relation of these fundamental constituent parts. The members of the government, as well as the estate of teachers and guardians, exist only {406} for the sake of these first three estates, and will not be included in the calculation. We will supply in the due place whatever must be said about such matters as their relation to commerce.

2.

I have said enough to be able to follow out the solution of my task—a solution that, at any rate, draws exclusively on what was already said. If only to avoid having it seem as though I have passed over things relevant to the matter at hand, leaving the reader to secretly suspect that one could discover arguments in what was passed over against the assertions I have set forth, I will carry the reasoning that I began a few steps further, while nevertheless explicitly reminding the reader that, strictly speaking, it does not serve my purpose to continue in this fashion. The producers, which up till now I have considered as one unitary and fundamental estate, in turn divide into several sub-estates: [59] the agriculturalist in the proper sense, the vegetable, fruit, and flower-gardener, the animal-husbander, the fisherman, and so forth. Their exclusive rights are founded on treaties just like those of the fundamental estates. "If you refrain from this branch of produce-extraction, I'll refrain from that branch. Promise to supply me with what you grow, and let me firmly count on this. In return I'll supply you with what is mine, and you'll be able to count on me." Since these sub-estates should not each be required to win from the earth every kind of produce, an obligatory exchange of produce for produce is now also negotiated. What follows from this for the estate of merchants is self-evident.

Each of these sub-estates, moreover, consists of individuals, and the rightful relation between these individuals is also founded on treaties. "You have been granted by the rest of the citizens, at any rate, the right to till the fields wherever you come. And this same right has also been granted to me," one agriculturalist will say to another, "but if we should meet upon the same soil, you will sow land that I have already sown, and another time I might do the same to you, and neither of us {407} will grow anything. So please leave me this piece of land to labor on—and may I never find you there!—and in return I will leave you that piece of land over there as your own, never treading on it. If you never cross over this common boundary from your side to mine, I will never cross over from my side to yours." These will be in agreement with themselves and with all the others who have also been granted the right to pursue agriculture, and this negotiating of treaties, common to all, is the rightful basis of their property—a property that consists merely in the right and the entitlement to win the fruit from this piece of land following their own insight and judgment [Ermessen] without being disturbed by anyone else.

The fundamental estate of the artisans divides into several sub-estates, and the exclusive right of one such guild to pursue a particular branch of art is founded on treaties with the other guilds. "If you renounce the practice of this branch of art, we will in return renounce the practice of another. Give us what we need of the goods that you manufacture, and you can count on receiving from us what you need of ours." An obligatory exchange of manufactured goods for manufactured goods is now also agreed on, and as a consequence the determination of the estate of merchants receives a new modification.

It is no different with the guilds among which the estate of merchants has distributed the warrant to pursue the trade in specific articles, and it would be wearying to say a third time what I have already said twice.

I will return now to what I intended to show.—All these treaties [60]—and for my intentions, indeed, it will suffice to consider only the above treaty between the three fundamental estates—provide an external justification for the expressly stated law of the state, and the government must make sure that they are observed.

It must put itself in a position to be able to do so. The question: What must the government {408} do with regard to public commerce? means the same as the following: What must it do to make sure that the treaties set forth above are observed?

First of all: the estate of producers should oblige itself to extract as much produce as is necessary not only for its own needs, but for the nourishment of the rest of the citizens and for the customary manufacture. It must be able to do this, and therefore more nonproducers must not be employed in a state than can be fed by its produce. The state will have to calculate the number of citizens that may exempt themselves from agriculture according to the number of producers, the fertility of the soil, and the present state of agriculture. Suppose, for example, that a producer in this state were able, through the labor expected of him, to gain nourishment for two people and about enough raw material for the labor of one. Such a state could count on having one nonproducer for every producer, meaning, to begin with, an artisan, merchant, member of the government or of the estate of teachers or guardians. Following this standard rule, this number will be lesser or greater under different conditions.—The extraction of produce is the foundation of the state. It is the highest measure toward which everything else is directed. If it stands under unfavorable natural influences, or if its art remains in its infancy, the state can permit itself only a few artisans. It is only when nature becomes milder, and agriculture—the first among the arts—progresses, that the other arts may grow and be encouraged.

The first clear consequence for the state is that it must limit to a set number the overall number of those who may devote themselves to the arts according to the standard rule just given, and never allow this number to be exceeded *as long as the circumstances remain the same.*

Things that can be dispensed with should always be ranked behind things that are either absolutely impossible or difficult to do without. And so it is in the great economy of the state. Those hands that can be withdrawn from agriculture and devoted to the arts must be directed, first of all, toward indispensable labors. Only as many hands as then remain may be directed toward the manufacture of goods that can be dispensed with, satisfying the need {409} for luxury. This would therefore be the second clear consequence for the state: it must not only determine the overall size of the estate of artisans [61], but also the number of those who devote themselves to each particular branch of art, always first taking care of bare necessities. Let all be sated and dwell securely before someone decorates his dwelling. Let all be comfortably and warmly clothed before anyone dresses himself sumptuously. A state where agricultural techniques have not advanced far and require many hands for their perfect application [*Vervollkommnung*], and that lacks even ordinary mechanical craftsmen, cannot enjoy any luxury. It does not matter if someone says: "But I can pay for it." It would not be right if someone could pay for something he can do without while his fellow citizen finds that goods that are absolutely necessary are either unavailable or unaffordable. And moreover, what the former would use to pay for these goods is not even, by Right and in a rational state, his own.

It is easy to see how the government could ensure and keep watch that the set number of artisans is not exceeded. Everyone in the already existing state who intends on devoting himself exclusively to any sort of occupation will, without exception, be required by Right to register with the government. As the representative of all and in the name of all, the government will issue the exclusive title of right to him and renounce whatever must be renounced on everyone's behalf. If someone wishes to register for a branch of art that is already occupied with the maximum number of workers permitted by law, he will not be issued the title of right, but will be informed of other branches where his help is needed.

3.

Here I shall pass over *that* point of the treaty that concerns the cost of manufactured goods, since farther down I will address the question of the value of things in general terms.

The estate of artisans, according to the above, obliges itself to deliver those manufactured goods permitted under the given circumstances of the nation, {410} in the requisite quantity and the degree of quality possible in this country. The state must provide a guarantee to the producer and all the rest of the citizens regarding this point of the treaty as well. What must it do for this to be possible for it?

First of all, in order that the manufactured goods are always available in the requisite quantity, the state must make sure that, just as, following what we said above, the number of workers determined for each of the branches of art that have been introduced, and the overall number of artisans derived from this number, should not increase, it also does not decrease. The balance must be continually preserved. If at some time there is reason to fear a shortage of workers in a certain area, we clearly cannot encourage citizens [62] to devote themselves to this branch by allowing its members to raise the price of the goods they have manufactured and thus cheat the other classes of people. Practically the only means of encouragement that remains is to pay premiums from the state treasury until the required num‑ ber of citizens—or, if need be, a few beyond this number, whose goods the state could then purchase in advance to prepare for the shortages feared in the future—have applied themselves to this branch of labor. Once these new workers have learned this trade rather than some other, they would be compelled from now on to practice it, protecting the state against such shortages for at least one generation.

Furthermore, to ensure that the manufactured goods are delivered in the highest possible degree of perfection, the state must have everyone who announces his intention to practice a certain branch of labor be examined by those who understand the art in question. If someone's work is not at least as good as that of his fellow artisans in the country, he will be forbidden the public practice of his art until he has learned it better and is able to pass a second examination. I have restricted what the residents may demand to the degree of perfection of manufactured goods *possible in their country*, with this possibility judged according to the best of the work that has actually been delivered domestically. I {411} hope that the fairness of this restriction, and this manner of judging, should be self-evident to everyone. Why shouldn't the goods I receive be as perfect as those manu‑ factured in some other country?—To ask this is like asking: "Why aren't I the resident of a different country?" And this means about as much as if the oak should ask, Why aren't I a palm-tree? or vice versa. Everyone must be content with the sphere in which nature has put him, and with all that follows from this sphere.

4.

Let us now proceed to the third chief estate of the nation, the estate of trad-ers. Just as the number of artisans in the state who can be granted the right to practice depended on the number of producers and the present state of the extraction of produce, the number of merchants depends on the number of members of both estates and their relation to one another. It is to be determined according to the quantity of goods found in circulation within the nation, and therefore, firstly, according to the general state of art, and secondly, according to the division of the arts into a number of branches, as well as the division of the extraction of produce into a number of indus-tries. As regards the first [of these factors], the further that the arts have advanced, the greater the number of their branches and, as a consequence, the greater the number of manufactured goods and the more produce—as nourishment and as raw material for the artisans—will have to be provided *as goods*. [63] As for the second [factor], one only barters for those things that one does not oneself produce or manufacture. It follows that, given the same quantity of goods, there will be more *exchange* the greater the *division* of general production and manufacture. The government therefore has to calculate the amount of exchange taking place in the nation as well as the quantity of hands it will occupy, both overall and in each of the different branches of trade, in case such a division is found to be necessary. Accordingly, it must limit the *estate of traders* to a certain number of people that this estate should neither exceed nor sink below. The means that the government has available in the case of every estate {412} to keep to this closed number have already been indicated in the case of the artisans, and, as should be self-evident, apply just as well to merchants.

Of greater importance is the positive treaty concluded between the estate of traders and the remaining estates. The latter renounce all direct trade among themselves, promising to sell whatever goods have been determined for public exchange only to, and purchase needed goods only from, the former. In return, the estate of tradesmen promises to purchase the goods being sold and deliver the goods that are needed at any time. It is clear that the treaty must include these conditions [*auf diese Bedingungen geschlossen werden müsse*], with the remaining estates renouncing all direct exchange among themselves, since otherwise the estate of traders would enjoy no property right it could securely count on, but would depend on chance and the good will of the other estates. They would conduct their trade through the estate of tradesmen only when it was more advantageous for them, trading directly with one another whenever they hoped thereby to gain a greater profit. And one can hardly think of any purpose for keeping goods determined for public trade from the market other than to bring about an artificial rise in price by causing their scarcity, thus unjustly profiting from the need of one's fellow citizens. In a state existing in accordance with Right this should simply never take place, and yet the only way to prevent it is by placing all trade in the hands of a single estate that it would then be possible to supervise in this regard, which is not the case, for reasons that shall be offered farther down, with the primary producers and manufacturers. It is clear that the estate of traders must oblige itself to buy and sell at all times, since every citizen should be able to live as comfortably from his labor as is in his power, and must not be endangered as a result of renouncing the occupations of others, as would indeed occur were he not able to receive in exchange for his goods, as soon as he desires, the products of the occupations that he has renounced and others now perform. [64]

It is easy to discover how the government can oversee the fulfillment of the obligation we just mentioned. It is {413} a positive law, given teeth through the threat of punishment, that the merchant put in charge of providing specific articles must purchase them from all who offer them to him, and must sell them to all who demand them from him. The citizen who is refused either the one or the other will register a complaint and the merchant will be punished. But, one will ask, how can he be punished for not selling the goods that were demanded when he does not even have them? This affords me an opportunity to show how the government could supervise the fulfillment of the positive obligation of the other estates toward the merchant. No merchant will be employed who has not filed an account of the sources from which he intends to obtain his goods. Knowing the extent of the business of the producers or manufacturers, the yield of goods at certain points of time, and how much of that yield will be delivered to him, he will be able to perform a passable calculation of the supply of goods to be found directly with them. He has the right to lay claim to this supply, and even, if need be, with the help of the authorities, since these estates are obliged by Right to sell. The government, as we said above, cannot directly observe the farmer or manufacturer who first grows or makes these goods. Yet the merchant, having himself been granted the right to count on their goods, is able to do this, and the government as well by means of him. At the same time, even if it were able to, the government would have no need to directly observe the merchant. The moment there arises a stoppage of trade, the citizen whose life is endangered as a result will without doubt report this to the government. So long as nobody complains, one can assume that everything is taking its due course.

And again one could ask: How can the merchant be punished for not accepting one thing in exchange for another when he perhaps lacks an equivalent for the goods in question? I answer: in a state organized according to the principles set forth, it is impossible that goods could be brought to a trading house whose quick sale the trading house wouldn't be able to count on, since indeed, in the very foundation of the state, the extent of production and manufacture permitted by the probable needs of the citizenry has been taken into account. The trading house in question can even {414} coerce this sale. Just as it has been assured specific sellers, it has also been assured specific buyers. It knows their needs, and if they don't buy from it, it may be presumed that they bought from somewhere else, and perhaps directly from the producer or manufacturer. This goes against the obligation of the buyer as well as the seller, and both should be indicted and subject to punishment. The merchant in this state will therefore always be presumed to have begun his trade with a reserve fund sufficient to cover the time between buying and selling, a reserve fund [65] whose existence he must likewise prove to the government before he receives the title of right.—He is, I thus say, always in possession of the necessary equivalent. In such a state, a thoroughly calculable outflux and influx passes through the hands of the merchant.

I do not wish to distract the reader with the solutions of petty difficulties. I will only present a single such problem here, as an example of how others can be resolved.—One should not take fright at the thought of the immense stock-holds of goods that would be required with trade being in this state [*Zustand des Handels*]. So long as the merchant knows where his goods are and can count on their being delivered at any time, it is not the least bit necessary that they lie heaped up before his eyes. The supply of grain, for example, that a grain trader buys from a large landholder can remain undisturbed in the granaries where it lay previously. When the nearby baker seeks grain from the grain trader, he need only direct the baker to the desired quantity in the granaries, deducting the freight from the payment. The baker, though, must never find himself forced to make inquiries among all the large landholders, visiting one after another and being turned away by all of them, even though they perhaps possess a sufficient supply, simply because they wish to coerce higher prices. Rather, he should be certain that, with a single trip to the grain trader and for the price that has been determined, he will either receive the goods themselves, or be directed to where he is certain to find them. {415}

5.

I still need to discuss more clearly my thoughts regarding the fixed prices of things in a state existing in accordance with Right, a topic which I have often mentioned above.

In the domain of the doctrine of Right, one must assume that the end of all free activity is the possibility and pleasantness of life. Yet the latter is based on personal taste and inclination, and thus is not suitable, in and for itself, to serve as a universally valid standard measure. And the objects of enjoyment, moreover, are only such as lie beyond, and can be spared from, what is needed merely to be able to live, and hence must be measured according to the measure of the former. We may therefore exclude the factor of pleasantness entirely from our calculations for the time being, until it should fall back into them of its own accord. Measured according to the possibility of living, the true intrinsic value of every free activity, or—to enter into the world of objects, where our reasoning can move about more easily—of the result of every free activity, is the possibility of living from it, and the result of this [66] one activity—or, in other words, this thing—will be *worth more* than another, the *longer* one is able to live from it. The measure of the value of things relative to one another would be the time during which we could live from them.

Yet one is not more sated, nor nourished for a longer time, by a specific quantity of oysters than by a piece of bread of a specific size. According to the measure indicated, both should thus have the same value. And yet the former, at least among us, has a much higher price than the latter. The cause of this difference is the supposedly greater pleasantness of the first means of nourishment. In order to provisionally exclude this pleasantness from the calculation, while nevertheless preparing a measure by which one can estimate it at a later point, one must find something in which one takes into account the mere possibility of life, mere nourishment, disregarding altogether the degree of its pleasantness—something that, *in the general* {416} *assumption of the nation*, everyone should and must have in order to live. Among those peoples who have become accustomed over the course of many centuries to its enjoyment, this is without doubt bread. Bread, or rather, since with bread a process of fabrication has already occurred, the produce from which it is manufactured—rye, wheat, and the like—would now have value absolutely, and it is by this measure that we estimate the value of everything else.

Applying this measure, one would now have to estimate the intrinsic value of the other means of nourishment. Meat, for example, has a higher intrinsic value as a means of nourishment than bread, since a smaller quantity of the former nourishes us for just as long as a larger quantity of the latter.

A quantity of meat that nourishes someone on average for a single day is worth as much grain as the same person would use to nourish himself for the same day, and, so far as we can tell at present, he would have to pay this quantity of grain in exchange for it. With the admission of a further principle, one will be able to apply this same measure to calculate the value of manufactured goods and of all work that is not directly applied toward extracting the means of nourishment, as well as of produce not grown to provide nourishment but as raw material. The worker must be able to live while he works, and in case he needs *a period of apprenticeship*, we must also take this into account, distributing [its costs] over the course of his working life. He must thus receive as much grain for his labors as he would require if, during this time, he were to live from bread alone. Since he also has need of other means of nourishment besides this, he may use what remains of his grain to barter for these according to the measure indicated above. Produce intended as raw material are worth as much grain as could be produced from the field [67] where they were grown with the effort expended in their cultivation. The manufacturer, however, is able to compensate himself for this value, for which he obtained his materials. His finished goods, as they pass from his hands into those of the merchant, are worth this value plus the wages of his labor.

In order to complete our estimation of the value of {417} things, we must still seek a measure for the pleasantness of life. The following considerations will lead us to a universally valid means of estimating this pleasantness, independent of the personal taste of each individual.

The means of nourishment that has been assigned an absolute value and is determined to serve as the measure of all other things could have only received this distinction because it can be gained most easily, which is to say, with the least expenditure of time, force, skill, and soil. A quantity of any other means of nourishment *with an equal intrinsic nutritional value* will require a greater expenditure of one or more of these factors. Yet a nation will make this greater expenditure, and hence the produce must itself reward it. Since this cannot result from its intrinsic value, its value as nourishment in general, it can only result from its extrinsic value, its value as *pleasant* nourishment. This greater expenditure is what, according to a universally valid estimation, the pleasantness of this means of nourishment among this nation is worth. This means of nourishment itself, it follows, is worth not only its intrinsic value, but, because of its pleasantness, *also that quantity of the primary means of nourishment that could be grown through the application of the same force, time, and soil were the extraction of the former not to occur.*

From the cultivation of what is pleasant it will necessarily follow that less nourishment overall is produced than could have been produced in the state. It is clear, then, that this cultivation may not advance further than the bare necessities of everyone allow, and must never extend so far that someone must do without the necessary nourishment. With this we have discovered the rightful limit of such cultivation.

This cultivation, indeed, amounts to having the forces of the nation spared from the production of indispensable goods. It is fitting, then, that this savings be distributed among everyone in a relatively equal fashion, and that all live equally pleasant lives. I said "relatively." This is to say: in such a way that each one will maintain the kind of force and well-being he needs {418} for his specific occupation. Thus, for example, a man who occupies himself with deep thought, and whose imagination should soar up toward invention, would lack even the bare necessities were he to feed himself like the farmer, who engages from day to day in a mechanical labor that only strains his physical forces. [68] It won't hurt the farmer to still his hunger during his workdays with a mass of vegetable foodstuff—a nourishment that he will without doubt gain by his labor out in the open air. In any case fine and clean clothing would soon be ruined with his sort of occupation. By comparison, someone who works with his hands while sitting inside a room needs nourishment that satisfies in smaller quantities. And the one who, whether it be in higher forms of art or in science, must invent, requires a more varied and revitalizing nourishment, and an environment in which the cleanliness [Reinlichkeit] and nobility that should rule him within is constantly placed before his eyes in the outside world. Yet even the farmer, on his day of rest, when he enters into a thoroughly human existence, deserves to enjoy together with the others the better things that the soil of his land grants, and wear clothing worthy of a free man.

Following these principles it is possible to measure the value that any ware brought into public trade is required by Right to have. The merchant must pay the producers and manufacturers from whose hands he receives these goods as much as both of them need to live for the duration of the process of cultivation or fabrication with the pleasantness appropriate to their occupation. Someone who does not engage in trade, and hence can only receive these goods from the hands of the merchant, must pay as much, over and above the original cost, as the latter requires in order to live during the time when the trade is taking place according to this same measure. When grain is regarded as the common measure of value, this means that they must pay enough grain for all the named parties to feed themselves, with enough left over to exchange for all the other needs belonging to their way of life. The government has to determine {419} through the law this doubled price of all the goods to be brought into public trade, following a prior calculation made in accordance with the principles set forth, and then maintain these prices through punishment. Only then is everyone assured of what is his—not what he has taken control of through blind luck, cheating others, or violence, but what belongs to him by Right. In the state, all are servants of the whole, and receive in return their just share of the goods [*Güter*] of the whole. No one can grow especially rich, nor can anyone become impoverished. All individuals are guaranteed that their present state of existence will continue into the future, and, through this, the whole is guaranteed its own quiet, steady continuity.

I have not paid any regard here to money as an artificial basis for measuring all value. For while the theory of money is of no consequence to the propositions we have presented, the latter are of great consequence for the former. Just as little have I taken into account taxes collected by the state, or the salaries paid [69] to those estates that neither produce, manufacture, or engage in trade, since an investigation into these questions should elucidate and confirm the theory that was presented rather than contradict it. All this in due time.

6.

The state is obliged to guarantee for all its citizens, through law and compulsion [*Zwang*], the state of affairs that results from this balance of commerce. Yet it cannot do this if there is any person able to influence this balance who does not stand under the state's law and command. Thus, it must cut the very possibility of such influence off at the root.—All commerce with foreigners must be forbidden to its subjects and rendered impossible.

It is not necessary to prove that there is absolutely no place for commerce between the subjects and foreigners in the system of trade set forth. The government should be able to count on {420} a certain quantity of goods entering into trade, in order that it may always guarantee its subject the continuing enjoyment of his accustomed needs. How can the government count with assurance on the foreigner's contribution to this quantity, when he does not stand under its command? It should fix and guarantee the price of goods. How will it achieve this vis-à-vis a foreigner, since indeed it cannot determine the prices that he must pay in his country to live and to purchase raw materials? If it proposes a price to the foreigner that he cannot keep, he will avoid its market in the future, and a shortage of goods satisfying the accustomed needs will arise. The government should guarantee to its subject the sale of his produce or manufactured goods, and the fitting price at which they are sold. How can the government do this if its subject should sell to foreign countries whose relation to the goods of the government's subject the government is able neither to oversee nor to regulate?

What follows from a correct proposition is itself correct. Let us suppose that the state is not completely indifferent to how its citizen comes into that which it recognizes as his property and protects for him. And let us likewise suppose that the citizen, with regard to acquisition, is not completely free [*Vogelfrei*] and dependent on chance up to a certain degree—say, that one may not commit armed robbery—so that one person is allowed to snatch away everything for himself while another gets nothing.[6] Let us suppose, in other words, that the entire duty of the government doesn't exhaust itself in guarding over everyone's private hoard, regardless of how it was accumulated, and in keeping those who have nothing from gaining anything. If, on the contrary, the true purpose of the state is to help all [70] obtain what belongs to them as partners of humanity, and only then to keep them in possession of what they have, all commerce in the state must be regulated in the way that was indicated; thus, it will be necessary, if this regulation is to be possible, for all foreign influence, incapable as it is of regulation, to be kept at bay. And thus, just as the rational state is a closed realm of laws and individuals, it is also an entirely *closed commercial state*. Every living human being is either a citizen of the state, or he is not. Likewise, every {421} product of human activity either belongs within the compass of its commerce or it does not. There is no third possibility.

If a state has need of barter with foreign lands, this can only be conducted by the government, just as it is alone the task of the government to conclude war or peace or alliances. The more precise reasons for asserting this will emerge farther down from considering the perspectives that the government must assume in the case of such barter, and cannot yet be presented in an illuminating way. Here it is enough to have shown from universal principles that, in a rational state, direct trade between the individual citizen and a citizen of a foreign country simply cannot be permitted.

Third Chapter

On the presupposed division of the branches of labor in a rational state

One or the other reader may believe that we have surreptitiously reached the conclusions of our theory by hiding them in our premises, since we do not posit property, as is customary, in the exclusive possession of an object, but rather in the exclusive right to a free act, with the free acts necessary to sustain human life being divided up in an entirely arbitrary way into several estates. Such a division, they might say, is something wholly accidental, wholly inessential to the state as such. States could exist in which every resident has his own piece of arable land on which he grows his food, keeps a few livestock, carves wooden shoes for himself, spends the winter days weaving the linen for his coat from the hemp he grew himself, and so forth. A state such as this would have neither a particular estate of artisans, nor a balance between these and the producers, nor {422} trade and merchants—not a single aspect of my theory would apply to it, and yet I should never wish, on this account, to deny it the name of a just state. Ordinances concerning trade and industry would then be only a matter of what is advantageous or prudent, [71] and, to this extent, entirely arbitrary and in no way a matter of rigorous Right.

In answer to this, I will remark first of all that even in such a state the right to property does not directly concern the arable land as such, but rather the exclusive right to use this as one pleases. I shall say more about this point later on. But it is of no consequence to our present investigation. I will further remark that a nation in the state of existence we described is an impoverished nation, remaining halfway in barbarism. If such a nation is governed from within [aus ihrer eigenen Mitte], and its rulers have only the degree of culture that one can obtain within it, there could hardly be any thought of having a wise legislation and a well-organized state. If I should refuse to call a state administration such as this—a state administration that, under these circumstances, counts, in its giving of laws, on the present and continuing existence of such a state of things—contrary to Right, it is only in consideration of the fact that one can no more be obliged to pass beyond the limits of one's *knowledge* than to pass beyond the limits of one's *capabilities*. But if a government that knows, or is able to know, something better than this should set this same goal for itself and make the same sort of calculations, not making the slightest effort to depart from this wretched state of affairs and wrest the nation from it as well, I would have no choice but to call it contrary to Right.

It is no mere pious wish of humanity, but the absolutely necessary [*unerläßlich*] demand issuing from its Right and its vocation, that it live on the earth as easily, as freely, with as much command over nature, in as truly *human* a way, as nature will permit. Man should labor, and yet not as a beast of burden who sinks into sleep under the weight {423} of its load and, having just barely refreshed its exhausted forces, is roused to bear it anew. He should labor without fear, with pleasure and joy, and have time left over to raise his spirit and eye to the heavens, which he has been formed to behold. He should not simply eat together with his beast of burden, but his meals should differ as much from its feed, his dwelling from its stall, as the build of his body differs from its build. This is his right, simply because he is a human being.

There is much and frequent talk of national riches, the national state of prosperity, and the like. It will be necessary for me to indicate in the course of this writing most of the meanings these terms can have. Here we hit on the following: the intrinsic essential state of prosperity consists in being able to procure for oneself the most truly human pleasures with the least [72] difficult and time-consuming labor. This should be the state of prosperity of the *nation* as a whole and not only of a few individuals, whose extreme prosperity is often the most obvious sign, and indeed the true reason, for the extreme sickness of the nation. It should be spread out in more or less the same degree among all.

Unless the forces of our own nature undergo a monstrous increase, or the nature outside of us transforms itself without our doing through a sudden miracle, annihilating its own, previously known, laws, we cannot expect this state of prosperity to come from nature, but only from ourselves. We must acquire it for ourselves through labor. The sole means of this are art and skill [*Kunst und Kunstfertigkeit*]. By means of these, the slightest force, through its purposeful application, becomes equal to a force one thousand times greater. Yet art and skill arise only from continued practice; they arise from each man devoting his entire life to a single occupation, directing all his force and all his thought [*Nachdenken*] toward this one occupation. Accordingly, there must be a division of the branches of labor necessary for human life.

Only under this condition would force work to the greatest advantage.—In some {424} village of the impoverished state we described above each man sits alone in front of his hearth, and slowly carves, with great effort and unsatisfactory tools, a pair of miserable wooden shoes. What if all these were to apply the same time and effort to the business of agriculture, and were to assign to one person among them, and the most skilled at that, the task of making shoes for everyone else, and doing nothing else but this? Then they would receive better shoes, and with the produce they had meanwhile gained by cultivating their fields, they would not only be able to feed their shoemaker quite well, but a tailor too.

In short: whoever has the right to an end also has a right to the means that alone leads to this end. Every people has the right to want an increase in its state of prosperity, and yet this is only possible through the division of labor. A people, it follows, has the right to want this, and it is the duty of the government—that institution [Anstalt] put in charge of obtaining and preserving all of the people's rights—to arrange [veranstalten] for this to happen.

Fourth Chapter

Whether the taxes paid to the state will change anything in the balance of industry

It will be necessary to employ some people who occupy themselves exclusively with handling the laws and maintaining public order, others with public instruction, and finally some who practice the use of weapons [73] and stand ready at all times to defend the nation against the violence of enemies from within and without. These can neither cultivate the land, manufacture goods, nor engage in commercial transactions, and yet they must nevertheless live just as well, each according to the nature of his occupation, as the rest of the citizens. There remains {425} no other choice than that the other estates also work for them, delivering to them the needed produce and manufactured goods, just as in any case each of the working estates must deliver its goods to the others. The only difference is that each of the working estates gives goods in return, whereas they do not have to give anything in return. The things they need must be delivered to them without any visible or palpable equivalent. Their concern for the governance, education and instruction, and defense of the nation is the equivalent that they pay.—This is the fundamental concept of tax, which should suffice here and everywhere.

The government, which has to calculate the number of these people— I will refer to these, in general terms, as *public officials*—who should be employed both in total and in each of the chief and subordinate branches, also has to calculate the manner in which by Right each should and may live, according to the nature of his occupation, given the specific degree of the prosperity of the nation. The magnitude of the tax that the nation must pay issues from these calculations. It is impossible to think to what end the government in a rational and well-organized state would demand more than it needs. Yet what is needed, the nation is required by Right to pay, since it cannot demand that those who protect the rights of all should alone be injured in their rights.

The introduction of taxes will in no way result in a disturbance of the balance set forth between the different estates and individuals, but only in an, at any rate unavoidable, curtailment of the general state of prosperity—a curtailment that will be borne no less by the public officials than by the rest of the citizens. Were it no longer necessary for some citizens to devote themselves exclusively to the public offices and business of the state, we could think of the following two opposed scenarios. If, on the one hand, the same quantity and the same kind of goods are delivered now as were delivered before, and which previously allowed {426} the entire nation to live in the manner it did, it follows that throughout the entire territory of the state exactly the same amount of work, and no more than this, will take place as before. The former public officials will now be reemployed at the common labor. The resulting reduction in the labor of the others will be divided equally among everyone, and all, it follows, will gain in rest and leisure. Or, on the other hand, those who previously worked—and whose work [74] kept the entire nation, including those who served up till now as public officials, in the manner to which it was accustomed—work just as much as before. Thus, it will be possible for a number of citizens, equal in number to the former public servants, to apply their labor to finer means of nourishment and manufactured goods. Since this at the same time will always also reduce the need for the bare necessities, a portion of the labor that previously went toward these can now be applied to finer things, and the nation will have gained not in leisure, it is true, but rather in good living. Let one suppose a case combining both these approaches, which without doubt is what would actually happen. Now everyone will gain more enjoyment from less work, and thus their state of prosperity will be increased. That the state of prosperity allowed by the given natural conditions never actually occurs is due to the existence of public officials who must themselves live without being able to contribute to the work required for this merely sensuous life. And they bear this reduction in public prosperity along with the others, since, in a well-arranged state, they will be paid a salary not according to the possible but rather the actual prosperity of the nation.

With the organization of commerce that I have described, this curtailment of public prosperity will affect all the working estates and each one of their individual members in equal measure, just as all stand to benefit in equal measure from governance, instruction, and defense. Each will pay his share, just as he should. The value of each thing entering into public commerce, one can say, is no longer to be determined merely according {427} to the measure indicated above—that the producer, manufacturer, and merchant should be able, each after his manner, to exist in an equally pleasant fashion. Besides this, the public officials should also be able to exist.

One can assume that whatever must be paid as taxes, and thus remains entirely with the public officials, has disappeared from public trade and is lost to a public engaged in commerce. Or finally we can assume that the producer or manufacturer will have to allow a deduction from their goods, and the merchant from his trading free, as though in payment of a debt. It all amounts to the same thing, and the result remains forever the same. The curtailment of public prosperity is the true burden, and this is borne by all in common.

Whatever method one may seize on to collect these taxes, the result remains forever the same. One may choose to take the contributions directly from both the producer and manufacturer, and likewise require the tradesman to deliver some portion of his purchases. Or we may take the merchant's contribution from the producer and manufacturer at the same time [that they pay their own contribution], [75] and then let him repay the latter two estates by raising the price at which he can purchase their goods. Or we might seize on that method which is simplest and most easy to supervise, collecting the entire tax from the farmer and letting him be repaid for the manufacturer's and merchant's contributions by raising the price of his produce. As long as the prices of goods are fixed according to the principles set forth above, and only after first deducting the quantity of goods paid as taxes to the state from the total sum of the goods found in public commerce and then determining from whose hands the state will collect these taxes, the balance will be preserved, and public justice upheld. {428}

Fifth Chapter

How this balance of industry is to be secured against the uncertainty of agriculture

The system being set forth, as we have seen, counts on the fact that the quantity of the articles of consumption and manufacture entering into public commerce, as well as the ratio of these quantities to one another, will remain forever the same, periodically canceling one another out [*und von Zeit zu Zeit durch einander aufgehe*].

With regard to manufactured goods, this can indeed be counted on, insofar as their quantity depends on the workers who are employed. This is not so with regard to articles of consumption, however, since the yield from agriculture does not remain the same from year to year. Moreover, manufacture, since it receives its raw materials from agriculture, will also be disturbed by irregularity in the extraction of produce.

Were the fertility of one year to exceed the calculation, this would be just as disruptive to the balance as another year's crop failure. We shall, however, direct our gaze solely toward the former occurrence, since, starting from this, we will be led automatically to a means to guard against the latter.

The producer should extract as much produce as is needed to provide nourishment for the nonproducers and, beyond this, raw materials for the manufacturer. He can be quite sure he will be able to sell such a quantity. Yet he won't be able to sell more than this. The merchant, unable to find a buyer for it, cannot take it from him. Nor could the manufacturer accept it. He has no equivalent he could give in return, since his work only takes account of his customary needs. There is no way to bring the surplus of extracted produce into public commerce. [76]

Now, indeed, the needs of the producer also only take into account what he usually sells. As long as he can sell this amount, he will receive the sustenance he deserves and has no need of the surplus allotted to him {429} through unaccounted fertility. This surplus can be regarded as if it simply did not exist. It could be eliminated not merely from the calculation, but could actually be eliminated from nature itself, and this would nowhere [an keinem Ende] cause any harm. On the one hand, however, it seems unfair to deprive the producer of a profit that he gained not by cheating his fellow citizens, but that nature's favor allotted to him. On the other hand though, and most importantly: How could the crop failure of a year in which the yield remains below the calculation be covered and endured [übertragen], if not through the excessive fertility of another year?[7]

It follows that the necessary yield of the extraction of produce and the ratio of this to the other goods must be estimated not according to one single year, but according to a series of years long enough for abundance to make up for the crop failure. Not: one year provides so much produce. But rather: say that five years provide so much produce, of this the average for one year will be so much, and this last quantity of goods should enter into commerce. The size of the remaining estates will be calculated in accordance with this last quantity, regardless of the current year's actual yield.

Only the state has the ability to balance the yield of one year against the other in this way. The most natural way of going about this is as follows. Whoever has cultivated more than the amount set for him will report it to the state. The state will not reimburse him for the surplus on the spot with an equivalent payment, since this would result in an increase in circulation together with all its disadvantages. Rather, it will only *credit* this surplus to him, providing him, if need be, with a certificate for the sake of his security.

Now perhaps in this same year there will be a shortage in other regions of the country. In this case, those goods that one has estimated will be needed for yearly consumption will be delivered to the merchants in these regions, and these, in turn, will pay these out to those *producers* who, according to the calculation, should have themselves cultivated and delivered these goods. The state now *writes up* these goods on its account as a *credit* owed by the producers, and if {430} they didn't even cultivate what they need for their own nourishment, the state will deliver this to them as well, adding it to the same account. Or, as the second possible case, in this same year there haven't been any crop failures anywhere within the state's limits, or at least none large enough to consume the surplus cultivated in other regions. If this happens, the surplus will be deposited with the merchants as a reserve to cover the possible shortages of future years. The merchant will not pay it out to the state until actual scarcity ensues and the sale of this surplus becomes necessary. To prevent the grain from spoiling [77] with age, it can be arranged that the merchant not give out anything from the fruits of future harvests until he has dispensed with the old stock. He will in turn keep the surplus of this new harvest for the following year, and will continue to do the same each subsequent year until finally, after a crop failure has occurred, the surplus is absorbed. If someone has a credit with the state, he will be repaid when he suffers his first crop failure. Or in the case that, within a specified period of years, his crops either never fail or never fail so badly as to absorb the state's entire debt, he will be reimbursed through an exemption from his taxes. And likewise, if someone owes the state, he will repay this sum in the first fertile years with the surplus he has cultivated.—The state must make sure that it always has some surplus on hand, and indeed must see to this well in advance. If one considers a newly arisen state, or a state that is just now beginning to comply with the rightful laws of commerce, this must happen in the following way: the state should not estimate as many manufacturers to be possible in the first years as it could in fact support were it to take no account of the possibility of a crop failure. And it must likewise devote a greater number of hands to agriculture than it would need were it not to take this necessary precaution.

With these measures, a situation of actual shortage can never arise. Should it happen, however, that the surplus grows smaller with every year, with there even being fear that the first bad year would cause a short-age, this would then prove that the ratio of manufacture and trade to the extraction of produce has not been correctly determined. {431} The state must quickly withdraw some hands from the former branches, and return them to agriculture. Were the opposite to occur—were the surplus to grow greater from year to year—this would then prove that the state can bear an increase in the number of factories and in the cultivation of finer produce. Arrangements must then be made for this increase, in order to preserve the balance and help the nation to the greater state of prosperity to which it has claim under these circumstances.

Sixth Chapter

Whether this balance would be endangered through the introduction of money, and changed through the constant progress of the nation to a higher state of prosperity

There are some readers, I suppose, for whom it will be difficult keeping a firm grip on their thoughts in a nexus of things grounded solely on concepts. They will return again and again to the accidental [78] reality familiar to them, mixing this reality in with this nexus, without considering that through this nexus the given reality shall itself be eliminated. Such readers have perhaps long harbored in silence the following objection to my argument:

Certainly the basis for measuring all value that has been presumed—grain—should not serve as the actual means of exchange. One certainly cannot in actual fact measure out a quantity of grain for every ware. Discounting all the other inconveniences, there would then have to be two supplies of grain in circulation passing from hand to hand: one quantity for yearly consumption and another for trade, with the latter incomparably more considerable than the former, since the sum of value found in public trade {432} far exceeds the amount of grain consumed in a year. It follows that a rational state will conduct itself in just the same way as any other civilized [*kultiviert*] state. A particular means of exchange and sign of all value—in short, *money*—will have to be introduced. Yet the value of money against goods is variable and subject to a high degree of fluctuation. Neither laws nor power [*Gewalt*] can fix this value and keep it as it is. If the state institutes compulsory prices with which the buyers or sellers are not in agreement, then those who possess money will hide their money and those with goods will hide their goods, destroying the trade between them. The former are entirely beyond the reach of the power [of the state], whereas the latter can only be influenced by odious and costly means. Thus, as long as the use of money is presumed, trade will allow itself neither to be calculated nor brought under laws. It will create its price and law for itself. So it has always been, and so it must always remain.

To this I answer that while money will by all means be introduced into the rational state, its value shall remain invariable, or at least it will be unable to change unless this is arranged by the state itself, which, here as elsewhere, must follow firm principles. I cannot prove this without going a bit deeper into the principles on which the theory of money depends.

All of the useful things that are found circulating throughout the territories of the state are continually being claimed for the use of the people. Their quantity decreases from the time of the old harvest up to the new harvest, and again increases with the latter. It follows that there must always be available an enduring representation, such as shall neither decrease nor increase, of its entire value—a sign of this value. The more useless this sign is in and for itself, the less intrinsic value it has, the more fitting it will be to serve as a mere sign, since [79] everything that can be utilized belongs to the nation's intrinsic wealth, and should be enjoyed by the nation and not applied to other ends. {433} Money should be manufactured from the material that is least useful.

As we said above: whoever has goods should be able to exchange them at every hour for whatever goods he pleases. With the introduction of money, this now means: he should be able at any hour to receive money for his goods and whatever goods he pleases for his money. A new medium of exchange has now interposed itself between goods. Yet this consequence is self-evident, and with the introduction of money, the ability to convert goods into money and money into goods with the requisite ease will follow automatically from the laws of trade set forth above.

A closed commercial state, whose citizen engages in no direct commerce with the foreigner, *can make absolutely whatever it wants into money.* All it has to do is declare that it will let itself be paid with this money alone and absolutely none other. When it comes to the possession of money, only one thing matters to anyone: everyone else with whom he engages in commerce must accept it from him for the same value at which he received it. The citizen of a closed commercial state can engage in commerce only with another citizen of the same state and with absolutely no one else. Yet all the citizens of the state are required to procure for themselves that form of money which they can use to pay the one to whom they pay the most money. This, now, will be the state. Everyone must pay taxes, whether directly or indirectly, to the state, which receives incomparably more income than any individual person or trading house in the entire country. In this way a *national currency* comes into existence. With this *national currency*, the question will never arise whether the money will be accepted abroad, since for a closed commercial state foreign countries are as good as nonexistent.

Such a state need only be sure that its national currency cannot be counterfeited, and that absolutely no man or power {434} other than itself is able to manufacture it. This is the sole limiting condition, the reason for which we will see further down.

For a closed commercial state it is a matter of complete indifference whether there is, in the customary manner of speaking, much or little money in circulation. Rigorously speaking, there can be neither a "too much" nor a "too little" here, since money, in and for itself, is nothing at all. Only through the will of the state does it *represent* something. The entire sum of circulating money represents the entire sum of goods found in [80] public commerce; the tenth part [*Teil*] of the first the tenth part of the value of the second, the hundredth part of the first the hundredth part of the second, and so forth. Whether this hundredth part is called a dollar [*Taler*] or ten dollars or a hundred dollars makes no difference. In every case, I can use it to purchase a hundredth part of the goods found in public commerce. How rich someone is depends not on how many pieces of money he has, but *how great a part of all circulating money* he possesses.

An earlier passage demanded that the state appraise the value of things relative to one another and then went on to describe how this would be done. I say: of things relative to one another. How much more should this finer—viz., costing a greater expenditure of time and force—means of nourishment, this produce intended as raw material, or this manufactured ware, be worth than some other ware, and what is the relation of all these goods to the primary means of nourishment, in which an absolute value is posited? Now, however, there is talk of an altogether different appraisal. *What part of the circulating representation of all value* should each thing cost? This calculation is also bound by strict laws, save in one single point where it depends on something arbitrary [*von der Willkür abhängt*].

Namely, following what was said above, the quantity of the sign that the state puts into circulation is entirely arbitrary. However large or small it may be, it will always have the same value. Let someone suppose that it would please him to set this quantity at one million {435} dollars, or, in other words, divide it into one million parts, which he shall call dollars. Through the appraisal described previously, the value, relative to grain, of meat, fruit, and the like, as well as flax, hemp, linen, and woolen cloth, has already been determined. Let one reduce the value of all goods other than grain found in public commerce to the value of grain, and then add the quantity of grain that, from one harvest to the next, is actually set to enter into trade. One can then say: the value of so many measures of grain is in circulation. Let one then divide the number of these measures by the money found in circulation. Suppose, for example, that this value equals one million measures. Given our above presupposition, each measure of grain is necessarily worth one dollar in money. A quantity of meat, fruit, flax, linen, or woolen cloth found in our previous calculation to be equal to the measure of grain would likewise be worth a dollar, and so forth. The prices found in this way would then have to be fixed through the law.

As long as the ratio of the value of goods found in circulation to the money in circulation remains the same, the prices cannot change. The nature of things, the necessary will of all, and the law are in agreement. They are founded on that ratio, and will necessarily remain [81] the same for as long as this ratio remains the same. The prices would only change according to the nature of things, and consequently need to be changed through the law, if this ratio should change, which happens either when the quantity or intrinsic value of the circulating goods increases while the quantity of money remains the same, or when the quantity of money increases while the value of goods remains the same. In the first case that was posited, each part of the circulating money would receive a higher value, since the whole of which it is a part represents a higher value. In the second case, each piece of money would receive a lower value, since it is no longer so great a part of a whole that, now as before, represents the same value of goods. Speaking in the usual manner, without exactly getting at the root of things, one would say: in the first case the times are more cheap, and in the second, more expensive.

With the continuing existence of the state, the goods found in circulation {436} should at any rate partly increase in number and partly become more refined. Since the prosperity of an industrious and well-governed nation will grow from year to year, an ever greater number of goods of an ever higher value relative to the primary means of nourishment will enter into circulation. The state will keep a precise watch on this increase, since it occurs under its own direction. Therefore, the state can and will determine the ratio of money according to this increase in the value of goods. If, on the one hand, the prices in money of the goods are to remain as they were, it will increase the amount of circulating money in proportion to the additional value of goods. If, however, the quantity of circulating money is to remain the same, the state will distribute the additional value of goods among the entire quantity of money, and reduce the prices in money of all things by as much as its calculations require. Just about the only way for the state to increase the sum of circulating money without causing irregularities and disparities elsewhere is to distribute the money to the family fathers, to each as much as suits his circumstances, without receiving anything in return. In this way it would provide them with nothing more than what is their rightful claim to the increased prosperity of the entire nation.—It would be wisest for the state to avail itself of both these means—the distribution of money and the reduction of prices—at the same time, so that each measure would assist and complement the other, restoring the disrupted balance between goods and money.

Thus, it is also self-evident in this instance that the balance will not necessarily be disrupted through the nation's progress to a higher state of prosperity or even through an increasing population. And we have likewise shown the means that the state has to employ lest such a disruption result on this account. A *decrease* in the value of goods in circulation is not possible in a state that is governed well, being regulated from the very beginning according to correct calculation.

The only way that the sum of circulating money could *increase* without the knowledge or calculation of [82] the state {437} is if others besides the state were able to manufacture the national currency. If the money were not recognized as counterfeit, its manufacturers would thereby withdraw themselves from the common labor, which had been calculated to include their forces. As a result of the money increasing while the value of goods remains constant, a disparity would arise that the state could only eliminate by decreasing the value of money, or in other words increasing the price of goods in money. In this way, then, whoever possesses money would lose a certain part of the property he has already acquired. If, however, the money was recognized as counterfeit and not accepted by everyone, then at the very least those who accepted it would have been robbed. It must therefore be impossible to counterfeit the money. The money must be of such a kind and such a nature that only the state could manufacture it. How will this be arranged? Here is not the place to say. And when we come to that place, I will still not say even though I might know, for this is not something that should be imparted to the public.

The *decrease* in the sum of money found in circulation caused by wear and tear to the pieces of money is of no significance, and is not hard to prevent. On the one hand: for the sake of public security, the money should be made of a durable material and thus never exposed to very much wear. On the other hand: when the worn-out coins enter into the state's treasuries, where they must be accepted without hesitation, the state must destroy them and give out new coins in their place, bringing these into circulation.—Of greater significance appears to be the reduction in the quantity of money caused by the citizens' hoarding and saving. A skilled and industrious worker does somewhat more work than one had counted on him doing, and thus also draws more than his share of money. Yet he buys only those necessities that one had counted on him buying, or perhaps not even these, scrimping here as well. Saving the product of his greater labor and thrifty way of life, he brings it out of circulation. If many now do the same, this will at any rate give rise to a considerable {438} reduction of the circulating sum of money—a reduction that will exert a noticeable influence on the calculation made before. Yet there are no preventative measures that can be seized on in response to this, and, moreover, to take such measures would be to limit the fitting and rightful freedom of the citizen. Such thriftiness, however, can only reasonably aim at two things. Either it provides us with the means of living when age or illness prevent us from doing all the work expected of us, or even indeed from doing any work at all, or it allows us to raise our [83] children, teach them something useful, and leave them with a good foundation for practicing a trade [Gewerbe]. In short, the purpose of all work over and above what we need to live is so that in the future we or our loved ones may live over and above the yield of our labor. It follows from the very intention of those who save money that whatever has been withdrawn from circulation will be brought back into circulation at some point in the future.

This then shows us the true and natural remedy for what one had feared would endanger the ratio of money to goods. If, in an already existing state, it has always been the custom to save for the sake of future spending, then the number of those presently saving money will be equaled by those presently spending what either they or their parents had once saved. Thus, those sums being brought back into circulation will suffice to cover the sums being withdrawn from the present circulation of money. A nascent state, or a state that is only now coming into a rightful order, would do best if, on the presupposition that its citizens will at first save money, it were to take this yearly savings into account when it estimates the quantity of money that is actually in circulation. It would then assume that a certain quantity of money has been stashed away, and in determining the money prices of goods it would simply presume that this money doesn't exist at all. Or, especially if it finds itself in the latter condition, it might oppose the nonworking pensioners from the old regime—it can't just let them {439} die from want, after all—as an artificial counterweight to the workers who are saving money. The former would be compelled to do something useful by maintaining the balance, and, as they gradually die off, the workers' savings would begin to come back into circulation, giving rise to the natural balance described above between the consumers and savers.

The state collects its taxes in money in order to secure the universal validity of the national currency. Hence, it will pay the salary of the public officials in that which it receives from the citizens: in money. One recalls from above the standard measure according to which they should live. Since the value of money relative to goods is determined by law and is permanent, the state can easily calculate the sum of money each official must receive as his yearly salary. If mainly for the sake of illuminating my propositions by applying them to a greater variety of situations, I must still add the following remark. This, however, only concerns the case where the state of public prosperity has increased noticeably, and the state has to restore, in the manner described above, the destroyed [aufgehoben] balance between the legal determination of the value of money and the natural value of the circulating goods. [84]

If the state leaves the existing prices as they are and restores the balance through an increase in the circulating sum of money, the official's salary must then be increased in proportion to the greater state of prosperity. His present salary will allow him to live as he lived before, and the salary increase is his share in the greater prosperity of the whole. If, however, the state leaves the circulating sum of money unchanged and restores the balance by reducing the prices of goods, then the official's salary is to be left unchanged. For indeed, with this same sum of money he can now live better than before, and the additional goods he is now able to buy with this money are his share in the increased prosperity of the whole. If the state combines both means, then it must likewise increase the salary of the public officials, though by as much less as the official gains through the reduced prices. In this case the salary increase and lowered prices together contain the public official's share in the public prosperity. {440}

Seventh Chapter

Further discussion of the principle set forth here concerning the right to property

As I intend to bring this section to a close, drawing together the most remarkable of its results into a single point, I feel that I must still provide some further elucidation of the chief proposition, since it is with this that the entire theory stands or falls. I have reserved this till the end, so as not to interrupt the quick progress of the previous investigations.

The chief results of the theory set forth are as follows: in a state existing in accordance with the law of Right the three chief estates of the nation are calculated in proportion to one another and each is limited to a set number of members. A relative share of all the country's produce and manufactured goods is guaranteed to each citizen in return for the work expected of him, and likewise to every public official, although in this case without a visible equivalent. To this end it will be necessary to fix and ensure the value of all things relative to one another and their price in money. And finally, if all this is to be possible, all direct trade between citizens and abroad must be rendered impossible. All these assertions are founded on my theory of property. If this theory of property is correct, then, without doubt, there will also be good reason for these assertions. If the theory of property is false, then that which claims to be nothing more than a consequence of the theory of property will no doubt fall together with it.

Yet it is precisely in the theory of property that concepts are in circulation [85] deviating very much from mine. Thus I must at any rate fear from many readers that they will not find my reasoning convincing, for there will certainly be many among them who openly profess these different concepts, or are at least darkly led by them. I must {441} once again invite these readers to submit to proof both my principle and those principles that either deviate from it, or are wholly contrary.

In my opinion the fundamental error of the opposed theory of property—the first source from which all false assertions about property derive;

the true reason for the obscurity and oversubtlety of many doctrines; and what is, properly understood, the cause of their one-sidedness and incompleteness when applied to actual life—is this: that one posits the first, original property in the exclusive possession of *a thing*. With such a view holding sway, it is no wonder that we have even experienced a theory claiming that the estate of large landholders, or the nobility, is the only true proprietor, the only citizen from which a state is formed, and that all others are mere accessories [*Beisassen*] who must buy the toleration of the former under whatever condition pleases them. This, I say, is no wonder, since of all things it is land and soil that most visibly become property and most rigorously exclude all foreign admixture.

In opposition to this theory, our theory posits the first and original property, the basis of all others, in *an exclusive right to a determinate free activity*. This free activity can be determinable, and determined (described, characterized, named), in one of three ways. *Either* solely *through the object that it acts upon*. This is the case, for example, with the right to undertake *whatever one may wish in and with a certain area* and keep the rest of the human race from modifying this area in any way. *Figuratively and derivatively*, this area could at any rate itself be called *the property* of the one who has been granted the right, though *strictly speaking* his property consists solely in *his exclusive right to every possible modification of this area*. In actual life I am not familiar with any example of such an unlimited right to property. *Or*, secondly, this free activity is determined only through itself, through its own form (its kind and manner, its purpose, and so forth), without any [86] regard to the object that it acts upon: the right to conduct exclusively a {442} certain art (to manufacture clothing, shoes, and the like for others) and to keep everyone else from practicing the same art. Here we have property without the possession of any kind of *thing*. Or finally, this free activity is determined through *both*: through its own form and through the object that it acts upon: the right to undertake exclusively a specific act upon a certain object, and to exclude all other men from the same use of the same object. In this case too, an object can figuratively and derivatively be called the property of the one who has been granted the title of right, although strictly speaking his property consists only in the exclusive right to a certain free action toward this object. The exclusive right of the farmer to cultivate grain on this certain piece of land is of such a kind.[1] This right does not curtail the right of another to put his herd to pasture on the same land, or the state to engage in mining beneath the surface.

In our theory there is no property of land [*Boden*], or at least not until those who assume that there is such a thing can make us understand how such a right to property might be *practiced* in actual life—if indeed these truly understand what they are saying, and really mean, as these words declare, a property of *land*, and not, as in our interpretation, a right that is exclusively one's own to a certain *use* of the land. The earth is the Lord's; to man belongs only the ability to cultivate it and use it in a purposeful fashion. {443}

Our theory is proved, and the opposing theory refuted, in the following way:

That one person should receive something as his own happens only to mediate the conflict of many over this same thing. We cannot speak of the property of a man living in isolation on an inaccessible island. The concept of property [87] doesn't apply to him at all, since he may take for himself whatever he wishes and is able to take.—How do these several men, between whom the right to property is to mediate, come into conflict, and what is the seat, properly understood, of their conflict? They clearly only come into conflict through the active expression of their force. Now if the conflict has actually been resolved, the seat of the conflict will without doubt also be the seat of the resolution of the conflict. One of them must desist from what encroaches on the other, who should now be the only one performing this activity. The former must not pick from the tree whose fruit the latter should pick, or harvest the field that the latter should harvest. Only then will each one have his *own*, *proper*, use of freedom.

Precisely this is presupposed, albeit silently, by the opposing theories. They are in agreement with our theory, and their consequences, so far as they are able to extend given the narrow concept from which they depart, nevertheless follow from *our* premises, and not from theirs.—Property should be an *ideal* possession of a thing that I do not immediately possess *realiter* by carrying it in my hands, covering it with my body, or the like. Yet if this possession is not to remain thoroughly ideal, consisting solely in the necessity that all men *think* that the object is mine and not theirs; if this possession is to have any sort of real consequence in actual life, this must consist in all men being bound to refrain entirely from all effects [*Wirksamkeit*] on this thing, not changing it in any way but leaving it as it is, with all activity upon this object likewise left exclusively for me to perform. This is what I will actually take it to mean, and all the courts {444} of the world will do the same. I do not understand what an ideal possession would be, but I believe that through my right to property I have received the right to keep all men from acting in a certain way toward the object of my ownership. Only when someone actually acts upon this object will I complain about an injury to my right to property and be able to prove the injury, and then every court will accept my complaint and help me defend my right [*und mir zu meinem Rechte verhelfen*].

It is evident from all this that no right to the property of things can take place without the right to keep all men from acting upon them. Whether others observe my right to property is revealed solely by whether they avoid this foreign activity. This right to exclude foreign activity is, it follows, the true seat of the right to a property of things. [88]

Conversely, an exclusive right to the property of an activity can take place without the ownership of any single thing. This is the case, for example, with the exclusive right that we mentioned above to practice an art or branch of industry. Here we need not consider the rather accidental ownership of the tools of the art or the object to which it is applied, since these are not even necessarily the property of the worker but could have been loaned and supplied to him.

The basis of all right to property, it follows, is to be placed not in the exclusive possession of objects [Objekten], but in the right to exclude others from a certain free activity reserved for ourselves.

We should not overlook, as external proofs for the correctness of our theory, either the clarity and universal intelligibility that it is able to give to all propositions concerning property, or its universal [durchgängig] applicability to actual life.

The *rightful basis*, the rightfully binding force of the right to property thus described, rests solely on the treaty of all with all (of all, this is to say, who can reciprocally influence one another). If we consider someone for himself, {445} disregarding, as must be done in the domain of the doctrine of Right, his responsibility before his own conscience, he may do whatever he wants. It is only because several people are there who should also exist that he must limit his free activity to such a degree that they can exist. And they, from their side, must do the same for him. Since all are equal, each rightfully limits the freedom of the other by as much as the other limits his. The *equal* degree that each limits the other rests in the law of Right, and does not depend on anything arbitrary. They must nevertheless negotiate *which determinate sphere of activity* should remain exclusively for each one, with the others having to refrain from this sphere of activity for his sake. It is only their free and arbitrary decision, and neither nature nor the law of Right, that determines anything in this regard. Hence, it is necessary to conclude a treaty. If one hundred farmers live together and have a specific piece of land in their power, then it clearly follows from the law of Right that this must be divided into one hundred equal parts, with one of these given to each farmer as his own. But why is it that I and none of the other ninety-nine farmers should have precisely this first piece of land to the south, and my closest neighbor this piece next to mine? No other rightful reason can be offered for this than the fact that all the others have left these pieces of land to us, just as we, in return, left to them the pieces of land that they now occupy. [89]

It is only in exchange for obtaining his share, and so as to hold on to it undisturbed, that anyone renounces the share of all the rest. If someone hasn't received anything as exclusively his own, he hasn't renounced his right to anything. With regard to Right, he is isolated, since he did not negotiate with the others over his rights [mit gerechnet], and retains the rightful claim that was originally his to do whatever he pleases wherever he wants. *For the sake of what* could he reasonably have to renounce anything? What could enable him to wish that everyone keep what is theirs when he has nothing? I clearly see that it would be possible for an allied multitude of proprietors to use their power to keep the {446} weaker, dispersed individual from either asserting or making good on his rightful claim. Yet I am not asking about power, but Right, and I find that such a multitude has no right to do so. Only a treaty could give them this right, and since they did not conclude their treaty with this individual, he is not bound by it.

It clearly follows that not only the farmer, but all the residents in the state must have some form of exclusive property, since otherwise one could neither oblige them to recognize the property right of the farmer nor rightfully keep them from forcing the latter from his field and robbing him of his fruit.

What then is the exclusive property of the one who is not a farmer, of the manufacturer or merchant? What did they accept in return for ceding to the farmer the exclusive right to the property of the land?

His art or knowledge of trade he owes to nature and to himself, but not to the state. In this regard he is not bound to the state as the farmer is bound to his piece of land. Tossed up naked on any shore, he can say: I carry with me all that is mine. What can the state still give to him? Clearly, only the guarantee that he will always be able to find work or sell his goods, and that in return for these he will receive his due share of the goods of the land. It is with this assurance that the state first binds him to itself.

Yet the state cannot guarantee these things if it doesn't close off the number of those who may conduct the same branch of labor, while providing for the cultivation of the sustenance needed by all. Only through this *closure* does a branch of labor become the *property* of the class of its practitioners, and only through *this provision of sustenance* a property *from which they could live*. And it is only in return for being granted this as their property that they could renounce the property of the land-cultivating class. Security, I say, should be given [90] to them by the state: it should give them a guarantee. To say: all this will happen {447} of its own accord, everyone will always find work and bread, and then risk everything on such good fortune, is not decent [*anständig*] in a thoroughly just constitution. Are we talking about a sparrow who, as long as it eludes the net, will no doubt also find its little piece of grain, though we don't in the least count on this happening and in fact would much rather see that it didn't? If the state abandons these classes of people to chance, then it gives them absolutely nothing. Whether they thrive is now just as much their own doing as their art or knowledge. And, consequently, they have in no way renounced the property of others. With regard to their industrious activities the state has no right to bring them under its laws and into a determinate relation to the other classes of people. In every respect they are free: divested of both law and Right, without rule and without guarantee, half savages in the bosom of society. Given the complete uncertainty in which they find themselves, they will cheat and rob—though, indeed, one doesn't call it robbery, but *profit*—they will cheat and rob, as long and as well as they can. And those whom they cheat and rob, having become the stronger ones, will cheat and rob them in turn. They will do this for as long as it works, and will put as much as they can aside in a safe place for the emergencies against which they are never secure. And in all this they do only what they have a most perfect right to do.

With the closure of the different branches of acquisition, and with the guarantee that everyone will be able to purchase what they usually need at a fair price, the closure of the commercial state to the outside will follow of its own accord. There is no need to add another word about this. {448} [91]

SECOND BOOK

History of the present time— the condition of commerce in the actual states of the present

First Chapter

Preamble

To wonder at nothing is the peak of wisdom, says one of the ancients.[8] So long as he is talking about the astonishment at the unexpected that robs us of our composure and disturbs our calm reflection, he is entirely right. Yet we wish to add that in the ability to wonder about something consists the predisposition to wisdom, thinking for oneself, and freely producing concepts.

Someone who is not a thinker, but who nevertheless has healthy senses and memory, grasps the actual state of things that lies before his eyes and makes a mental note of it. He need do nothing more than this, since, after all, he only has to live and conduct his business in the actual world, and doesn't feel the least bit drawn toward thoughts that, as it were, not being needed right on the spot, are stockpiled for the future. He never either transcends this actual state of affairs with his thought or thinks of another, but rather, through the habit of only thinking this state of affairs, there arises in him gradually, and without him properly becoming conscious of it, the presupposition that only this state of affairs is and only this could be. The concepts and customs of his people and his age seem to him to be the only possible concepts and customs of all peoples and all ages. He certainly does not wonder at the fact that everything now is just as it is, for according to him it simply cannot be otherwise. He certainly will never raise the question of how it has come to be this way, since according to him it was this way from the beginning. If he is confronted with a description of other peoples {449} or ages, or a philosophical sketch of how it has never been but everywhere should have been, he will always drag in the pictures of his world, from which he cannot tear himself away, seeing everything [92] in terms of this world and never grasping the entire sense of what is presented before him. It is his incurable illness to regard the *accidental* as *necessary*.

He, on the other hand, who has become accustomed to using thought not only to copy what actually exists, but to freely create within himself what is possible, very often finds that entirely different nexuses and relations of things are just as possible—indeed far more possible, natural, and rational—than those that are given. He not only finds the given relations to be accidental, but at times wondrously strange [*wunderlich*]. And so he raises the question: How and in which way did everything come to be the way that it is, since it surely could have been otherwise in countless different ways? The history of the past answers this question for him, since indeed all historical research of deep penetration neither can nor should be anything else than a genetic answer to the causal question: How has the present state of things arisen, and what are the reasons that the world formed itself into what we find before us?

Here our only concern is with commerce. My readers have already seen that, with regard to commerce, the author holds that a state of affairs entirely different from what we find in the actual world is not only possible, but indeed demanded by the law of Right. Thus, he may at any rate wonder why it is not the latter state of affairs, but that which we actually see before us, that came into being. At present we need only describe the state of affairs that actually came into being. Such a portrayal is part of the history of the present time, and yet perhaps we can make this description even clearer by casting a glance at how the given state of affairs emerged from that state of affairs immediately preceding it. Here too we will count on the reader having the ability and the willingness to wonder at things and the adroitness to look away from the present {450} and enter with his thought wholly into the past or the future.

Second Chapter

The known world considered as one great unitary commercial state

The peoples of the ancient world were very rigidly separated from one another by a multitude of circumstances. For them, the foreigner was an enemy or a barbarian. The peoples of modern Christian Europe, in contrast, may be considered as [93] one nation. Already united by the same descent and same customs [*Gebräuche*] and notions indigenous to the forests of Germania, they also came to be bound together, after their dispersal throughout the provinces of the Western Roman Empire, by a single common religion and the same submissiveness to its visible head. The peoples of different descent who later joined them acquired, along with the new religion, the same basic system of Germanic customs and notions.

Were one to apply our concepts of state, authority, and subject to these individual settlements of half-barbarians, one would be led completely astray. For indeed they lived in the state of nature. Only for the sake of war were they united by their king who, following the custom of the German forests was, properly speaking, just the leader of armies. Otherwise, being in most respects without political alliances, they were their own judge and defender. It is only through the relation of the serfs to their masters and the vassals to the feudal lord that these crowds of people were connected to one another. The few judicial actions that took place—and these were, properly speaking, only acts of arbitration—were merely a *consequence* of these relations. They were far from being an *end in itself*, {451} with *the laws the true and proper means of binding together* the nation. Even the bond of the feudal system bound them so loosely that the same man could be vassal of one king and freeholder in the lands of another, so that, in the case of a war between the two kings, he would be required to fight in person for the very king *against* whom, as a freeholder, he had sent his man.

These tribes were united by everything, and were not separated from one another by what usually separates men—namely, a state constitution—since they didn't even have one. No wonder that they considered and conducted themselves as one nation, interbreeding, traveling throughout one another's lands, trading and trafficking, and enlisting in one another's service, with everyone always still feeling at home even when he arrived at another's domain.

It is only later that proper political concepts and institutions came into circulation. This took place through the introduction of Roman law [Recht] and the application of the Roman concepts of emperors [Imperatoren] to the modern kings and the modern Kaiser, who was originally only thought of as the military leader of Christianity, and was *supposed* to be for the entire Church what the church bailiffs were for individual bishoprics or cloisters. The relation of serfs and vassals to their lords gradually changed into the relation of subjects to their authority and judge. So, for example, there arose, first of all in France, [94] a monarchy in the old style. Now for the first time the tribes were separated from one another through state constitutions. This separation was made even easier by the fact that the Reformation had destroyed the clerical power that previously held the Christian church together as a whole.

In this way the modern states were formed: not as the doctrine of Right is wont to describe the emergence of a state—through the collection and unification of unattached individuals under the unity of the law—but rather through separating and dividing into pieces a large, unitary, though only weakly bound, mass of men. {452} The individual states of Europe are just such pieces torn away from a former whole, with the extension of their boundaries for the most part determined by chance.

It is no wonder that this process of separation, having begun not long ago, is not yet finished, with still-noticeable traces of the former circumstances remaining, and that a good part of our notions and institutions still seem to presuppose the continuing existence of this state of affairs, even though it has been abolished.

During that period of the unity of Christian Europe there was also formed, among other things, the system of trade that, at least in its basic features, continues to the present time. Every part of the great whole—every individual—cultivated and manufactured and acquired by trade from other parts of the world whatever was most expedient given its natural situation, and brought its goods unhindered to market through all the parts of the great whole, with the prices of things arising of their own accord. In this region one was the exclusive master of this branch of agriculture, and in another region of another branch. If someone was not exclusively allotted a branch of agriculture, he would live more wretchedly, though without altogether perishing. In these days, to refer to a ware it was enough to name the place where it was manufactured, and merchants selling certain articles were nicknamed after the country from which they came, since it went without saying that these goods weren't manufactured anywhere else and that people only ever came from the country being referred to with the aim of selling these goods. A common means of exchange was valid, namely gold and silver money, having more or less the same value in all parts of the great commercial state, and circulated unhindered from one region to another. There could be no thought of calculating the extent of this trade relative to the total inland production, since there was not any common sovereign in the proper sense and everything was in a state of anarchy. Yet since the arts had spread so little, there was no reason to fear that the markets would be glutted and the manufacturer [95] and merchant {453} would suffer or that they would experience a shortage of the means of nourishment. Given the simple way of life and limited needs of men, there was also no reason to fear the producer having to do without the goods to which he had grown accustomed.—Under this state of affairs trade was entirely free, without being either calculated or restricted.

If one merely leaves out of the equation the lack of calculation, which was neither possible nor much needed, such freedom was entirely in order under these circumstances. The citizens of the same state should all trade and traffic with one another. If Christian Europe was a whole, then the trade of the Europeans among themselves must be free.

It is easy to apply this same reasoning to the present state of affairs. If the whole of Christian Europe, with its new colonies and its trading centers in other parts of the world, still remains a whole, then the trade between all its different parts must certainly remain free, just as it was originally. If it is, in contrast, separated into a number of states, each forming a whole and each standing under a different government, then it must be separated off into just as many thoroughly closed commercial states.

We have now arrived at the source of the greatest part of the still-existing abuses. For a long time there were no states at all in modern Europe. At present, one is still attempting to form them. Moreover, one has up till now only one-sidedly, only half comprehended the task of the state, conceiving of it as an institution that, through the law, should preserve the citizen in whatever state of possession it finds him in. Yet one failed to see that the profounder duty of the state is to put each in possession of what is his due. Yet the latter is only possible by eliminating the anarchy of trade, just as one gradually is eliminating political anarchy. The state must close itself off as a commercial state, just as it has already been closed off in its legislative apparatus and judiciary.

All institutions that either allow or presuppose the direct commerce between a citizen and the citizen of another state {454} consider both fundamentally as citizens of one state. Such institutions are the remnants and results of a constitution that was abolished a long time ago. They are parts of a past world that have no place in our own world. Those systems that demand free trade, those claims that one must be able to buy and market one's goods throughout the known world, have been passed down to us from the way of thinking of our forefathers. Such ideas were suitable for them. We accepted them without proof, and have become accustomed to them, and putting other ideas in their place will not be without difficulty. [96]

Third Chapter

The reciprocal relation of the individuals in this great commercial state

To investigate how it came about that men agreed to grant the validity of gold and silver, and nothing in their place, as the sign of all value would take us too far afield. At the very least the reason offered by a famous writer will not do.[9] He claims that because the extraction of a certain amount of gold or silver costs just as much time and effort as the extraction or manufacture of some other specific ware, we are able to accept the one as an equivalent for the other. The man who is left to his own devises will value the other's produce not according to the effort expended on it but rather according to the utility that he intends to draw from it. Hence, even if we presume that there actually was such an equality in the effort expended, we must still ask why the farmer would equate the effort that the miner put into extracting a piece of gold with the effort expended in producing some bushels of grain. Why would he regard this effort to be as well employed as his own? While the miner couldn't live without grain, the farmer naturally {455} can't do anything with the miner's gold. If someone employs his efforts to no purpose, would the human race then regard itself as obliged to repay him for this with purposeful labor?

I must, however, explicitly recall that the value of these metals rests merely in the general agreement about their value. Each person accepts these at a certain ratio to his goods since he is certain that everyone with whom he can engage in commerce will accept them in turn from him at this same ratio. The true intrinsic value of these metals, their usefulness as raw materials, is far from equal to their extrinsic value, which rests merely on opinion. The goods manufactured from them obtain their value only in consideration of the fact that one can, or at least should have been able to, again make money out of them. The money material that they contain must also be paid for.

Precisely because, as I recall in passing, the value of world currency to goods has no other guarantee than public opinion, this ratio is just as fluctuating and variable as public opinion itself. It is really only through spreading the view that [97] goods become cheaper or more expensive, in place of the more correct view that the value of money rises or sinks, that one has been able to shut the eyes of the great public to this variability. The national currency described above would, in contrast, have an entirely different guarantee, since it would have to be a fundamental law of the state that it will forever accept the money it gives out at the same value in relation to commodities and maintain it at this value among the fellow citizens.

If all this is presupposed, the relation of the money circulating in the great commercial state to the goods found in its public trade will be just the same as in the rational state described above. The entire sum of money represents and is worth the same as the entire sum of goods, and so much of a part of the former value represents so much of a part of the latter. With the quantity of the goods remaining constant, it makes absolutely no difference whether {456} a greater or lesser quantity of money is in circulation. Here too, wealth rests not on how much money someone has, but rather on how much of a part of all existing money he possesses. It is at least to be accepted, as the one firm principle amid all this unceasing fluctuation, that so much of a part of the circulating money is equal to so much of a part of the value of the goods (I speak here of the intrinsic value, the value for the maintenance and pleasantness of life), despite the fact that, since one never rightly knows how much gold and how many goods are in circulation—this or that ware can be brought out of circulation and thus made more expensive through artificial means, or a multitude of similar circumstances can also intervene—this ratio is fluctuating, dependent on chance, and exposed to cheating.

I still presuppose it to be the case that trade is completely free throughout the entire great commercial state, standing under no limitations at all. In this case every individual is a free and independent member of the commercial state. It is not yet possible to see any common interest of a plurality, through which this plurality would be unified as one body, a unitary greater whole within the commercial state. Possessing a piece of gold, each individual can lay claim to whatever goods throughout the great commercial state form a part of all the goods found in it as great as his part of all the money. Yet each one, in making this claim, is independent of the others. It is a matter of complete indifference to him whether someone else does or does not have money, since in no case will his money rise or fall in value.

The most that could unite a plurality of individuals under the same fate and show them all to be a particular commercial body [98], with common advantages or disadvantages, is their geographic situation—the greater or lesser distance separating them from the place of the extraction or manufacture of a ware. Here, however, we shall ignore this possibility.

Suppose that the sum of money circulating in the commercial state is distributed equally among all the individuals {457} participating in it. These would then all have an equal claim to an equally large quantity of the available goods. All are equally rich, meaning no one is relatively rich or poor. Whether, with the goods that they can buy for their money, they will live pleasantly, with only the bare necessities, or even quite wretch-edly—the question, in other words, of their *intrinsic* wealth or prosperity—is not at issue here.

If someone's share of the available money exceeds what he would have obtained through an equal division, then he is relatively rich. The more his share is in excess, the richer he will be. And, likewise, someone who has less than he would receive through an equal division is relatively poor.

Yet that stock of money only has value insofar as we count on giv-ing it out in exchange for goods. Should we lack the means to replace the outflow, it would soon all be given away. Properly speaking then, someone should only be called relatively rich if he periodically earns a quantity of goods whose value in money exceeds what he would receive through an equal division of all goods, and then knows how to convert these goods into money and the money obtained thereby into goods that he has not himself earned. Perhaps he will even carry out these exchanges to his advantage, making *his* effort worth more to others than their effort is worth to him and having them work more for him than he works for them.

Everyone naturally wishes to profit as much as possible from the other while allowing the other to profit as little as possible from himself. Everyone wishes to let the other do as much work as possible for him while he works as little as possible for the other. If no law and no authority should hinder him, he will employ every possible means to accomplish this. Every dollar that he obtains is now worth two. The first, because he has it, and with it a claim to the services of others. The second, because no one else, having it, has a claim to his services.

An unceasing war of all against all, of buyers and sellers, will arise among the trading public. {458} This war will become ever more fierce and unjust and dangerous in its consequences as the world's population increases, the commercial state grows through additional acquisitions, production and the arts advance, and finally, as a result, the quantity of goods coming into circulation, and with this the needs of the population, increase and mul-tiply. When the way of life among the nations was simpler, this had gone on without great injustice or oppression, but now that needs have grown greater, it has turned into the most screaming injustice, a source of great misery. The buyer seeks [99] to extort the seller's goods from the seller, and thus demands freedom of trade—the freedom, in other words, for the seller to glut the markets and, finding no outlet for his goods, be compelled to sell them for far below their value. And likewise he demands strong competition between the manufacturers and traders, so that, by making it harder for them to sell their goods and obtain the cash they need to survive, he can compel them to give him their goods at whatever price he may still offer in his generosity. Should he succeed in this, the worker will grow poor and industrious families will either waste away in want and misery or emigrate from an unjust people. The seller will defend himself against this oppression, or even indeed will himself seize control of the supply through the most varied means—buying everything up, artificially raising prices, and the like. In this way he puts the buyers in danger of suddenly having either to forgo their usual needs, or to purchase them at an unusually high price and suffer want in some other regard. Or else he will lower the quality of the goods in response to the lower price being paid for them. The buyer will not receive what he thought he would. He is deceived, and in most cases poor and hasty labor will also give rise to a pure loss of public force and time and of the produce subjected to such shoddy workmanship.

In short, no one will be provided with the slightest guarantee that, if he continues to work, he will continue to enjoy his present state of existence. For men wish to be completely free that they may destroy one another. {459}

Fourth Chapter

The reciprocal relation of the nations as wholes in this commercial state

As long as the governments of the particular states of which the commercial state consists do not directly collect taxes from their citizens, but defray the costs of the administration of the state through demesnes and other such means, the relation of the individual to the commercial state will remain just as we have described. All the individuals are free members of the commercial state, existing for themselves, and whether they become rich or poor is of no interest to any other member of the commercial state, and is of just as little interest to its government. The government likewise represents a member of the commercial state that exists for itself, administering its wealth and using it to engage in commerce both abroad and at home. [100]

Yet as soon as the government begins taxing its citizens directly, and indeed in the commercial state's common means of exchange—in world currency—this gives rise to new considerations, and the relations in the commercial state become more complicated.

The rational state, according to the above, collects as much taxes as it *needs*. With the majority of actual states, one will proceed very safely if one assumes that each will collect as much as it *can*. Nor can this be held against them, since they are as a rule unable to collect as much as they need to accomplish those purposes that, mostly for want of wealth, still remain to be accomplished.

The governments collect taxes in world currency, since they pay residents and foreigners alike only in this currency, as if they have no closer relation to the former than to each of the latter. Nor could it be otherwise, if the particular juridical state does not form a particular commercial society, and every individual citizen can end up engaging in commerce with the most distant foreigner as easily as with his neighboring fellow citizen, depending as much, with respect to the prices for which he buys and sells goods, {460} on the former as the latter, who in this regard is not even his fellow citizen, but an entirely free individual. Everyone must therefore be equipped with the universally valid means of exchange for use in every situation, and can use none but this.

The more of this world currency that its subjects possess, the more the government can collect from them as taxes; the less, then the less. It therefore will become in the government's interest that all those who pay taxes have quite a lot of money, so that the government can take quite a lot from them. Thus, *the government conceives* of these tax-paying citizens as unified into one entity, a single body, whose affluence is its concern, even though the individuals, *as they conceive of themselves*, remain separate from one another and without a common interest. For the government there is only one wealth, one source of potential power [*Ein Vermögen*]: the tax-paying body.[10] Now, for the first time, the concept of national wealth, and of a nation having wealth, has some sense. Previously—or indeed for as long as this perspective is disregarded and the state guards only against one person taking from another, without seeing to it that everyone has something—we could only speak of a nation united through laws and a common judiciary, and not, however, of a nation united through common wealth.—In this way, nature leads governments for their own advantage beyond the narrow boundaries that they have set to their administration, [101] giving them, on account of its utility, an interest they should already have had for the sake of what is right.

If several or all of the governments found in the commercial state introduce taxes paid in money, then from their perspective there will arise several national-wealths, and a relation of these wealths to one another.

This relationship can be of three kinds.

Let us disregard, for the moment, the intrinsic state of prosperity of the citizens—whether their way of life is easier or more toilsome. Since the true source of riches indeed rests solely in the supply of goods, it follows that we should call neither relatively poor nor rich a nation that periodically imports goods that cost the same amount of money, {461} and have the same intrinsic value, as the goods that it exports. It would be in a state of complete equilibrium with all the other foreign countries considered as a single entity (for nothing prevents that it could lose to one nation and gain back an equal amount from the others). It will keep its money in circulation undiminished, and the government could continue to collect the same taxes as it was wont to collect before.

I also count the government's treasury among the wealth of the nation, thinking of this as one of those individuals of the nation who are engaged in trade. And I presuppose that it too does not spend more money abroad than it draws, since it is only under this condition that the above case will occur.

Or—this is the second case—a nation produces, manufactures, and works far more, and far more advantageously, to satisfy the accustomed needs of foreign countries than these work in return to satisfy its needs, selling the results of its work for more money than the latter receive for their work. Such a nation is relatively rich. The money circulating within its borders increases periodically. It is rich in a pecuniary sense. As long as its sources of goods do not dry up, and the need of the foreign countries remains the same, this wealth will be sound [*gegründet*] and enduring.

Money has value only under the condition that it is given out. It only obtains its representative value when it circulates throughout the entire commercial state and helps determine the prices of goods in all regions, and not when, in contrast, it is concentrated in one nation, where it would necessarily lose value in relation to the nation's goods. The rich nation described above, it follows, must and will necessarily spend its periodically gained surplus of money abroad, with the result that the income of these foreign countries would again enter into equilibrium with their expenses. The great difference [102] between the two nations consists only in the fact that the rich nation exchanges this surplus {462} for goods that it could do without, and compels the foreigner, who can scarcely pay for the bare necessities, to work for its pleasure. The rich nation, in other words, unceasingly increases the state of its intrinsic prosperity at the expense of the foreigner, whose condition becomes ever more miserable.—The meaning of this will first become evident when we cast a glance at the opposite case, a nation that is growing poorer.—Yet there is also another possibility, which is indeed the more probable result of pecuniary riches. The government of such a nation, following the maxim to take as much as it can, will take the profit from foreign trade and use it to hire foreign forces toward its own ends.

The third and final case is when a nation continually loses its money in foreign trade. This nation is poor, and becomes ever poorer.—Let one suppose that ten million dollars are in circulation within a single nation, and that with every year one million of these are lost in trade for foreign goods. In the first year these ten million dollars will represent not only the goods that the country either gains within its territories or acquires in exchange for these, but also and in addition to these a quantity of goods from abroad that can only be acquired in exchange for money. In the following year only nine million dollars will still remain in the country. Here I am completely disregarding the possibility that previously accumulated state funds, or the considerable fortunes collected by individuals, could flow back into circulation, since this does not offer a fundamental remedy. Of these nine million, one million will represent, now as before, those goods that can be obtained from abroad only in exchange for money, while the remaining eight represent the same quantity previously represented by nine. Since there is less money for the same quantity of goods, the prices, according to our rule, should change and the value of gold increase. Yet, on the one hand, according to our presupposition, all the foreign countries will purchase its goods using their money as a means of exchange. On the other hand, it is perhaps possible that the residents of the country, who indeed exchange goods for goods, and also the foreigner, when he is expecting goods in return, will trade without money, on credit, or let goods be represented by goods, or the circulation will become quicker, and the shortage of money {463} will be covered by the [faster] time of its circulation. It is not impossible that the prices will remain the same. Yet this much is nevertheless clear: that, according to our calculation, in ten years there will be no more money in the country. Farther down we shall consider what keeps this total impoverishment at bay, putting experience in apparent conflict with calculation.

Every tax is a curtailment of the intrinsic prosperity of the nation; this is its constant effect. Whatever the citizen pays to the state, he must earn without enjoying the fruits of his labor. If the taxes remain the same as a nation grows poorer, the prosperity of this nation will be curtailed with every year. Were this not to happen, or were the poverty to reach such a degree that the state of prosperity could decrease no further, it will become necessary [103] for the taxes, and with them the state's income, to be reduced, and, as a result, the government will lose power.

Why don't we actually see nations become completely without money, when what was just described seems to have been happening to many of them for a long time? Quite many, to be sure, have ended up poorer in money than before. Yet complete impoverishment, and its obvious spectacle, is concealed by an ever worse national economy, where everything possible is offered for sale and transformed into a commodity, and where the capital, the nation itself, is consumed once the interests on this capital, the work of the nation, no longer suffice. The actual result of such an economy is that, since the country's population is continually depleted, what little remains of the national wealth will be divided up among ever fewer men, who will hence receive a greater part than would happen without this depopulation.—Men will emigrate, seeking refuge under another clime from the poverty they could not escape on patriotic soil. Or the government will turn them into commodities, drawing money from foreign countries in exchange for them. With fewer hands working on the raw produce, this produce can also be sold. This trade {464} will expand, and whatever manufacturers still remain in the country will no longer be able to get ahold of the produce they need and will perish from want. What had previously gone to nourish these manufacturers is once again exported for a pure profit. If some of the crop should fail, then, in a country such as this, where everything is sold and nothing saved for emergencies, a great many men will die. Through a decrease in the number of domestic consumers, ever more goods will be gained for foreign trade. The farmlands will either fall in price or lie deserted in a desolate country. For a time foreigners will speculate on these lands, thus discovering a new branch of trade.—And there is yet one more ware that one should hardly have had to resort to: the state sells itself, its very independence. It now continually collects subsidies, thereby turning itself into the province of another state and the means to whatever end this other state pleases.

This progression, in which each evil is remedied through a still greater evil, will continue without cease. When the depopulation has reached its peak, even more land will be gained for wild growth needing neither tillage nor tending. Now mast trees and other wood, animal-skins, dried fish, and the like will be the chief articles of trade for the wild descendants of a civilized people. They will find these kinds of goods in abundance, and will always be able to exchange these for the few things they need.

In short: whoever lives there will find what he needs in this meager fashion; he would not live at all [104] if he could not do so. The true victims of the state's impoverishment have died, perhaps one or two generations ago. Because these no longer even exist, no one asks why these have nothing. {465}

Fifth Chapter

The means that governments have employed up till now to steer this relation to their advantage

Every government that has opened its eyes to this relation of its nations to the other nations within the great commercial state, and that, with respect to this circumstance as well, is not content to let everything turn out as God pleases, has seized on nearly the same measures, hoping, through artificial means, to make this relation as advantageous as possible for it. The usual maxims expressing this intention are as follows: money should remain in the country; the foreigner's money should be drawn into the country. Without wishing in the least to diminish the generally patriotic and beneficent sentiments of so many governments toward their subjects, one may nevertheless assume that, at least in the case of such provisions, these governments are more concerned with maintaining or increasing the taxes they are to collect, and by means of these taxes, their military might relative to other nations, than with securing the state of existence of their subjects.

Sufficient light has not yet been cast on the universal concepts of Right for governments to regard it as their duty to secure the state of existence of their subjects. And it is also incomprehensible how one could have thought of the measures customarily in use as means to this end.

It makes no difference to our investigation whether a nation is losing in trade, and the government's intention is to reduce this loss and, little by little, eliminate it entirely, or whether a nation is gaining, and the government wishes either to maintain or increase this profitable state of affairs. The end remains forever the same—namely, to steer the ratio of trade to its advantage. And everywhere more or less the same means are used to attain this same end. {466}

The first of these is to increase exports, and thus, through this, the money that one draws from foreigners. Agriculture is encouraged, so that there is produce to export, and its exportation is promoted, perhaps through

153

premiums. Special circumstances must prevail for it to be advantageous to export raw produce. [105] If the exported produce is intended as raw materials, it must either be impossible to draw into the country those who will labor on such raw materials, or inadvisable because of other considerations. If, however, they are intended to serve directly as nourishment, it must be impossible to find workers who would consume them within the country. For whether the workers are consuming the produce or using it as raw materials, in either case they would also be earning the wages of their labor for the nation. Otherwise, the export of both raw produce and the primary means of nourishment are with right forbidden in such a system of political economy. This same system, in consequent fashion, will unconditionally promote both domestic factories and the foreign export of their manufactured goods.

The next method then consists in hindering or burdening the import of foreign *manufactured goods,* with a resulting reduction in the money flowing abroad: either by completely banning these goods, or through the imposition of considerable tariffs on them. One could hardly think that it would be either necessary or advantageous to burden the import of foreign *produce* except in the case of those intended for mere luxury [*Wohlleben*]. The primary means of nourishment will not be permitted to come from abroad at a loss of the costs of freight when there is no shortage of these within the country. Yet if the nation imports raw materials, assuming that the foreigner permits their export and we have the means to labor on them domestically, the wages of labor that it thereby gains will increase the national wealth.

Finally, the third method is the encouragement of trade for and in place of foreign countries, with the nation offering itself as a go-between and shipping agency for the individual nations of the great commercial state, setting itself up as their navigator and driver over land and sea and once more profiting from its effort and its trade advantage. {467}

Sixth Chapter

The result of using these means

We now have to answer two questions. First, to what extent will the purpose that one had pursued with these means actually be reached through them? And second, is this purpose itself purposeful? Is it the purpose that one should have pursued?

As for the first question, it is immediately clear that if a sum of money now remains in the hands of residents, from whom the state can collect taxes, rather than going to a foreigner who will pay no taxes on it to the government, or likewise if a tax-paying resident now receives a sum of money from a foreigner who would have paid the taxes on it to another government, then the national wealth, in the sense of the word established above, would certainly either increase or at least decrease by less, with the government realizing the increase in its strength intended through these measures. [106] What we stated above in general application is true in an even higher sense for governments. Every dollar earned by its nation is worth double for it: insofar as it is thereby in its command, it can be used against the goals of every other government, and insofar as no other government has it in its command, it cannot be used against its own goals.

Yet it is also clear that when even only one government has publicly pursued these measures, seeking to draw exclusive advantages for itself and its nation from living together [with other nations] in a common commercial republic, all the other governments that are suffering as a result, if they are the least bit wise, will feel the need to pursue the same measures. It is likewise evident that once one nation has achieved superiority in trade, the other nations that are oppressed as a result must employ every possible means to weaken {468} the first nation's superiority and bring themselves back into equilibrium, and that when they are not immediately able to do so at the expense of the predominant nation, they will just as gladly do this at the expense of a nation even weaker than themselves. With all the states at any rate already tending toward reciprocal hostility on account of their territorial borders, a new tendency toward enmity will arise on account of their trade interests, resulting in the eruption of a secret trade war of all against all. The interest in one's own advantage will be joined by an interest in the other's loss. Sometimes a nation will be happy to satisfy the latter without the former, causing pure damages. So it was when the Dutch extirpated all the spice plants that they found beyond the islands set aside for their cultivation, burning part of the harvested spices, just as in war one burns the supplies that cannot be brought along for one's own use.

This secret war will pass over into acts of violence [*Tätlichkeiten*], and such as are not honorable. One will foster smuggling into neighboring lands, and indeed openly encourage it.—Conflicting trade interests are often the true cause of wars that have been given another pretext. Thus, one buys [107] half continents at the price of a people's political principles, as one says, since the war is actually directed against the people's own trade, and indeed is to the disadvantage of those who have been bought.

Trade interests ultimately give rise to political concepts that could not be more perilous, and these concepts in turn give rise to wars whose true cause one no longer conceals but parades in open view. Thus will arise dominion over the sea, which, beyond the range of a shot fired from the shores of inhabited lands, should no doubt be as free as air and light. Thus will arise the exclusive right to trade with a foreign people—a foreign people that [considered for itself] doesn't concern one trading nation more than another: and over this dominion and this right there will arise bloody wars.

In the long run, the efforts made by the nations {469} who are los-ing at trade will not be without favorable result. We can only wish them luck in this. But what will be the result for the states that, till now, have enjoyed superiority in trade? With each new step the foreigner takes toward independence from them, they lose a corresponding amount of the national riches to which they are accustomed. And if the government continues to collect the same taxes, they will also suffer a decline in their intrinsic state of prosperity. If, however, the government reduces taxes in proportion to the loss of national wealth, then it will lose in equal measure its military might relative to other countries. Perhaps it had only wished to possess this might for a time and to attain a temporary goal, which, reasonably speaking, could not justifiably be anything other than attaining its natural borders, thereby securing itself against every war. If it had used this passing moment of pecuniary and military superiority to actually attain this goal, then it could quietly let this decline come to pass. It has everything it needs, and could even close itself off as a commercial state and be sufficient unto itself. Yet could we ascribe such modesty to any of the states now in existence? If the government presumed by us had counted on the continuing existence of its former superiority, and indeed it has to count on this since it has not yet attained its goals—be they rational or contrary to reason [*vernunftwidrig*]—

then the progress of foreign countries would put it at a great disadvantage. Its neighbors would soon notice its decline, and this state, weakened already in trade, would now also be weakened through war.

This system appears in a yet far more disadvantageous light if one considers the true goal that governments should pursue in arranging [108] their trade, which is to secure for their subjects the state of existence to which they are accustomed. This is demanded by prudence as well as by justice, although we wish [in the present considerations] to completely disregard the latter. Maintaining domestic tranquility is necessarily the first goal of government and {470} must always take precedence over the promotion of its power beyond its territorial limits, since indeed the latter is conditioned by the former.—It is only through the precise calculation of the reciprocal relation of the different estates of the nation in the way described in the first book, and the complete closure of trade with foreign countries, that a government would be able to secure for all its subjects the state of existence to which they are accustomed. In no way would the incomplete measures be able to achieve this. No state that counts on selling its goods abroad, fostering and guiding its domestic industry with a view to this expectation, can ensure for its subjects that these sales will continue into the future. If a citizen of the neighboring state applies himself to this same branch of agriculture, or if a government-issued ban should suddenly compel the citizen of the neighboring state to dispense with these goods, then the worker will be without food and will perish from want. The only ground for consolation that one can give in this case is that this stoppage of the accustomed trade will not occur suddenly, that it will be possible to find an outlet somewhere else to replace the one that was lost, and that we can devote ourselves to another branch of agriculture if with this one there is no longer real progress to be made. Yet even if we disregard the fact that sudden bans on goods in foreign countries can indeed also bring forth immediate and rapid difficulties, one will be spared nothing through the slow rate of decline save the too noticeable and startling appearance of impoverishment. Those who are going to perish there will still perish, and it makes no essential difference for the nation whether this happens in one year or twenty.—Regardless of all the burdens placed on the import of goods from abroad and how many tariffs have been imposed on them to make them more expensive, no manufacturer who only counts on domestic sales and indeed relies on these to survive can be sure of his sales if it is still in any way permissible to import an indeterminate quantity of goods. The market can be glutted, compelling both him and the foreigner to sell under value. Or his countrymen may travel abroad to purchase foreign goods that are more expensive, yet also more desirable or even in fact better {471} than the cheaper domestic items. Or the foreigner will discover new advantages putting him in the position to sell his goods at a lower price than the native citizen despite the impost placed on them. An attentive government will no doubt intercede in this case and [109] once again raise the impost. Nevertheless, those manufacturers who were unable to cover the loss will already have been ruined in the meantime, and all the manufacturers will have been harmed.—The other side of the disadvantages is immediately clear, and few words need be spent on its analysis. However much it may promote domestic industry, no state that depends on a supply of goods from foreigners—a supply that is neither regulated nor in its power to control—can guarantee to its subjects that they will always be able to have at a fair price the goods they are accustomed to having. Should some accident keep the foreign tradesmen away, then there will be a shortage of their goods. Or they may bring a smaller quantity of the goods, and the cost of the goods will increase.

Let one not say—I will touch on this matter here merely in passing—let one not say that, following philosophical principles that have not been granted, I expect of governments a function that they would never recognize as belonging to them, since I presuppose that they should provide the worker with work and outlet for his goods, and the buyer with a sufficient supply of the goods that he is accustomed to having at a fair price—all things that each one should have to take care of himself, not troubling the government about such matters. Yet in states enjoying civil order [poliziert], manufacturers whose workshops were forced to come to a sudden standstill for lack of sales or raw materials, or a people in danger of doing without its primary means of nourishment, or compelled to pay for it at a rate out of all proportion to past prices, have always turned to the government with an obscure feeling of their right. And their governments never dismissed these complaints as if they did not pertain to them, but offered council to the best of their abilities, with an obscure feeling of their duty and a clear view of the dangers {472} posed by the uprising of mobs of people whom direst need has left with nothing to lose.

Nor will the incomplete measures that have been described—measures that involve neither a calculation made of the number of goods that should be brought to market given the needs of the buyers, nor the fixing of prices—end the war described above between buyers and sellers.

Thus, not only will the halfways and incomplete restriction of trade retain all the disadvantages of completely free trade, but it will bring about new disadvantages.

Bans or tariffs on foreign goods will necessarily cause the prices of these goods to rise, and as a consequence everyone will suffer a reduction either of his previous state of prosperity or at least of that state of prosperity that [110] he would have achieved without those restricting laws. Now, strictly speaking, and *in a merely rational state*, no man may lay claim to a greater state of prosperity than issues from the climate where he lives and the culture of the nation of whom he is a member, unless something happened previously to provide him with such a claim. In all the states now in existence, however, we find just such a precedent. All of them arose, whether recently or long ago, from a constitution where trade is entirely free. Each individual had a claim to all the advantages that his strength could grant him within the immense commercial republic of which he was an independent and free member. He has grown up enjoying these advantages, and has become accustomed to this enjoyment, since he was able to count with good reason on their continuing throughout his life. His government, also a witness to all this, remained completely silent, guaranteeing through its silence that, to the extent that it was in its power, these pleasures would continue to be available.

Were a confluence of natural causes either to deprive him of these pleasures, or render them prohibitively expensive, {473} he would have to bear this just like every other accident stemming from will-less nature. Yet that a free being would freely and consciously deprive him of these things, and that his government would take back its silently given word, is at any rate an injury to his right.

This injustice—it is indeed unavoidable, and protects against manifold other injustices, but it nevertheless remains, strictly speaking, an injustice—is dimly felt by the nation, even if it perhaps cannot yet clearly explicate it in rational terms [*aus Gründen entwickeln*]. It feels that it has been deprived of something whose secure possession it had counted on. This feeling of injustice is compounded by the general ignorance of the great crowds about the true goals that every sensible government intends with such trade restrictions. They believe that one takes these things from them only to keep them for oneself, thereby becoming rich, in order to increase the state income in this way when no other way can be found. Hence, taxes of this kind are always much more deeply despised than all those ancient and customary taxes raised from landed property, and thus the public is forever inclined to blame every increase in the prices of things, though this can have a number of different causes, simply on the taxes.

There will arise hatred of the government in the hearts of the subjects, and driven by this hatred, they will wage war against the government through cunning ruses and, ultimately, open violence. There will arise smuggling, and an artificial system of fraud. In the opinion of the people, cheating the government is no longer a crime, but instead becomes a permissible and laudable act of self-defense against a common enemy. For the man who does not wish to join in this [111] universal practice [*Sitte*], it will be impossible to continue at his trade.[ii]{474}

Faced with the hostility of its subjects, the government, from its side, will now seize on harsh and hostile countermeasures that will be carried out even more harshly by its embittered subordinate officials. The word and assurances of the subjects will no longer be valid, since these measures have publicly declared them one and all to be a nation of cheaters or even public enemies of the government. Searches will be employed everywhere, and treachery encouraged by offering rewards; the cunning ruses and lies of the subjects will be opposed with new ruses and new lies on the side of the officials. Since smuggling will nevertheless not be eliminated through all these measures, the one unfortunate creature who gets caught will be punished with disproportionate severity while a thousand who are more cunning mock all these provisions. The embitterment grows, and from now on we will even see armed crowds of smugglers taking to the field against the government troops that guard the borders, or tariff officials, dispatched into rural lands, falling prey to a wild rabble whose pranks will go undiscovered and unpunished.

Administering the state incomes in this way will, moreover, require an army of chief and subordinate officials and state servants of all varieties, thus removing, once again, a multitude of hands from the national industries that these measures should have promoted, and costing the government the very sums that should have been saved or earned.[iii] {475} [112]

In short, this system, where foreign trade is closed incompletely, without precise calculation of what goods ought to be brought into trade given the nation's needs, not only fails to achieve what it should, but in fact brings about new evils. [113]

THIRD BOOK

Politics—how the commerce of an existing state can be brought into the arrangement required by reason; or, on the closure of the commercial state

First Chapter

More precise determination
of the task of this book

We know the goal that states must strive toward with regard to commerce, and we know the point where they stand at present with respect to the same. It cannot be difficult, then, to discover and indicate the path that will lead them from the latter to the former.

It is a matter of complete indifference for our investigation whether trade and industry are entirely free within a given state, standing under absolutely no restrictions, or whether the state has made incomplete attempts {476} to close itself off through bans on goods and other restrictions placed on foreign trade. These attempts are nowhere to be found on the path that leads from the anarchy of trade to its rational arrangement, since in all systems of this sort, the first false presupposition, which we will *specify* farther down, remains untouched. These incomplete restrictions could at best have the advantage of accustoming the citizen, who desires to retain his natural freedom of commerce even in the bosom of regularity and laws, to restrictions as such—if indeed there were need, with the measures we are about to indicate, to habituate him and prepare his mind in this way. In a word: what we are about to say is just as valid for a state that has not previously known trade restrictions as it is for a state that has, and can be carried out just as well in the one as in the other.

The proper point of transition from all the present political [114] systems of trade and industry—which, as much as they may diverge from one another in secondary matters, nevertheless agree on the main point and are to be regarded as one and the same system—to that system that, in our opinion, is alone true and that reason itself demands, is as follows. The *state must close itself off entirely to all foreign trade*, forming from this point on an isolated commercial body, just as it had already previously formed an isolated juridical and political body. Once this closure has been brought about [*zu Stande gebracht*], everything else will follow quite easily, and the measures that should be pursued from this point on no longer lie within the domain of politics but rather of the pure doctrine of Right, and have already been set forth by us in the first book. Among these matters, only the doctrine of the closure of the commercial state is the object of politics, and it is this doctrine alone that we must present in this book.

If the individual citizens as well as the state as a whole are not without previous relations, as the idea of a rational state presupposes, but have instead {477} emerged, respectively, as free citizens of a great commercial republic and as a part torn off by chance from the great whole, then they may well have obtained special claims that, while rightful, are enjoyed neither by the citizens of the rational state nor the state itself, and that must be secured before the complete closure of the state and its perfect separation from the rest of the inhabited world. Before all else, it is necessary to investigate whether there are indeed such rightful claims originating in the previous state of affairs, and what these claims are. Without further ado, let us attend to this matter.

Second Chapter

The rightful claims of the citizen, as a hitherto-free participant in world trade, on the closing commercial state

By dint of his labor and the piece of money that he earns through this, the citizen obtains a claim to all the things that either nature's favor or human art brings forth in any part whatsoever of the great commercial republic. When it is about to close off the commercial state, the government finds its citizens in precisely this state of existence, and we can at least presuppose this state of existence as the fixed [115] point of departure for our investigations, since indeed, in all the present European states, trade was at one point entirely free, even if perhaps it was later brought under incomplete restrictions.

The citizen has acquired the right to remain in this state of existence, since, from his side, he contributed something to the flourishing of this great commercial republic and the enlivening of its overall commerce. It is a right granted to him by the state, whose silent consent, as we recall from {478} before, led him to count on the continuing existence of this state of affairs. It is a right that could not be refused to him but at his great disadvantage. Strictly speaking, it is true, everyone should be content with what is yielded by the climate in which he dwells and the art of his fellow citizens among whom he lives. And everyone would be content with this, neither suffering hardship nor craving for foreign things, had not so many become habituated to such goods, perhaps even from their earliest youth on. This habituation has turned these goods into needs that are indispensable to their well-being. The government silently looked on as they grew accustomed to these things. With its silence it guaranteed to them that, at the very least, it would do nothing to deprive them of these goods or render their possession more difficult.

Hence, it follows that, with the closure of the commercial state, the citizen emerging from participation in the great system of world trade [*am großen Welthandel*] will have a rightful claim to the continuing enjoyment of all those goods of the great European commercial republic that he was previously able to provide himself with, *insofar as they can somehow be cultivated or manufactured in the country where he dwells.* As regards the latter, we cannot think of any reason why, presuming the possession of the raw materials, it should not be possible to manufacture everything in every country, or why any people would be so naturally unteachable that it could not become skilled at any mechanical art and make it its own. Yet, as for the former, it is certainly agreed that there are certain produce that can either never be cultivated in certain climates, or at least not advantageously and not without greater disadvantages for the natural produce of the land. Yet in every climate, so long as it is temperate and we don't shy away from effort and expenses, we will be able to discover and cultivate produce to substitute for the foreign crops. {479} [116]

Thus, a government that is about to close off the commercial state must first introduce and implement, in the quantity needed for the country, both the domestic manufacture of all the manufactured goods that its citizens have come to need, and the domestic cultivation of the authentic or substitute forms of all the customary produce as well as whatever is needed as raw material for the factories.

Even those goods whose cultivation or manufacture will prove altogether impossible, and that in the future should be dropped from trade, need not be brought out of circulation all at once. Rather, this can be done little by little, in such a way that periodically an ever-smaller quantity of these goods is distributed, and at last none at all. The citizens should be informed beforehand of this arrangement, and in this way their rightful claim to the continuing enjoyment of those goods, derived as it is from the silent consent of the state, would vanish.

Yet both with regard to transplanting foreign industries into the country and to gradually weaning the nation from those pleasures that, in the future, will no longer be satisfied, a distinction must be made between those needs that can actually contribute something to well-being and those that only take opinion into account. We can quite well suppose that it would be hard for someone to suddenly do without Chinese tea, or have no fur coat in the winter and no light dress in the summer. Yet it is hardly clear why the coat must be of sable or the dress of silk, when the country produces neither sable nor silk. And it is even less clear why it would be so terrible if one day our clothing suddenly lacked all that embroidery through which it is made neither warmer nor more durable.

In short: the closing off of the commercial state, of which we are speaking, would not involve renouncing [what we once enjoyed] and modestly restricting ourselves to the narrow circle of produce previously cultivated in our country, but rather appropriating vigorously, so far as we are able, {480} our share of all that is good and beautiful upon the entire face of the earth. This share is due us, since our nation, through its work and its artistic sense, has without doubt also contributed for centuries to this common possession of humanity. [117]

Third Chapter

The claims of the state, as a self-sufficient whole, during its complete separation from the rest of the earth

Certain parts of the earth's surface, together with their inhabitants, have been visibly determined by nature to form political wholes. They are isolated all around from the rest of the world by giant rivers, oceans, or inaccessible mountain ranges. The fertility of one tract of land within their circumference compensates for the infertility of another. The produce that is most naturally and advantageously extracted in one tract of land belongs together with the produce of another, indicating an exchange that nature itself demands. Rich pasturage is matched by cropland, woodland, and so forth. None of these tracts could exist for itself alone, and yet united they produce the highest state of prosperity for their inhabitants.—These hints given to us by nature of what should stay together and what should be sundered are what is meant when, in more recent political thought, one speaks of *the natural boundaries* of empires [*Reiche*], a consideration that should be treated as far more important and serious than it usually is. Here too one must not only consider the borders that are fortified and guarded by the military, but pay much more attention to productive independence and self-sufficiency. {481}

Since the pieces into which the modern European republic has been divided have not been determined deliberately and in accordance with concepts, but through blind chance, then even if we had no historical knowledge about this, one may already suspect from the nature of the matter that the states that arose were not able to obtain their natural borders, but that, instead, over here two ruling families are striving side by side to form their separate states within a circumference determined by nature to be a single state, while elsewhere a third family expands its holdings across disjoined and severed borders.

169

What will result from this can just as easily be foreseen. The governments will dimly feel that they are missing something even if perhaps they
don't clearly see what this, properly understood, is. They will speak of the
necessity of *arrondissement*.[11] They will protest that for the sake of the rest
of their lands they cannot do without this fertile province or these mineral
and salt mines—always aiming obscurely at the acquisition of their natural borders. All will be driven by the thirst for conquest—be it blind and
indefinite, or indeed clear in vision and [118] very definite [in its aims].
And thus they will find themselves unceasingly in a state of war—be it
direct or indirect, actually declared or merely in preparation. Those states
that properly should be one, since they lie either wholly or partially within
the same national borders, are in a natural state of war. The states, and
not properly speaking their peoples, since, as long as the latter are united,
it is a matter of complete indifference under what name and what ruling
family. The states, and of course the ruling families themselves. These have
completely opposed interests, which, if imparted to the people, become
national hatred.[iv] In contrast, two states that between themselves {482} have
no natural conflict over their borders, but that each from its side makes
demands on one and the same third state, will be natural allies. And so a
state of affairs will necessarily ensue in which peace is concluded only to
prepare for a new war.

It has forever been the privilege of philosophers to sigh about wars.
The author loves them no more than anyone else, but he believes he sees
that they are unavoidable in the present circumstances, and does not think
it serves any purpose to complain about things that cannot be avoided. If
war is to be eliminated, the reason for war must be eliminated. Each state
must obtain what it aims to obtain through war, and which, reasonably, is
the only thing it can aim at: its natural borders. When this is accomplished,
it will have nothing more to seek from another state, since it possesses [119]
what it wanted. Since it has not advanced beyond its natural borders into
the borders of another state, no other state has anything to seek from it.

A state that is about to close itself off as a commercial state must first
assume its natural borders, advancing toward or restricting itself to these as
the case may be. On the one hand, if it is to satisfy the demands of the
citizens {483} explained in the previous chapter, it will need an extensive
land containing within itself a complete and closed system of the necessary production. Yet on the other hand, with a general order holding sway
and with a fixed state of intrinsic prosperity, the citizens no longer can nor
should be oppressed by the hoard of taxes needed to keep a giant standing
army in constant readiness for war. And finally, as will first be clearly demonstrated farther down, when a state is closing itself off it will lose all ability
to have a powerful effect on foreign countries. What it does not do before

closing itself off, it will not be able to do afterward. If it tolerated foreigners within its natural borders, these will later seize territory with impunity and thoroughly rout the inhabitants of the state from their lands. And if, in contrast, it retained some territory beyond its own true borders, it will not afterward be able to defend itself against the attacks of the natural owner, and will provoke them to seize even more surrounding territory.

Such a state must provide, and be able to provide, its neighbors with the guarantee that from now on it will not expand itself in any way. Yet it is only able to give this guarantee on the condition that it also closes itself off as a commercial state. The closure of the region and the closure of commerce influence each other reciprocally, and each requires the other. A state that pursues the customary system of trade and aims at superiority at world trade will retain a continuing interest in expanding itself even beyond its natural borders, so that it may thereby increase its trade and by this means its wealth, applying this new wealth in turn to new conquests, which will then be put to the same use as before. A new evil is forever chasing the feet of the old, and the greed of such a state knows no boundaries. The neighbors can never trust its word, since it retains an interest in breaking it. For the closed commercial state, in contrast, no advantage can accrue from extending itself beyond its natural boundaries, for {484} its entire constitution only takes account of its given circumference. [120]

Fourth Chapter

Decisive measures for achieving both the closure of the commercial state and the conditions for this closure that have just been set forth

Let us now set aside the goals we set forth in the two preceding chapters until we automatically strike on the means for achieving them, and simply recall the task, presented above, of closing off the commercial state.

What is demanded is the complete elimination of all direct commerce between the citizen and any foreigner. One can only say that something has been eliminated completely when it has been rendered impossible. The direct commerce between the citizen and any foreigner must be rendered completely impossible.

The possibility of world trade rests on our possessing the means of exchange valid in all the world, and being able to put this to use for us. The foreigner will not sell to someone who does not possess the same sign of value—which is to say, gold or silver money—as he himself possesses. And he for whom the money that the foreigner could give him is worth nothing cannot sell anything to the foreigner. Trade by means of money is, from this point on, not possible between them. There only remains the possibility of exchanging goods for goods. Yet such trade will not get out of hand, if only because of its inconvenience. The state would be able to supervise it more easily, and, as we will see farther down, a state that is closing has at its disposal the most {485} infallible means of eliminating all need and all desire for it.

Hence, the solution of our task is as follows: all the world currency that is found in the hands of the citizens, viz., all gold and all silver, should be brought out of circulation and converted into a new national currency, a money—this is to say—that would be valid only in the country, and yet would be exclusively valid in it.

The validity, and indeed the sole and exclusive validity, of the new national currency, would be provided and guaranteed in the following way: the government, which, by means of the taxes, is already the recipient of the largest payments, and could, in addition, use an artificial provision during the introduction of the new national currency to temporarily make itself into the largest and indeed nearly the only seller, would accept payments only in this money. [121]

It is clear that the government must be the one who manufactures and gives out this money and provides it with general validity by announcing that it will henceforth be the only means of exchange, and that the government will accept only it in its pay-offices. It is also clear that, through specially erected currency exchanges, the government would have to give out the new money in exchange for gold and silver, first at equal value, and then, after some time, at a loss in its value in gold and silver.—It is obvious why the government must erect special currency exchanges and cannot accept direct payments of gold and silver, despite the fact that it is at any rate one and the same government that must first disburse the new money from the currency exchanges before it can accept it at the pay-offices, accepting at the one the gold and silver that it refuses at the other. It should not depend on the subjects' good will whether they procure for themselves the new national currency right away and willingly trade in their gold and silver. They should be compelled to make this exchange.

As for the material from which this new money should be manufactured, I will at present say only this much. Lest it offend the imagination of the people [*Einbildungskraft des Volkes*], this material must not have been previously familiar to them in any context, {486} having become known to them now for the first time with the new money. And from now on it must only be used for money. It is material for money and nothing else than material for money, and the people need know nothing more than this. For keep in mind that the gold and silver in circulation should be exchanged for this and brought back into the hands of the government. If now, say, paper or leather or any other material already familiar from before and already possessing a determinate intrinsic value is made into money, the unthinking public will then ask: How can this little piece of paper or leather be worth my good money, and how can they demand that I sacrifice the latter for the former?

There is, to be sure, no sense in these words: since the silver piece in itself is worth just as little to me as this piece of paper marked by the state. The bushel of grain that I need, however, is worth something to me. And from now on, I no longer will obtain this for the piece of silver, but rather for the piece of paper. And if things were reversed, so that gold and silver, previously merely valued as goods according to their intrinsic utility, are now introduced as money and offered in exchange for the paper money that had been exclusively in circulation, the same public would still ask: How then can this piece of silver be worth my good paper? Yet this public has now already become accustomed to holding gold and silver in such high esteem. This habit should be indulged, and we must not do violence to it by using a material for this new money that is at present valued less than gold and silver. The public now knows absolutely nothing about this material, and thus has no idea what it is worth. The government tells the public that this material has such and such a value, [122] and the public need do nothing more than trust the government, just as before it had trusted the general opinion about the value of gold and silver. And it will actually turn out to be so in experience that a certain piece of this material is worth a bushel of grain or the like; or in other words, that one obtains the latter in exchange for the former. {487}

The new money should commend itself to the imagination even more than the old. It should strike the eyes as beautiful. What sparkles and shimmers is much sooner believed to be of great value.

The manufacture of the new money should cost the government as little as possible of the previous world currency, since it will need this for other purposes outside of the country that shall be discussed farther down. The new money must have as little true intrinsic value as possible, since all that is actually useful should be used as much as possible as a thing and not as a mere sign.

For the reasons indicated above, it must be impossible for either another man or another government to counterfeit this new money. Every possible form—and thus, in the case of money, everything that is a feature of the mold from which it is cast—can be counterfeited. If this material is to be inimitable, it must be impossible either to reduce it to its constituent parts by artificial means, or hit on it by trial and error, or for it to be betrayed through the accounts of others. Some essential constituent part of the compound must be a state secret. In a monarchic state this means it would be known only to the governing family.—From this it should be evident why I cannot express myself more clearly on this point, even supposing that I knew how this would be carried out.

The government must ensure for all time the value of the money distributed by it—viz., the value with respect to goods that it attains at the time of its introduction. It will thus be necessary to introduce, together with the national currency, fixed prices for goods, calculated according to the principles set forth above, and to continually maintain these fixed prices.

The government will solemnly agree to forever renounce the right to increase the quantity of circulating national currency arbitrarily and for its advantage, either by accepting equivalent goods in exchange for newly created money or by using it to pay salaries and defray other expenses. It will cover public {488} expenses with the fixed yearly taxes that are drawn from and returned into actual circulation. With every change in the relation of money to goods, with every reduction of prices [123]—an increase can never occur—and with every increase of the quantity of circulating money, the government must strictly hold itself to the principles set forth in Book I, Chapter 6. These, as well as everything set forth in Book I, Chapters 3,4,5, and 6, will be fundamental laws of the state, to which, if, for example, the state were a monarchy, the monarch will irrevocably bind himself and all his successors, with every new monarch renewing this obligation upon attaining the throne. It would be most fitting for the government, when it issues the act introducing the new money, to at the same time openly instruct the entire nation regarding the new system of administration, indicating the true reasons for its existence and assuming the obligation we have just discussed.

From what we have said it is clear that the system set forth here, should it ever actually be carried out, must either be accepted or rejected in all its parts, and that no government may, say, merely undertake the described monetary operation as a convenient means of enriching itself, while omitting to close off the commercial state, regulate public commerce, fix the prices, and guarantee everyone's state of existence—regarding all these as burdensome occupations while at the same time even reserving for itself the right, at the first occasion that it should again need money, to mint and put money into circulation at its pleasure. Such a way of doing things would cause property to become insecure and give rise to immense disorder, very quickly bringing the people to feel despair and outrage against a thoroughly unjust government.

A state that has been organized entirely according to the principles set forth, as we will see even more clearly farther down, can never end up in a position where it would need or even desire an arbitrary increase in the quantity of circulating money as a means {489} of enriching itself.

The actual act of promulgating and introducing the new money and collecting gold and silver in return will, however, necessarily require certain artificial provisions, and could be made very much easier through others. As regards the actual plan for this introduction, and the sequence of individual steps that need to be taken toward this goal, I will, as is appropriate, remain silent before the public. I recall only this much: there is no need to seek council with the public and inform them in advance before carrying these things out, since doing so would only arouse doubt, questions, and mistrust, all of which are most fittingly removed through the visibly good result of these measures. The actual introduction of the new money must happen all in one stroke, although the effectiveness of this one stroke will be increased through preparatory regulations that can be applied just as well toward some other goal. [124] There is no need here for severity, bans, or penal laws, but only for a very easy and very natural provision. *In one moment, through this provision, all silver and gold will become completely useless to the public for every purpose save exchanging it for the new national currency, whereas the new national currency will become completely indispensable even just to live.*

Fifth Chapter

Continuation of the preceding considerations

The assertion that a state, having dared remove itself from all commerce with foreign lands, will have no need of silver and gold, and can make whatever it wishes into a universal sign of all value, *seems* to me so clear, and to lie so near to everyone's feet, {490} that I cannot make myself believe that I have thus said something paradoxical or astonishing. Yet I know that men usually discover last of all precisely what is nearest to their feet. And I also know that the heads of some are organized in such a way that conclusions, which should properly always rest on the root of their premises, drive down their own roots through mere force of habit, and continue to exist long after the premises have been extirpated. Thus, I must still fear having offended some readers, and find it advisable to say yet a few more words for their sake, while urging all those who have not found anything astonishing in the previous chapter to skip over the present discussion.

Hopefully none of my readers will deny that, with regard to money, the only concern of anyone is that this particular piece of money is accepted again by everyone with whom he trades at the same value for which he obtained it. Now, in the present circumstances, it is possible for us to engage in commerce, either indirectly or directly, with every resident of the known European commercial republic. Hence, in these circumstances, it is of course necessary that we have that sign of value which is accepted by everyone. Yet if we are relieved of this possibility, we will also without doubt be relieved of the need [125] that results from it. Whoever guarantees to us that from now on, in matters of money, we will only have to deal with our government and our fellow citizens, certainly relieves us of having to care about having other forms of money than those which these accept. It is no longer a question of what the foreigner accepts, since I will never have to trade with him.—If I must travel to the Society Isles, and know beforehand that over there one will only let me have food in exchange for red feathers, then I would of course do well to procure red feathers. If I don't want to travel

179

there, what use are these red feathers for me? Likewise, if I have to engage in commercial transactions {491} in a place where only gold and silver are accepted, I must of course get my hands on the latter. If, however, I don't have to engage in commerce there, but only at places where these are not accepted, what use will I have for gold and silver?—Although a number of governments have closed themselves off to foreign trade as best they could, and it is only to their detriment that they could not do an even better job of it, they have continued to consider themselves, even in relation to their own subjects, as free members of the great commercial state, and indeed so much so that they even pay their citizens with the same world currency that they collect from them as taxes in the course of the year, while at the same time worrying and fretting about not having more of this world currency. And princes, in times past, have sought to make gold, not thinking that, without making actual gold, they could simply give out anything that came into their hands in its place.

The only reason for this sort of astonishment, therefore, is habituation to the circumstances that are to be eliminated.

Another reason for fear could arise from confusing the sign of value proposed by us with another similar yet in no way equivalent sign of value— confusing it with the paper and leather-money, banknotes, assignates, and the like that have been attempted from time to time in nearly every state. Someone might say: one knows from the most frequent experience that, save under special conditions that we will not find in a state that is closing itself off, this kind of money always tends to lose value in relation to gold and silver, sinking deeper and deeper, just as in many cases it ultimately becomes worthless, with those who possess it losing their property.—My reply to this is that all these previous representations of money are completely different from the money that I have proposed, and that what is true of the former in no way applies to the latter. Those signs of money [Geldzeichen] circulate *besides, and at the same time as, the cash.* Apart from the rare case where a {492} nation enjoys great superiority in world trade and has debt claims on practically every foreign country, [126] such signs of money are accepted only within a certain circumference, most often only in the country itself. The latter is accepted there, and at the same time throughout the entire world. It is understandable that someone would prefer something serving two different purposes and covering every possible need to something that can only be used in one way. Not so in our system. Only the national currency is in circulation, and *none other besides it.* It cannot lose value against something that is not the least bit present, and that never enters into comparison or collides with it. Moreover, as follows from this first point, those other forms of money indeed always relate to cash and are supposed to be *realized* (as one puts it) in cash at some time and in some way. Cash always lies midway between these forms of money and the goods, and it follows that they are in fact not *money* at all, not an *immediate sign of goods*, but rather only a *sign of money*. They are not money in the first, but only in the second power [*Potenz*], and could in turn be represented were a money in the third power to arise. And so on ad infinitum. Thus, in all these systems the first false presupposition—that only gold and silver can be proper, true money—remains standing. The credit afforded to the sign-money now depends precisely on the general belief in the possibility and ease of its realization in cash. Not so in our system. Here the national currency relates to no other, and—save in one single very infrequent case that we shall discuss farther down—should not be converted into any other money. It stands in a direct relation to goods, and will be realized only in these. It is, it follows, the true, immediate, and only money. The entire false system is already contained in the mere expression "realize something in money." Nothing can be realized in money, since money itself is nothing real [*reell*]. The ware [*Ware*] is the true [*wahre*] reality, and money is realized in it.

There is only one objection that could be made {493} to our proposal that seems important. It is as follows: until now, property in money—the source as well as the final result of all other property—has been independent of the governments, who, no less than the least of their subjects, have been subject in this regard to general necessity, and has been guaranteed by the agreement of nearly the entire human race. It has not stood in any government's power to make the dollar that someone possesses worth less than it is now worth. In our system, where it would stand in the power of every government to make as much money as it could ever wish, releasing the rulers from the bridle of necessity, even the citizen's property in money would become dependent on the unlimited free license of their rulers. These would from now on even be able to steal the property of those who possess money from out of [127] locked safes, since by increasing the quantity of money in circulation without limit, they can cause its value relative to goods to decrease without limit. Drawing the government's attention to its ability to do this is neither a philanthropic nor just way to begin, and the best we could wish for is that everyone will scorn and mock these ideas as vacuous dreams, incapable of being carried out, and that no one would ever convince himself that there might in fact be something to them.—I had indeed added that the rulers should not arbitrarily increase the quantity of money for their own advantage, and that they should solemnly oblige themselves not to do this. Yet who could compel him who holds all the power in his hands even merely to assume such an obligation, or afterward keep his word? Who could watch over him, making sure that he keep his word, when indeed he might quietly increase the quantity of circulating money without anyone noticing? And if he does so immoderately, and at last the abundance of money becomes noticeable to everyone, who will call him to answer for his deeds and refer him to the authorities?

I reply to all this: the most certain guarantee against illegalities and transgressions of every kind is that the need does not arise for them, that they {494} do not bring an advantage for the transgressor but rather are sure to cause harm and disadvantage for him. Whether one needs fear that a government that has accepted the proposed system will arbitrarily increase the quantity of circulating money depends on whether, given the constitution that would necessarily emerge following the introduction of national currency and the complete closure of the commercial state, there could ever arise a case where the government had need of such an increase, where it would draw an advantage from it, or where it could expect anything else from it but harm and disadvantage? And this question will answer itself in the course of our investigation.

Sixth Chapter

Further measures for the closure of the commercial state

Through the measure described above the government will come into possession of all the world currency that previously circulated within the country.

From now on it will no longer need this money domestically, since it
won't give out any of it to anyone living within the country. It will only
be able to use the money toward foreign countries, and, since it has already
covered its internal needs and is thoroughly self-sufficient, it will indeed
become a considerable and dominant monetary power [*Macht*] toward these.
It should avail itself of this power quickly, while it still remains power, to
accomplish the goal set forth above and vigorously appropriate for the nation
its share of all that is good and beautiful upon the entire face of the great
commercial republic.

One sees that I presuppose the country is not yet {495} completely
impoverished and bereft of world currency. The more that is still in circulation, the better. A fully impoverished state will of course be compelled to
introduce a national currency, perhaps of paper, so that it should still have
some means of exchange. In so doing, it may even link it to the world currency—once again a mistake that will prove to its own disadvantage—as
though it wished to again procure this for itself, and redeem its paper money
with it. In this way the state will indeed also close itself off automatically,
since an extensive trade is scarcely still possible between it and foreign lands.
Yet its closure is not an appropriation of the advantages of other countries,
but rather a resignation under compulsion of necessity to its own poverty.
Such a state is led and driven by daily need. For this state, everything will
automatically turn out the only way it can. It has no need of our rules, and
our words are not aimed at it.

I will set forth in sequential order the measures that must be taken by
a state that is still in possession of cash and introduces a national currency
not from need but from wisdom.

1.

In one and the same stroke, the state will introduce the new national currency and also gain control of all active and passive trade with foreign countries. This happens as follows: immediately before promulgating the new national currency, the government will purchase all the foreign goods available in the country, employing officials who have been commanded to do this through sealed orders that are all to be opened on the same set day throughout the entire country. The aim of this purchase is, on the one hand, to gain a precise knowledge of both the available supply of and present need for these goods, and, on the other hand, to take control of the legislation of their prices.—The goods, understandably enough, will remain where they are and will be sold through the same people who would have sold them before. Only, from now on, they will no longer be sold on the account of the one who possessed them previously, but instead on the account of the government. This means: for whatever price {496} the government sets for them in accordance with its more distant goals. For example, the prices of those goods that in the future should disappear from the market can be raised, and from time to [129] time may be raised even more. Other prices, however, will be reduced. The government will settle accounts with the merchant, using the national currency, immediately after its promulgation. If its determination of the prices caused a loss for the merchant, the government will compensate him for this. And if, however, the determination of prices brought the merchant a profit, the government will collect this.

The correct declaration of these supplies of foreign goods, being of great importance for the state, will at any rate be enforced with inspections—the very last that will be necessary from now on—and the threat of heavy punishment for incorrect declarations. At the same time as this monetary action is being undertaken within the country, a manifest of the government will appear in every foreign land requesting all foreigners to inform the government within a certain time of all their monetary dealings with residents of the state that is to close itself off, and to settle accounts with the government, lest they be punished with the loss of their claims. Likewise, the residents of the country are requested to hand over to the government whatever claims they have on a foreigner, allowing them to be settled through the government. In addition, the foreigner will be warned that, starting with the day of the appearance of the manifest, they should not enter directly, without explicit permission and interposition of the government, into commercial dealings with any resident of the state that is to close itself off, for if they do so, the government will turn them away together with whatever debt claims have arisen in this way.—When dealing with foreigners regarding past transactions, the government will assume all the obligations of the private man with whom the foreigner first entered into a contract. It will render and collect whatever payments should have been rendered to and collected from it. Should the private man happen to be insolvent, the government is of course not bound, strictly speaking, to fulfill its obligations, since indeed the foreigner originally had dealings only with the private man and was a creditor not to the government but to this man alone, from whom he would not have received any money, {497} and has no right to draw advantages from the interposition of the government—an interposition that is, with regard to him, purely accidental. It remains for the government to act as it would wish to act for the nation's honor, especially since, although it will not be compensated for this loss, it will lose little by satisfying the foreigner, and the few cases of this kind that could occur would be extremely trivial compared to the rest of its business.

The government, in this settlement, renders its payments to and collects its payments from the foreigners in *world currency*, while rendering payment to, or collecting payment from, the citizen using *national currency* in its place.

There is another important matter: the total amount of trade that is to be conducted provisionally [130] with foreign countries will be fixed. That is to say: it will be determined which kinds of goods, how much of each for every year and for how long in total, and how much in each district and for each trading house, will still be imported from abroad or exported to there. From now on this trade will no longer be conducted by private individuals but by the state. The merchant, who has correspondents abroad and is best informed about the sources of his goods, may, now as before, order the foreign goods that are permitted to him by the calculation just mentioned. Yet his order must include the approval of the government, perhaps through a special trade commission established for this purpose, and the foreigner would know through the above-mentioned manifest that he will only be able to rightfully demand payment on the condition of and through this approval. The foreigner draws his payment from the government in world currency as soon as the goods have been delivered. The resident pays the government for them in national currency, also as soon as they are delivered, for the government does not grant credit, and all trade swindles, which in any case run counter to a well-ordered political economy, should also come to an end with the closure of the state.

However much or little the government pays the foreigner for the goods, it is not this price that will set the measure {498} for what the resident must pay, but rather the selling price dictated by the law of the land, with consideration given to what is necessary for the native merchant's own adequate sustenance while he is selling them. Here the government must not think of enriching itself, but always keeps a view to its higher purposes, periodically raising the prices of those goods that in the future will disappear from the market, while selling goods for even less than it would cost to buy them from abroad when the subjects could be tempted to obtain them through smuggling directly with neighboring lands. It would thereby lose nothing more than a little bit of the money that it has made so easily, and could gain nothing more than just such a little bit of the same.

It is just the same with the domestic goods that will still be exported abroad. The foreign merchant, who knows the sources of the domestic goods, may, now as before, order these directly from his past correspondents. But let him know that he must first send this order to the trade commission mentioned above, enclosing a bill of exchange for the payment in world currency. It is only when the order has passed through this commission and is furnished [131] with its consent, that it can go on to the domestic trading house, which will receive payment for the goods from the government in national currency after delivering them to the seaport or the trading town on the border. However dearly or cheaply the government will be paid for these goods from abroad, the resident will receive from the government the legally determined national price.—To oversee these export laws, strict supervision of the seaports and border towns will be necessary. Nothing may be allowed out of the country if the consent of the trade commission for its exportation cannot be produced. The nation will be all the better able to comply with this measure since it is now being employed for the last time, and the state of affairs that makes it necessary is only temporary. {499}

2.

The government took control of foreign trade with the aim of periodically reducing such trade, allowing it to cease entirely after a certain time. The government must accordingly take measures to ensure that this goal is reached quickly. It must advance toward this goal following a plan, and not let a moment pass without gaining ground toward its purpose.

With every year the imports from abroad must become fewer. From year to year the public will need fewer of those goods that can be produced domestically neither in genuine or substitute form, since it should indeed wean itself entirely from these goods and will even be actively urged to do so through their ever-increasing prices. The import and use of those goods that only take account of opinion [die nur auf die Meinung berechnet sind] may even be banned right away. In just the same way, there will be less need for those goods from abroad that in the future will be produced domestically in either a genuine or substitute form. Since, indeed, the domestic production and manufacture, being conducted according to a plan and through calculation and no longer abandoned to blind chance, will continually increase, foreign goods will be replaced by domestic goods.

Likewise, exports will decrease. First of all, the export of produce, if any produce was indeed exported before, will decrease, since the number of manufacturers either using this produce domestically as raw material or consuming it themselves will continually grow, and at the same time production will be guided toward substitutes for the foreign goods that will be abolished. Similarly, the export of manufactured goods will decrease, since the government, in accordance with its plan, will reduce the number of those factories that had counted [132] on foreign sale, and devote, in a fitting manner, hands that once worked for the stranger to labors on behalf of the resident. Its aim is not {500} indeed to attain trade superiority—a very dangerous tendency—but rather to make the nation entirely independent and self-sufficient.

3.

The withdrawal of world currency offers the government the most effective means of providing the nation with independence from abroad without suffering deprivation but instead while enjoying the greatest possible state of prosperity, since it can use this money to borrow and purchase as much of the foreign forces and equipment as it could ever need. Paying whatever is necessary, it would lure away from foreign countries great minds in the practical sciences, inventive chemists, physicists and mechanics, artisans, and manufacturers. It would pay as no other government can, and thus one will throng to serve it. With these foreigners it will enter into a treaty lasting for a certain number of years, during which they will bring their science and art into the country and instruct the residents in these, receiving on their departure compensation in world currency in exchange for the national currency that was previously paid to them. May they then return to their fatherland, enriched with what is valid there! Or if they wish to remain and become citizens, this is even better: just leave them with a free choice, and solemnly guarantee them this from the beginning.—One would buy machines from abroad and make copies of them within the country. The promise of money vanquishes every ban.

As soon as it has been agreed what branches of art can be introduced into the country, the government should promote production, paying special regard to the raw material needed by these branches of art, both encouraging the cultivation of substitutes when the genuine produce cannot be grown in this climate at all and refining those materials already in use. Almost every climate has its own substitutes for foreign produce—it is just that at first their cultivation does not reward the effort.ᵛ The government {501} of which we speak can reward this effort, since it [133] need not shy away from any expense. It should introduce into the land every produce whose advantageous cultivation, and every one of the more noble sorts of animals whose domestic breeding, is likely. Nor will it fail {502} to conduct every possible experiment in either raising these animals and growing these crops, or in the refinement of the already existing domestic produce—and even conducting these on a large scale.

In these matters, there is a specific goal that the government must aim at reaching before the complete closure of the state. Namely, whatever is produced anywhere upon the face of the great commercial republic in the moment when the state closes itself off must henceforth be produced within the country, insofar as this is at all possible in the given climate. The government should have an eye to this goal right from the beginning, working toward it according to a plan, and, with this goal as its measure, guiding the trade that, for the time being, is still permitted with foreign countries. Has this goal been reached, then the state will close itself off. After such a good beginning, the further perfection of all human occupations will advance within the state, isolated as it is from the rest of the world, [134] at a rapid pace.

4.

At the same time as these measures are being carried out, the state should advance into its natural boundaries.

I will refrain from certain investigations touching this point that could easily become odious and that philosophers have almost always conducted one-sidedly, and will just observe the following:

By virtue [vermöge] of its monetary riches, the government of which we speak has the ability [Vermögen] to arm itself so well, and to purchase and hire to this end such a great quantity of equipment and forces from abroad, that it would be impossible to offer it any resistance. Thus, it could attain its intention without bloodshed, and nearly without striking a blow—its operation being more of a march of occupation than a war.

Immediately after the occupation, the same monetary operation should be undertaken in the newly added provinces as was undertaken in the motherland, followed by whatever improvements in agriculture and factories prevail in the latter. {503} Through the first means the new citizens will be bound to the motherland with the strongest of bonds, since they will be deprived of the means to engage in commerce with others. Through the second means, which manifestly intends and fosters their greater state of prosperity, they will become friends of the new government.

It may be expedient to use friendly means to attract part of the residents of the new provinces into the motherland, and send others from the motherland into the new provinces to take their place, thus amalgamating the old and new citizens. This amalgamation should also be beneficial with regard to agriculture and industry, since it was indeed presumed that the new provinces, because of their natural difference, also belong together with the motherland, constituting, together with it, a complete system of production. May these new subjects bring into the motherland those aspects of their methods of agriculture and art that are first-rate, while the old residents of the motherland convey to the provinces what they understand better!

Once this occupation is complete, a manifest from the government to all the other states will appear, in which it will give an account of the reasons for the occupation according to the principles set forth here. With these very principles, which now no longer apply to the government, providing a guarantee, it will [135] solemnly bind itself to these obligations and assure that, from this point hence, it will no longer participate in the political affairs of foreign countries, will not enter into any alliance, will not serve as a go-between, and will not overstep its present boundaries under any pretext whatsoever. {504}

Seventh Chapter

The result of these measures

Within the country agriculture and the factories have now been brought to the intended degree of perfection, and the ratio of each to the other, of trade to both of them, and of the public officials to all three, has been calculated, ordered, and fixed. The state has advanced into its natural borders in relation to foreign countries and has nothing either to demand from its neighbor or cede to it. Once all this has happened, the commercial state will be completely closed, and the constitution of public commerce will be just as was described in the first book. As a consequence of the improvements made before closure, the people will find itself in a state of considerable prosperity, and all will receive their fitting share of this prosperity. Whatever a citizen needs and should have, a fellow citizen of his, who has taken his needs into account, will certainly have, and the former can receive it as soon as he wants. If someone has anything left over, then another citizen, whose needs take the other's surplus into account, will surely need it, and the former can deliver it to him as soon as he wants. Every piece of money that someone earns for himself will quite certainly remain forever worth these specific goods—e.g., this measure of grain—for him and his grandchildren and great-grandchildren, and he will be able to exchange it for these goods at any time. The value of this money against these goods may indeed rise, but it can never fall.—Everyone can be sure that, as long as he continues to work, he will continue to enjoy the state of existence to which he is accustomed. Nobody can grow poor and suffer want, nor could this happen to his children and grandchildren—as long as they work as much as the common custom of the country demands of them. No one can be cheated, and no one will need to cheat another. And if he wished to do so out of a pure {505} love of fraud, he would not find anyone whom he could cheat.—I shall refrain altogether from looking at the consequences of such a constitution for the lawfulness and morality of the blessed people that [136] finds itself under it, but I will allow myself to invite the reader to such considerations.

From this point on, as I said, the commercial state will be completely closed. Everything that is used or sold within the country will have been cultivated or manufactured there, and, conversely, whatever is cultivated or manufactured within the country will also be used and sold there. Whereas in the period from the introduction of the national currency up to complete closure, the government was involved in foreign trade, now neither the private man nor the government will engage in even the most limited commerce with foreign countries. We can only think of one case in which foreign trade will be retained. The cultivation of one produce, say, wine, is in one climate, for example in countries located very far to the north, not altogether impossible, but nevertheless very disadvantageous. In another climate, however—say, in southern France—it can be grown most advantageously. On the other hand, in the northern climate the cultivation of, say, grain is highly advantageous. Between such states, determined by nature itself to a continuing barter, a trade treaty could be set up in which the former would cultivate in perpetuity this set quantity of wine for the latter, and the latter in turn this set quantity of grain for the former. Neither of the sides entering into such a treaty may have a view to profit, but only the absolute equality of the value of the goods. Hence, this trade, which must be conducted by governments and never by private individuals, does not need any money, but only the keeping of a balance [*Abrechnung*]. That the prices will stay the same is guaranteed to the citizen by the government, and the continuation of the exchange itself is guaranteed by nature, since it indeed follows from our presupposition that this exchange is advantageous for both states, and that each needs the other. {506}

There still remains a case where, both during the process of closing off and after the state is completely closed off, the residents could have need of world currency: namely, emigration and travel into foreign lands. While promulgating the new money, the government would have to give the assurance that, if its citizens wanted to travel or emigrate, it would exchange the national currency for world currency at the same ratio that both stood to each other at the time of the promulgation.

We would at most have cause to fear a considerable amount of emigration in the beginning, from people to whom the new order, which alone is true order, appears burdensome, oppressive, and pedantic. The state will lose nothing with the loss of their persons. The money withdrawn from the government through their emigration would not be considerable in relation to the whole. They will only be able to collect as much money as they had available as cash at the moment of the conversion of the currency. The government, however, collects what is in everyone's hands, and since the émigrés are in the minority, their money is by far the least [137] part of what is available.—They will be limited, as I have said, to the cash that they actually had at hand, since they should not be allowed, after the conversion of the currency, to sell their produce or their lands and then withdraw from the government its value in world currency. The government will know if something of this sort has happened from its trade books, and the yield from such a sale will not be exchanged. At most they could have the interest on this sent abroad for the duration of their lives. The principle, as a constituent part of the national wealth, will remain in the land, and fall to the nearest kin of those who did not emigrate.

Only the scholar and the higher artist will have to travel outside of a closed commercial state. Idle curiosity and the restless hunt for distraction should no longer be allowed to tote their boredom from land to land. The travels of the scholar and the higher artist happen for the benefit of humanity and the state, and the government, far from trying to prevent these trips, should even encourage them, sending scholars and artists on {507} trips at public expense. While closing itself off, the government will still conduct trade itself, and, maintaining an account with foreign countries, can easily dispense bills of exchange payable from those. That it will be the only banker for abroad follows automatically from what was said above. After the closure is complete, and as long as gold and silver are still accepted abroad and the government still possesses this form of money, it would either have to disburse them directly or give bills of exchange for use abroad.—But regardless whether these are still accepted or if they have been abolished everywhere, the best remedy offers itself of its own accord. It is to be expected that this closed country, the seat of the most flourishing agriculture and factories and arts, will indeed be visited by as many foreigners who know what to look for when they travel as there are residents traveling abroad. These foreigners will require the national currency during their stay in the country, and they will only be able to obtain this through payment orders on the government. In this way, the latter will acquire debt claims abroad, and can direct its traveling citizens to these. It is to be expected that, on the whole, the two would cancel each other out.

The relation of the people to the government, or, in a monarchic state, to the governing family, is entirely happy. Since the government won't have need of much money, it will not have to collect many taxes. It will no doubt continue to have a multitude of business dealings, calculations, and inspections to conduct, in order to keep the equilibrium in public commerce and in the relation of all the citizens to one another from shifting—none of which is necessary for the governments of the present. But one should not believe that its personnel will be so numerous as under the circumstances that have traditionally prevailed. The ease of the administration of the state [138], and indeed of all work, depends on setting to work in an orderly fashion, with an overview of the whole, and following a fixed plan. What is accomplished must actually be accomplished, and not need to be begun anew, and one must not put one's sights on anything that will only excite resistance and {508} yet can never be put through. This fixed order of affairs exists in the state that we have described, and nothing will be commanded that cannot be compelled by the most natural means.

This state, moreover, will require no more standing troops than are necessary to maintain internal peace and order, since it does not wish to conduct wars of conquest and, having renounced all participation in the political relations of other states, hardly has to fear an attack. To be ready for this latter, extremely improbable case, the state will provide weapons training for every citizen fit to bear arms.

As a consequence of this arrangement of public trade, the government will be able to raise the few taxes it needs for these purposes in a way that is easy, natural, and not the least bit oppressive for the subjects.

For these same reasons, one need neither fear nor suspect that the government will ever avail itself of an arbitrary increase of the quantity of circulating money as a means of enriching itself. Why in the world would it wish to avail itself of this increase in its wealth? It will already be able to acquire whatever it needs, not only for bare necessities but even for superfluous luxury, in the easiest manner. Such a means of enriching itself, however, would necessarily bring forth disorder, incalculable deviations from the calculations that are the basis of the state's administration, and, precisely in this way, insecurity, confusion, and difficulty in the administration—the burden of which would fall, first of all, on the government itself.

The chief source of the subjects' displeasure with their government—the size of the taxes, the often oppressive way in which they are collected, and the obligation of military service—have thereby been diverted and annulled.

The government of such a state will seldom have to inflict punishments or employ odious investigations. The chief source of the transgressions of private individuals against one another—the pressure of actual need, or the fear of {509} future need—has been removed, and a great number of transgressions have been rendered entirely impossible through the strict order that has been introduced. There is just as little reason to fear crimes against the state, the fomenting of rebellion, and revolt. The subjects are doing well, and the government has been their benefactor.

The first state that dares to undertake these operations will enjoy such [139] striking advantages that the rest of the states will soon follow its example. Yet only the state that comes first will have the greatest advantages from them. When it pours its gold and silver money out into the rest of the world, this money will diminish in value abroad because of the increase in quantity. And when a second state follows the first state, this money will lose even more of its imagined value, and so forth, until all states have their own national currency, and gold and silver no longer serve anywhere as money but only as goods, and are only esteemed according to their true intrinsic value. For this reason, the first state that closes itself off need not be sparing with its gold and silver. The sooner it spends it, the more it will receive in exchange. In the future, gold and silver will sink all the way to their inner, true value. The one who is first gains the most, and the longer the latecomers wait, the less they will gain.

It is clear that in a nation that has been closed off in this way, with its members living only among themselves and as little as possible with strangers, obtaining their particular way of life, institutions, and morals [*Sitten*] from these measures and faithfully loving their fatherland and everything patriotic, there will soon arise a high degree of national honor and a sharply determined national character. It will become another, entirely new nation. The introduction of national currency is its true creation. {510}

Eighth Chapter

The actual reason why one will take offense at the theory we have presented

In the course of this investigation I have tried to remove whatever objections one could raise against individual parts of our theory. Yet with a great part of mankind, it is fruitless to go into the reasons of things with them, since their entire way of thinking has not arisen in accordance with reasons but through blind chance. With every passing moment they will once again lose hold of the thread offered to them, forgetting what they just knew and had insight into, and from which a conclusion is now being drawn, and thus are ever again torn back to their customary manner of thinking. Even if such people can offer nothing against any of the parts of which the whole consists, they will nevertheless remain averse to the whole itself. [140]

It is often more useful to search for the reason, itself hidden from them, for their way of thinking, and then place it before their eyes. Even if this will not improve men who are already formed, one can nevertheless hope that those who are still developing, and the generations of the future, will avoid the mistakes and errors of their predecessors.

Thus, I regard the following as the true reason why the ideas set forth here are most profoundly displeasing to so many, who cannot bear to think of the state of things at which they aim. It is a characteristic feature of our age, standing in sharp relief to the seriousness and sobriety of our ancestors, to wish to play and madly swarm to and fro with its fantasy, and since there are few other means available to satisfy this play-urge, it has a strong inclination to turn life itself into a game. Some contemporaries, having also noticed this tendency, and not themselves of a poetic or philosophical {511} nature, have blamed poetry and philosophy for this phenomenon, whereas in fact the former diverts that urge toward something else than life, and the latter challenges it to the extent that it concerns itself with life. We believe that it is a necessary step, induced through nature alone, on the path that leads our species forward.

As a consequence of this tendency, one never wishes to obtain anything by following a rule, but instead to have everything through cunning ruses and luck. Acquisition and all human commerce should resemble a game of chance. One could allow these men to have, keeping to the straight and narrow, the very things they hope to gain through intrigues, cheating, and chance, save on the condition that they now be content with it for the rest of their life. They would then not want it. It delights them more to strive for things cunningly than to possess them securely. It is these people who incessantly call out for freedom—freedom of trade and acquisition, freedom from supervision and policing, freedom from all order and morality. Whatever aims at strict regularity and at things taking a firmly ordered, thoroughly uniform course will appear to them as an infringement on their natural freedom. Such people must be repelled at the very thought of an arrangement of public commerce in which swindling speculation, accidental profits, and sudden wealth would no longer occur.

This tendency alone gives rise to that frivolity which is more concerned with the enjoyment of the passing moment than with the security of the future, and whose chief maxims are: things will take care of themselves, who knows what will happen in the meantime, what kind of stroke of fortune will occur. Its life wisdom for individuals, and its politics for states, consists only in the art of getting out of the present jam, with no care given to the future difficulties that one is thrust into through the remedy that was taken. For such frivolity the security of the future [141], which one {512} promises to it and which it never itself desires, is no valid substitute for the unbridled freedom of the moment that alone entices it.

A way of thinking that is contrary to reason does not easily dispense with a seemingly rational pretext. This is true here as well. And thus, in the case of the present extensive system of world trade, one has praised to us the advantages of the acquaintance of the nations with one another that comes about through travel and trade, and the multifaceted culture to which this gives rise. All well and good: if only we were first to exist as peoples and nations, and somewhere a solid national culture were present, which, through the mutual intercourse of different peoples, could then pass over and melt into an omnifaceted, purely human civilization. Yet it seems to me that, in striving to be everything and at home everywhere, we have not become rightly and wholly anything at all, and find ourselves nowhere at home.

The only thing that entirely eliminates all differences between peoples and their circumstances and that belongs merely and solely to the human being as such and not to the citizen, is science. Through science, and through this alone, men will and should continue to be connected to one another once their separation into peoples is, in every other respect, complete.

This alone will remain their common possession when they have divided up everything else among themselves. No closed state will eliminate this connection. Instead it will encourage it, since the enrichment of science through the unified force of the human race will even advance the state's own isolated earthly ends. Academies financed by the state will introduce the treasures of foreign literature into the country, with the treasures of domestic literature offered in exchange.

Once this system has become universal and eternal peace is established among the different peoples, there is not a single state on the face of the earth that will have the slightest interest in keeping its discoveries from any other, since each will only use these for its own needs inside its boundaries, and not to {513} oppress other states and provide itself with superiority over them. Nothing, it follows, will prevent the scholars and artists of all nations from entering into the freest communication with one another. The public papers will no longer contain stories of wars and battles, peace treaties or alliances, for all these things will have vanished from the world. They will only contain news of the advances of science, of new discoveries, of progress in legislation and the police, and each state will hasten to make itself home to the inventions of others.

Fichte's Notes

i. The right of pasturage may be quite uneconomical, I grant. But a trespass of another's property it is not: for the property right depends only on treaties, and, where explicit treaties cannot be demonstrated, on acquired possession and established tradition (the status quo). Only an incorrect theory of property would call something like this a trespass of property.

ii. I know a region in Germany where a certain foreign good, upon which lies a heavy impost, is generally sold for *less than* the purchase price and the impost combined. This price is only possible because the impost is most often not paid. It is clear that any single merchant who did not wish to commit fraud would be unable to maintain the current price, and would have to altogether forgo trading in this article.—Such is probably the situation with many goods in many regions.

iii. It is commonly said—I cannot vouch for the truth of this rumor, but even only as a rumor it will serve to explain my thought—with regard to a certain German state of the second rank, that the yield from an excise tax that was introduced is not the least bit greater than the costs of its administration, and that one has only retained it in order to employ old servants of the state, soldiers for example, and thereby provide them with a pension.—If this were so, should it not be possible to find a more fitting and less oppressive way of letting these pensioners earn their pension from the people?

iv. So it has—as a German writer, I will give an example from abroad, and avoid those that lie closer at hand—it has been dimly felt since the most ancient times that an island-state (especially for as long as the other realms are not yet in possession of their natural borders, and there is still talk of a balance of power between them) is not properly speaking a self-sufficient whole, and that such a whole requires a firm footing on the continent, with the islands considered only an appendix, so that, for example, the British Isles would, properly understood, belong to the mainland of France. The only matter for dispute, in this regard, was whether the ruler of the mainland should extend his rule over the islands, or the more powerful ruler on the islands should extend his own rule over the mainland. Both have been tried. French princes have taken control of England, and English kings have taken control of France, and till this day the latter prosecute their claims at least in title. And to this was added, in more recent times, a further, and not so natural, striving after superiority in world trade, and the equally unnatural colonial system of both realms. Hence, war from the most ancient times till this day. Hence, a national hatred among both people that is all the more vehement since both were destined to be one.

v. For example, our age has become quite accustomed to cotton fabrics. They provide some comforts, and to abolish them completely might well cause some hardship. Yet true cotton does not grow in northern lands, and it cannot be counted on that the residents of the lands in which it grows will continue to let us have it unprocessed. Accordingly, I would certainly demand that a northern state that is closing forbid the import of Indian, Levantine, and Maltese cotton, yet without depriving us of cotton fabric. But don't many kinds of grass, shrubs, and trees in our climate yield wool that is just as pure, and that can be refined even further through cultivation? I recall having heard that a number of years ago in the Oberlausitz a piece of fabric was manufactured purely from domestic produce that was equal to or better than the best foreign cotton.—"But hunting for these scattered wools, preparing them, and so forth, will cost far more than the foreign cotton, if we can obtain it." I don't doubt this, so far as things stand at present. But if, for example, you were to regularly sow the variety of grass that you know to be richest in wool, and refine it through all the means that stand within human power, and invent suitable tools for the harvest and preparation of this kind of wool, you would perhaps, with the passing of some years, gain a wool that is just as cheap as the foreign cotton, and also, perhaps, acquire a new, healthy, and pleasant-tasting means of nourishment in its seeds. Is there anything man could not make, with cultivation [Kultur], from even the most insignificant plants? Are not our customary varieties of grain originally grass—having been so refined and changed through their cultivation over thousands of years in the most diverse climates that one is no longer able to find their true ancestor among the wild vegetation! Indeed; but our generation is caught in such a throng of true and artificial needs that we have neither the time nor effort to expend on year-long operations, and on attempts that ultimately, indeed, could fail. We must stick with that which is entirely familiar, secure, and which will reward our effort on the spot. The state will rescue itself from this throng of needs through the measure indicated: it will have enough wealth to try everything at its own expense and quietly wait for the result. Within the country it will cost it nothing more than an easily manufactured piece of money: outside of it, a piece of another kind of money, that, with time, will lose all its value.

Translator's Notes

Translator's Introduction

1. *SW* 7: 311–44; GA I.10, 143–70.
2. *SW* 3: 498; GA I.7: 130.
3. Kompetenzzentrums für elektronische Erschließungs- und Publikations-verfahren in den Geisteswissenschaften an der Universität Trier, *Das Deutsche Wörterbuch von Jacob und Wilhelm Grimm auf CD-ROM und im Internet*, 5: 3921–23.
4. Ibid.
5. Ibid.
6. *SW* 3: 447; GA I.7: 90.
7. *SW* 3: 436; GA I.7: 81.
8. *SW* 3: 391–92; GA I.7: 43.

Interpretive Essay

1. For a particularly illuminating schema of division, cf. Julius Drechsler, *Fichtes Lehre vom Bild* (Stuttgart: Kohlhammer, 1955); Christian Maria Stadler, *Freiheit in Gemeinschaft* (Cuxhaven: Traude Junghans Verlag, 2000), 28–31.
2. Martin Heidegger, *Gesamtausgabe* (Frankfurt: Vittorio Klostermann, 1997), 28: 50.
3. *SW* 7, 311–44; GA I.10, 143–70.
4. For a penetrating analysis of the incompleteness of Fichte's system, cf. Sven Jürgensen, "Die Wissenschaftslehre als System der unvollendeten Vollendung," *Fichte-Studien* 16 (1999): 19–38.
5. For a concise account of the relation of Fichte to Kant, cf. Frederick Neuhouser, *Fichte's Theory of Subjectivity* (Cambridge: Cambridge University Press, 1990), 11–31.
6. In Peter L. Oesterreich's words: "The dominant picture of the pure transcendental philosopher has, in the last decades, put Fichte the philosophical rhetorician, cultural critic, and political teacher far in the shadows. That Fichte belongs to the few philosophers who were able, with their public lectures, talks, and speeches, to intervene in historical life and collaborate in the spiritual revival of their time seems today hardly worthy of attention. By thematizing applied philosophy, we therefore

enter into a region of the philosophy of Johann Gottlieb Fichte that remains little known and little investigated" ("Die Bedeutung von Fichtes Angewandter Philosophie für die Praktische Philosophie der Gegenwart," *Fichte-Studien* 13 [1997]: 223). This translation, and all translations from the German, are my own.

7. *SW* 3, 387; GA I.7, 37.

8. The scholarly understanding of German idealism has traditionally often presented a rather simplistic picture of a development leading from Kant through to Fichte, Schelling, and finally Hegel, who represents the culmination of the idealist project. Fortunately, in the last decades, this picture, which is derived in part from Hegel's own self-assessment, has been challenged, and a much more nuanced understanding of German idealism has emerged, stressing not only the importance of early readers of Kant such as Salomon Maimon and Karl Leonhard Reinhold, but also the diversity of the different philosophical perspectives that would develop within, and in conversation with, the idealist tradition. Of particular significance, in this regard, is the work of Dieter Henrich, a number of whose writings are now available in English.

9. *SW* 3, xxxviii; cf. GA I.7, 4.

10. *FIG* 3, 147.

11. GA 1.7, 17–18.

12. Ibid., 21.

13. GA II.1, 104.

14. Ibid., 103.

15. Ibid.

16. *SW* 6, 80; GA I.1, 235.

17. *SW* 6, 108; GA I.1, 258.

18. *SW* 6, 109; GA I.1, 259.

19. *SW* 6, 109–10; GA I.1, 259–60.

20. *SW* 6, 115–16; GA I.1, 264–65.

21. *SW* 6, 117; GA I.1, 266.

22. *SW* 6, 117–18; GA I.1, 266.

23. Cf. Jay Lampert, "Locke, Fichte, and Hegel on the Right to Property," in *Hegel and the Tradition: Essays in Honour of H.S. Harris*, ed. Michael Baur and John Russon, 40–73 (Toronto: University of Toronto Press, 1997).

24. *SW* 6, 119; GA I.1, 267–68.

25. Cf. Zwi Batscha, *Gesellschaft und Staat in der politischen Philosophie Fichtes* (Frankfurt am Main: Europäische Verlagsanstalt, 1970), 36; Manfred Buhr, "Die Philosophie Johann Gottlieb Fichtes und die Französische Revolution," in *Fichte— die Französische Revolution und das Ideal vom Ewigen Frieden*, ed. Manfred Buhr and Domenico Losurdo, 26 (Berlin: Akademie Verlag, 1991).

26. *SW* 6, 178–89; GA I.1, 315–24.

27. We need not suppose, however, that this apparently statist turn in Fichte's thought implies a rejection of the possibility of justified revolution. Rather, it marks a shift toward a different concept of the revolutionary class, and a more radical grounding of revolution. In the *Closed Commercial State* the right to revolution no longer belongs principally to those whose rights and property have been violated, but rather to those who have been excluded or expelled from the sphere of reciprocal treaties.

These, excluded from the sphere of recognition, are *Vogelfrei* (free as birds, and free game). No political bonds, but at most an inner ethical conscience, prohibits them from committing acts of violence. And since they have no property to begin with, the considerations presented in the *Contribution* are completely irrelevant.

28. *SW* 3, 441; GA I.7, 85.

29. The 1813 *Doctrine of the State*, while not articulating an economic theory per se, also reveals the extent to which the problem of economics has assumed a fundamental place in Fichte's concept of the political. Thus, in characterizing the false (bourgeois liberal) understanding of the state, he stresses, above all else, how it arises from a false conception of property: the belief, namely, that property can preexist the state, and thus that the state could exist merely to protect a property that is already there (*SW* 4, 403).

30. In this brief sketch of Fichte's life, I follow Anthony J. La Vopa's *Fichte: The Self and the Calling of Philosophy, 1762–1799* (Cambridge: Cambridge University Press, 2001).

31. Nevertheless, in the case of Fichte, as with Hölderlin, it would be wrong to regard these experiences as irrelevant to his philosophical development, or to believe that he did not regard the rearing of children as closely related to his intellectual concerns. Indeed, as Frank Aschoff persuasively argues, the time Fichte spent as a *Hofmeister* played a vital role in his passage from determinism to transcendental philosophy ("Zwischen äußerem Zwang und innerer Freiheit: Fichtes Hauslehrer-Erfahrungen und die Grundlagen seiner Philosophie," *Fichte-Studien* 9 [1997]: 27–45).

32. For a concise account of the significance of Jena in the development of German idealism, see Terry Pinkard's *German Philosophy 1760–1860: The Legacy of Idealism* (Cambridge: Cambridge University Press, 2002), 87–90.

33. We are reminded of Leo Strauss's suggestion that the Athenian stranger of Plato's *Laws* is a Socrates who chose exile rather than death.

34. Notable examples of discussions of the *Closed Commercial State* in monographs on Fichte's political philosophy include: Hansjürgen Verweyen, *Recht und Sittlichkeit in J.G. Fichtes Gesellschaftslehre* (Freiburg: Karl Alber Verlag, 1975), 113–23; Zwi Batscha, *Gesellschaft und Staat in der politischen Philosophie Fichtes*, 174–211; Manfred Buhr, "Die Philosophie Johann Gottlieb Fichtes und die Französische Revolution," 47–54; and Manfred Buhr, *Revolution und Philosophie: Die ursprüngliche Philosophie Johann Gottlieb Fichtes und die Französische Revolution* (Berlin: Deutscher Verlag der Wissenschaften, 1965), 72–93. In every case, however, the discussion of the *Closed Commercial State*, and of Fichte's economic theory in general, is subordinated to the explication of his political philosophy as a whole, or narrower aspects thereof. Similarly, the very few articles published on the *Closed Commercial State* are almost all concerned principally with the reception or contemporary applicability of Fichte's theory. A recent, felicitous exception is the work of Isaac Stone Nakhimovsky. In his "Fichte's 'Closed Commercial State' and the Problem of Perpetual Peace" (Dissertation, Harvard University, 2008), he argues that Fichte's theory of the state, like the work of Sieyès and Kant's essay *Of Perpetual Peace*, seeks to "improve upon Jean-Jacques Rousseau's description of constitutional government and institutionalize his Hobbesian account of popular sovereignty" (iii). For Fichte, however, Kant

"greatly underestimated the potential for conflict unleashed by heightened economic competition." In his *Closed Commercial State*, Fichte tries to remedy this failure, drawing specifically on "Sieyès's efforts to engineer a French-led restructuring of the European balance of power" (iii–iv).

35. Thus, Joseph Schumpeter writes "Fichte's *Geschlossener Handelsstaat* (1800) must not be considered as the work of an economic expert, since by doing so we would do gross injustice to the high but narrow ideal of its author" (*Economic Doctrine and Method: An Historical Sketch* [New York: Oxford University Press, 1954], 74).

36. For an account of the rhetorical quality of Fichte's writings in general, see Anthony J. De Vopa, *Fichte: The Self and the Calling of Philosophy* (Cambridge: Cambridge University Press, 2001), 1–20.

37. *SW* 3, 389; GA I.7, 41.

38. For an examination of the political significance of the opposition between publicity and secrecy in Fichte's thought, see Faustino Oncina Coves, "Geheimnis und Öffentlichkeit bei Fichte," *Fichte-Studien* 6 (1994): 321–44. Suggestive, in this regard, are Fichte's lectures on Freemasonry, which were published, with heavy editorial distortions, in 1802 (GA I.8, 409–62).

39. Cf. De Vopa, *Fichte: The Self and the Calling of Philosophy*, 368–424. Fichte, not unlike Kant and Hölderlin, was quite concerned with the relation of tone to philosophy and history, as we see, above all, in the popular and critical appendix of 1797, *Annalen des philosophischen Tons* (*SW* 2, 459–89; GA I.4, 293–321; *EPW*, 341–54).

40. *SW* 3, 389; GA I.7, 41.

41. *SW* 3, 390; GA I.7, 42.

42. Karl Marx and Friedrich Engels, *Werke* (Berlin: Dietz Verlag, 1958), 3: 7; For a detailed inquiry into the parallels between Marx and Fichte, see Tom Rockmore, *Fichte, Marx, and the German Philosophical Tradition* (Carbondale: Southern Illinois University Press, 1980), 62–71.

43. *SW* 3, 390; GA I.7, 42; Fichte's emphasis.

44. *SW* 3, 391; GA I.7, 42.

45. *SW* 3, 391; GA I.7, 43.

46. *SW* 3, 392; GA I.7, 43.

47. *SW* 3, 393; GA I.7, 44.

48. Ibid.

49. *SW* 3, 397; GA I.7, 51.

50. Cf. *SW* 6, 80–105; GA I.1, 235–55.

51. *SW* 6, 336; GA I.3, 60; *EPW*, 178.

52. *SW* 6, 337; GA I.3, 61; *EPW*, 178–79.

53. *SW* 6, 337, 342; GA I.3, 61, 65; *EPW*, 178, 182.

54. Cf. *SW* 6, 71; GA I.1, 229; "Rousseau, whom one after another of you name a dreamer, even while his dreams become reality under your eyes, conducted himself much too gently with you empiricists" and, in contrast, *SW* 4, 436: "The presupposition is thus that Right is something purely *a priori*, lying entirely in reason;—not something concerning which all would first have to arbitrarily reach an understanding, in that each already possesses something before the existence of Right, and gives part of it up:—thus according to Rousseau's *contrat social*, [some-

thing] empirical, arbitrarily conceived; a brooding over speculative tasks that puts its trust in luck, lacking speculative principles. As a result, the French revolution: no wonder that, taking its departure from such principles, it turned out the way it did."

55. The most important of these is language, which (as for Rousseau and Herder) has a specifically historical dimension. In the *Addresses to the German Nation*, Fichte famously argues for the superiority—not only for philosophy but for life—of the German language (and every other "original" language) over French. Because German evolved continuously together with the people, and was not forced on them by conquest, it allows for a continual mediation between notions belonging to higher and lower degrees of culture, and thus ultimately allows for the highest philosophical ideas to saturate and penetrate life in its entirety (SW 7, 311–44; GA I.10, 143–70).

56. By the time that Fichte wrote the *Closed Commercial State*, he had already had a falling out with Schiller, the cause of which was Schiller's refusal to publish in the *Die Horen* Fichte's *On the Spirit and the Letter in Philosophy*, itself written as a response to the *Aesthetic Education*, refuting its main arguments (De Vopa, *Fichte: The Self and the Calling of Philosophy*, 270).

57. Friedrich Schiller, *Sämtliche Werke: Säkular-Ausgabe*, ed. Eduard von der Hellen (Stuttgart: J. G. Cotta'sche Buchhandlung Nachfolger, n.d., ca.1900), 12: 9.

58. SW 3, 398; GA I.7, 51.

59. For a discussion of Fichte, and Marx's, debt to Aristotle, see Tom Rockmore, *Fichte, Marx, and the German Philosophical Tradition*, 62–71; Aristotle *Politics* 1.1.10–12.

60. Cf. Fichte's 1795 *Concerning the Capability for and Origin of Language* (SW 8, 341; GA I.3, 91–127). For Fichte, the question of the origin of language is not to be answered, as Herder attempted, through speculation into the possible circumstances under which it arose, but rather by deriving the necessity of its invention from the nature of human reason. Language is, in this sense, itself a work of human reason.

61. Quite different in this regard, and closer to Fichte, is Schiller's conception of history as the free creation of a harmony originally granted by nature.

62. Cf. Edmund Burke, *Reflections on the Revolution in France* (London: Walter Scott Ltd., n.d.), 74–76: "The science of constructing a commonwealth, or renovating it, or reforming it, is, like every other experimental science, not to be taught *à priori* . . . .The science of government being therefore so practical in itself, and intended for such practical purposes, a matter which requires experience, and even more experience than any person can gain in his whole life, however sagacious and observing he may be, it is with infinite caution that any man ought to venture upon pulling down an edifice, which has answered in any tolerable degree for ages the common purposes of society, or on building it up again, without having models and patterns of approved utility before his eyes. . . . These metaphysic rights entering into common life, like the rays of light which pierce into a dense medium, are, by the laws of nature, refracted from their straight line. Indeed in the gross and complicated mass of human passions and concerns, the primitive rights of men undergo such a variety of refractions and reflections, that it becomes absurd to talk of them as if they continued in the simplicity of their original direction. The nature of man is intricate; the objects of society are of the greatest possible complexity: and therefore no simple disposition or direction of power can be suitable either to man's nature, or to the quality of his affairs. . . . The pretended rights of these theorists are all

extremes: and in proportion as they are metaphysically true, they are morally and politically false. The rights of men are in a sort of *middle*, incapable of definition, but not impossible to be discerned."

63. *SW* 4, 394–95.

64. *SW* 2, 299–300; GA I.6, 293; VOM, 108; Fichte writes: "The absolute freedom of will, that we likewise take down with us out of the infinite into the world of time, is that principle of this life of ours—I act."

65. *SW* 7, 8; GA I.8, 198.

66. That Fichte would conceive of historical time as a product of artifice is a natural extension of the theory of temporality that Fichte develops in the *Foundations of the Doctrine of Science*, according to which time is synthesized through the imagination (*Einbildungskraft*) as it hovers between elements that cannot be united with one another. For indeed in the "practical field," Fichte explains, "the imagination proceeds into infinity, up until the wholly indeterminable idea of the highest unity, which would only be possible after a completed infinity, which itself is impossible" (*SW* 1, 217; GA I.2, 361; SOK, 195). Also significant in this regard is the assertion in the *Doctrine of Science nova methodo* that time mediates between the intelligible and the sensible (cf. Peter Rohs, "Über die Zeit als Mittelglied zwischen dem Intelligiblen und dem Sinnlichen," *Fichte-Studien* 6 (1994): 95–116).

67. *SW* 4, 395.

68. The malleability of the matter of politics, already suggested in Plato, is, as Leo Strauss has argued, essential to the modern understanding of politics, beginning with Machiavelli (cf. *What is Political Philosophy?: And Other Studies* [Chicago: University of Chicago Press, 1988], 43). Fichte's *Foundations of Natural Right*, by grounding the state in the assumption that, without the compulsion of law, men will act badly, and further by regarding the state as an artwork, seems to follow Machiavelli—a debt that he indeed makes explicit in his essay on the Italian author and "modern heathen." With Schiller, however (perhaps following Burke and his organic concept of the state), a very different notion of the "political matter" and the political art begins to emerge. Whereas the mechanical artist need not respect his material at all, and whereas the beautiful artist need only grant his material the appearance of freedom, the pedagogical and political artists are faced with a material that contains its end in itself, and thus cannot be merely subordinated to a purpose outside of itself, but must truly and objectively indulge its particularity and personality.

69. *SW* 3, 399; GA I.7, 53.

70. Ibid.

71. *SW* 3, 400; GA I.7, 53–54.

72. Thomas Hobbes, *Leviathan* (New York: Penguin, 1968), 223.

73. For a comprehensive discussion of Fichte's relation to Hobbes and the Hobbesian tradition, see Gary B. Herbert, "Fichte's Deduction of Right from Self-Consciousness," *Interpretation* 25, no. 2 (1997): 201–22; and Nakhimovsky, "Fichte's 'Closed Commercial State' and the Problem of Perpetual Peace."

74. Regarding the importance of temporality in the *Foundations of Natural Right*, see Faustino Oncina Coves, "Das Tempo in Fichtes Jenaer Rechtsphilosophie: Der Zeitrhythmus des Rechtsgesetzes," *Fichte-Studien* 16 (1999): 213–35.

75. *SW* 3, 400; GA I.7, 54.

76. Aristotle *Nicomachean Ethics* 1.7.

77. *SW* 3, 400; GA I.7, 54.

78. *SW* 3, 400–401; GA I.7, 54.

79. *SW* 3, 401; GA I.7, 54.

80. *SW* 3, 10; GA I.3, 320–21. For a comprehensive discussion of this aspect of Fichte's thought, see Hansjürgen Verweyen, *Recht und Sittlichkeit in J.G. Fichtes Gesellschaftslehre*.

81. Cf. Virginia López-Domínguez, "Die Idee des Leibes im Jenaer System," *Fichte-Studien* 16 (1999): 272–93.

82. *SW* 3, 8; GA I.3, 319.

83. *SW* 3, 92; GA I.3, 389.

84. *SW* 3, 56; GA I.3, 361.

85. *SW* 3, 61; GA I.3, 365.

86. *SW* 3, 61–63; GA I.3, 364–67.

87. *SW* 3, 68; GA I.3, 370.

88. *SW* 3, 74; GA I.3, 375.

89. Ibid.

90. *SW* 3, 74–75; GA I.3, 375–76.

91. *SW* 3, 79–80; GA I.3, 379; This understanding of the body, Virginia López-Domínguez suggests, represents both a reception and critique of the anthropology developed in Herder's *Ideen* (283).

92. The affinity between Fichte's concept of the encounter with the body of the other and Lévinas's ethics is the subject of Hans Georg von Manz's "Selbstgewißheit und Fremdgewißheit: Fichtes Konzeption des Anderen als Konstituens der Selbsterfassung unter Berücksichtigung der Perspektive Lévinas,'" *Fichte-Studien* 6 (1994): 196–213.

93. Jay Lampert, "Locke, Fichte, and Hegel on the Right to Property," 40–73.

94. Lampert, 56.

95. Hegel, *Werke* (Frankfurt am Main: Suhrkamp, 1986), 2: 84–85.

96. *SW* 3, 402; GA I.7, 56.

97. Here I refer to producers in the modern, all-encompassing sense, and not in the narrower meaning used by Fichte.

98. While gold and silver, as money, play a vital role in the argument of the *Closed Commercial State*, Fichte says little about mining itself, and never seems to suggest that it would belong to the activities of the estate of producers, despite the fact that they are generally responsible for extracting the products of nature. Assuming that, in Fichte's time, mining was conducted not by private individuals but was a special right of princes, as Fichte himself, in the one instance in which he refers to mining in the *Closed Commercial State*, seems to suggest, then his reluctance to grant an estate of private individuals the right to mine seems understandable. Moreover though, mining, especially for precious metals, involves an element of chance, and sudden profit, that would be hard to integrate into a closed commercial state. Yet Fichte's silence here perhaps also has deeper grounds. On the one hand, as Chad Denton suggested in a private conversation, almost all the copper mines in central Europe were depleted by the beginning of the seventeenth century. If a continuing supply of copper was necessary, then Fichte's notion of the "natural boundaries" of a state would no longer be viable, unless one extended Europe's own national

boundaries far into the colonies. On the other hand, the principal uses of nonferrous metals, as Chad Denton also suggested, were military.

99. *SW* 3, 407–408; GA I.7, 60.

100. Cf. *SW* 1, 150–53; GA I.2, 305–309.

101. *SW* 3, 408; GA I.7, 60.

102. *SW* 3, 413; GA I.7, 64.

103. *SW* 3, 410; GA I.7, 62.

104. For the Physiocrats only agricultural labor counted as "productive," whereas every other form of labor, including manufacture, was essentially sterile (Charles Gide and Charles Rist, A *History of Economic Doctrines from the Time of the Physiocrats to the Present Day*, tr. R. Richards (Boston: D. C. Heath, n.d.), 13).

105. *SW* 3, 404; GA I.7, 57.

106. *SW* 3, 419–21; GA I.7, 69–70.

107. *SW* 3, 441; GA I.7, 85–86.

108. *SW* 3, 442; GA I.7, 86.

109. *SW* 3, 414; GA I.7, 65.

110. *SW* 3, 415; GA I.7, 66.

111. *SW* 3, 416; GA I.7, 66.

112. Ibid.

113. Ibid.

114. *SW* 3, 416; GA I.7, 66–67.

115. *SW* 3, 417; GA I.7, 67.

116. *SW* 3, 479; GA I.7, 116.

117. In contrast to Schelling and Hölderlin, Fichte rejects conceiving of nature as organic.

118. *SW* 3, 448; GA I.7, 91.

119. Aristotle *Metaphysics* 1.2.8–11.

120. Fichte's invocation of wonder in the *Closed Commercial State* may be understood as the beginning of the attempt, culminating in the 1813 *Doctrine of the State*, to integrate Aristotle's metaphysical concept of wonder with the Christian notion of the miracle, in all its historical and eschatological dimensions. What allows this is the conviction that Christianity is a religion of understanding. Whereas the ancient world issues in a cult of genial individuality, in which geniality is conceived as inspiration and compulsion through an unconscious religious principle, the Christian world begins in faith (and even with the charismatic geniality of Christ), but ends with the reign of understanding and freedom.

121. *SW* 3, 449; GA I.7, 90–91; Fichte's emphasis.

122. *SW* 3, 449; GA I.7, 92.

123. *SW* 3, 450; GA I.7, 92–93.

124. *SW* 3, 451; GA I.7, 93.

125. *SW* 3, 451; GA I.7, 94.

126. *SW* 3, 452; GA I.7, 94.

127. *SW* 3, 453; GA I.7, 95.

128. *SW* 3, 455; GA I.7, 96.

129. Cf. *SW* 4, 573–81. "The second prophecy of Jesus concerned the certain execution of his work. Jesus's calling was to be founder of the heavenly empire on earth, and not merely a teacher; to already institute eternity here below universally

and actually. . . . Whatever he might have thought about the time of this founding at the beginning of his work, it could hardly escape him later on, as he became familiar with how the existing men stood toward his initiative, that such a task had to lie beyond the limits of every single human life, not to speak of his own life, whose quick, violent end he could easily foresee. Yet he alone had to do it, and no one else. This could only be reconciled in the following way: he would have to do it through his continuing effect, through the consequences of his existence that he left upon the earth; yet he himself [would have to do it] in his own selfhood, since he couldn't be represented through anyone else. Certain of this, he said to them: he is with them all the days, until the end of the earth, first of all accompanying them in the business of teaching, and teaching others through them; but at the end of this epoch of teaching he would again appear not in the shadowy form of doctrine, but in all the force of real effect, and begin upon earth, in fact and visibly, the empire that had been bestowed to him by his father. Then all the peoples would be assembled before him; this would be the end of the world, of the empire that is of this world, the remnant of the state, which, although of heathen origin, had been preserved up till then in Christianity, and was also able to exist next to this, as a merely preparatory institution."

130. *Allegory* is not a term that appears in the *Closed Commercial State*, but it is also not altogether foreign to Fichte's thought. In particular, in the *Fundamental Characteristics of the Present Age* he speaks, in his critique of Schelling's philosophy of nature, of how, in place of empirical investigation, it merely forces its material into an "allegorical form" (*SW* VII, 125; *GA* I.8, 293).

131. *SW* 3, 455; *GA* I.7, 97. Here Fichte seems to speak very roughly, not taking into account the rate of circulation.

132. *SW* 3, 457; *GA* I.7, 98.

133. *SW* 3, 458; *GA* I.7, 99.

134. Fichte's analysis of the changing attitude of governments toward their citizens, and the emergence of an interest in the economic life of the people, anticipates Foucault's extremely influential analysis of the emergence of biopower.

135. *SW* 3, 461; *GA* I.7, 101.

136. *SW* 3, 462; *GA* I.7, 102.

137. *SW* 3, 463; *GA* I.7, 103.

138. *SW* 3, 464; *GA* I.7, 103.

139. *SW* 3, 465–66; *GA* I.7, 104–105.

140. *SW* 3, 469; *GA* I.7, 107–108.

141. Charlton T. Lewis, *Elementary Latin Dictionary* (Oxford: Oxford University Press, 1891), 515.

142. For the etymological connection between the German *Muster* and the Latin *monstro* and *moneo*, see the *Etymologisches Wörterbuch des Deutschen*, ed. Wolfgang Pfeifer (Berlin: Akademie Verlag, 1989), 1142.

143. *SW* 7, 164–65.

144. *SW* 3, 471–72; *GA* I.7, 109.

145. *SW* 3, 473; *GA* I.7, 110.

146. *SW* 3, 481; *GA* I.7, 117–18.

147. *SW* 3, 475; *GA* I.7, 113.

148. *SW* 3, 476; *GA* I.7, 114.

149. *SW* 3, 476–77; GA I.7, 114.
150. *SW* 3, 476; GA I.7, 114.
151. *SW* 3, 479; GA I.7, 116.
152. *SW* 3, 418; GA I.7, 67–68.
153. *SW* 3, 479; GA I.7, 116.
154. It would be interesting to consider Hannah Arendt's reading of Kant's third critique and the political significance of taste in this context.
155. *SW* 3, 479–80; GA I.7, 116.
156. *SW* 3, 480; GA I.7, 117.
157. Ibid.
158. *SW* 3, 481; GA I.7, 117–18.
159. *SW* 3, 482–83; GA I.7, 119.
160. *SW* 3, 483; GA I.7, 119.
161. Ibid.
162. Even the *Addresses to the German Nation*, Fichte's most explicitly nationalistic work, ultimately subordinates nationalism to cosmopolitan values; Marc Maesschalck ("Fichte et la Question Nationale," *Archives de Philosophie* 59 [1996]: 355–80) tries to recover the forgotten nuances of Fichte's nationalism, arguing that he envisions "un patriotism 'déterritorialisé' grâce à la construction multiculturelle d'une indentité politique commune."
163. *SW* 3, 485; GA I.7, 120.
164. *SW* 3, 485; GA I.7, 121.
165. *SW* 3, 494; GA I.7, 128.
166. *Elementary Latin Dictionary*, 566, 937.
167. *Elementary Latin Dictionary*, 937.
168. While Fichte does not refer explicitly to the Latin *opinio*, I do not think it is spurious to draw attention to this connection, since academic German in the eighteenth century still retained a very close connection to Latin, which was only just beginning to lose its status as the common language of academic discourse. The authoritative German dictionary of Jacob and Wilhelm Grimm, begun in 1838 and not finished until almost a century and a half later, commonly includes Latin translations of German entries, suggesting that into the nineteenth century and beyond Latin kept its status as a point of reference for German.
169. *SW* 3, 486; GA I.7, 121–22.
170. *SW* 3, 485–87; GA I.7, 121–22.
171. Plato, *Republic* 414b.
172. Plato, *Republic* 416e-417a.
173. Plato, *Republic* 414e-415b.
174. Plato, *Republic* 416e-417a: ". . . since many unholy things have come to pass around the coin of the multitude, whereas the coin that dwells among the guardians is uncontaminated" (My translation).
175. GA I.7, 122.
176. For a rich discussion of the relation of money and thought in German idealism, though from quite a different angle, see Marc Shell, *Money, Language, and Thought: Literary and Philosophical Economies from the Medieval to the Modern Era* (Berkeley: University of California Press, 1982), 131–55.

177. Cf. Wilhelm Metz, "Die Weltgeschichte beim späten Fichte," *Fichte-Studien* 1 (1990): 121–31. Metz shows that there are two historical schemas presented in the *Fundamental Characteristics of the Present Age,* and that whereas the first of these is further developed in the *Addresses to the German Nation,* the second resurfaces in the *Doctrine of the State.*

178. *SW* 4, 532.

179. *SW* 3, 512; GA I.7, 141.

180. *SW* 4, 514.

181. Yet Christianity is not, for Fichte, a product of the ancient world or of Judaism. There is even a sense in which Christ is, for Fichte, spiritually if not racially, a German.

182. In this way, we may also compare Fichte's money operation to the old motif of the grail, whose relations to coinage and money Marc Shell brings to light (*Money, Language, and Thought,* 39–46).

183. *SW* 3, 509; GA I.7, 139.

184. The only treatment of this question, to the best of my knowledge, is Karl Hahn's "Die Relevanz der Eigentumstheorie Fichtes im Zeitalter der Globalisierung unter Berücksichtigung Proudhons und Hegels," *Fichte-Studien* 24 (2003): 156–63.

185. Cf. Barry J. Eichengreen and Nathan Sussman, "The International Monetary System in the (Very) Long Run," *IMF Working Paper* (2000): 23–29. Of special significance, with regard to Fichte's argument, is their emphasis on the role of the "politicization" of the monetary system in this transformation.

Translation

1. Karl August von Struensee (1735–1804), the Prussian finance minister, was a scholar in his own right, who had studied theology, mathematics, and philosophy, and written several important works on military science and economics. His approach to questions of political economy was more pragmatic than doctrinaire: he supported the free trade of gold and silver, yet also advocated protective bans on imports. He generally resisted innovation, yet frequently intervened for the sake of the poor. In his writings on military science, however, he stressed the importance of theory. Cf. Herman von Petersdorff, "Struensee, Karl August von," in *Allgemeine Deutsche Biographie* 36 (1893), 661–665 (Onlinefassung); URL: http://www.deutsche-biographie. de/pnd117348295.html.

2. Isaac Casaubon (1559–1614) was a philologist, widely regarded as one of the most learned men of his age, who was born in Geneva to French Huguenot refugees. Casaubon had found favor with Henry IV, who called him to Paris, though Casaubon's refusal to convert to Catholicism prevented him from occupying the professorship that had been promised him, and eventually, with the ascendance of the Ultramontanes that followed Henry IV's assassination, he was forced to emigrate to England. His edition of the works of the Greek historian Polybius (ca. 200–118), on which he devoted much of his labors, remained unfinished (*Encyclopedia Brittanica,* 11th Edition, 5:444).

3. The German *ausführen* is rather ambiguous in this context, since it can mean both to bring to completion the merely theoretical construction of a system, and to realize a theoretical construction in practice.

4. The German *Kunst* has a wider range of meanings than the English "art." It can refer to both the fine arts and everyday crafts, and indeed to any form of human artifice.

5. Fichte uses both *Kreis* and *Sphäre* in similar contexts, referring to both a circle of efficacy and a sphere of efficacy. As far as I can tell, there is no difference in meaning.

6. *Vogelfrei*, like the English "free game," means existing outside of legal protection. The one who is *vogelfrei* is thus an "outlaw" or "bandit."

7. *Übertragen* in this context can mean both to "endure"—a usage that is now obsolete—and to "carry over."

8. According to the editors of the *Gesamtausgabe*, Fichte is referring to the first verse of the sixth letter in the first book of Horace's *Epistles:* "Nil admirare prope res est una, Numici, solaque quae possit facere et servare beatum." H. Rushton Fairclough translates: " 'Marvel at nothing'—that is perhaps the one and only thing, Numicius, that can make a man happy and keep him so" (cf. I.7, 91).

9. This is a reference to Book I, Chapter 5 and Book II, Chapter 2 of *An Inquiry into the Nature and Causes of the Wealth of Nations*, by Adam Smith (1723–1790).

10. *Vermögen* can mean both ability or capacity to perform an action, and the total wealth that one possesses.

11. The German expression *sich zu arrondieren*, derived from the French *arrondir*, means to "round out" a territory by merging together different pieces of land.

German-English Glossary

Abgabe	tax
Abrechnung	deduction, keeping of a balance
Absatz	outlet, sale
Absicht	aim, intention, regard
Ackerbau	agriculture, cultivating the fields
Ackerbauer	agriculturalist, farmer
Anbau	cultivation, tillage
Anforderung	claim, demand
anschaffen	procure
Anteil	participation, share
Anweisung	bill of exchange, instruction, payment order
Arbeit	labor, work
aufgeben	forgo
aufgehen	absorb, cancel out
aufhalten	keep at bay, keep in check
aufheben	eliminate, nullify
Auflage	tariff, tax
Aufsicht	inspection, supervision
aufstellen	propose, set forth
Aufwand	expenditure, expense
Ausbeute	exploitation
ausschließen	exclude

austeilen	distribute
ausüben	practice
bares Geld	cash
bauen	cultivate, till
beabsichtigen	aim at, intend
Beamte	official
bearbeiten	labor, labor on, work out
Bedingung	condition
Bedürfniss	need
beeinträchtigen	encroach on, infringe
begnügen	be content, be satisfied
Begriff	concept, notion
berechnen	calculate, count on, settle accounts, take into account
berechtigen	grant the right
Berechtigung	title of right
Beschließen	bring to a close
beschränken	limit, restrict
besitzen	possess
bestimmen	determine
bestimmt	certain, destined, determinate, set, set aside, specific, specified
beurteilen	judge
bevorteilen	cheat
bewerben	procure
Bewohner	resident
Bezirk	area
Bilanz	balance
bilden	develop, form
Bildung	culture
billig	adequate, fair

Boden	land, soil
Botmäßigkeit	command
Bürger	citizen
darstellen	present
Defraudation	fraud
eigen	own, proper
Eigenschaft	quality
eigentlich	actual(ly), proper(ly), properly speaking, properly understood
Eigentum	ownership, property
eingebildet	imagined
einheimisch	domestic, resident
Einkünfte	income
Einmischung	admixture
Einnahme	income
Einrichtung	arrangement, institution
Einsammlung	harvest
Einschränkung	limitation, restriction
Einteilung	division
Einwohner	resident
Elend	misery
entrichten	pay
entschließen	resolve
entwöhnen	wean
erbauen	cultivate, grow
Ernährung	nourishment
Ersatz	substitute
Ersparnis	savings
erteilen	issue
Ertrag	yield

erwerben	acquire
erzeugen	cultivate, produce
erzwingen	coerce
Fabrik	factory
Fabrikant	manufacturer
Feldbau	agriculture
festsetzen	fix
frei	free(ly)
Freiheit	freedom
Fruchtbarkeit	abundance, fertility
Gebrauch	custom, use
Gegenstand	matter, object
Geld	money, currency
Geldstoff	material for money, money material
Geldüberschuss	surplus of money
Geldveränderung	conversion of currency
Geldvorrat	stock of money
gelten	be accepted, be valid, be worth
Gemeinbesitz	common possession
gerecht	just
gerechten	negotiate over rights
Gerechtigkeit	entitlement, justice
Geschäft	business, business dealings, function, matter, occupation
Gesetzgebung	giving of laws, legislation, legislative apparatus
gesetzlich	legal
Gesetzwidrigkeit	illegality
Gesichtspunkt	perspective
Gewalt	power, violence

Gewalttätigkeit	violence
Gewerb	branch of industry, industrious activity, industry, trade
gewinnen	earn, extract, gain, profit, win
Gleichgewicht	balance, equilibrium
Grundeigentum	landed property
Grundlage	foundation
Grundmaß	basis for measuring
Grundpreis	basis price
Grundsatz	principle
Grundstand	fundamental estate
Güte	quality
Gutsbesitzer	landholder
Handel	trade
Handel und Wandel	trading and trafficking
Handels-Republik	commercial republic
Handelschaft	trade
Handelskollegium	trade commission
Handelsleute	traders
Handelsmann	tradesman
Handelsschwindelei	trade swindle
Handelsstaat	commercial state
Handelsverkehr	commerce
Handlung	act, action, commercial transaction, trade
Herrschaft	dominion, rule, sway
Inländer	resident
juridisch	juridical
Kaufleute	merchants
Kaufmann	merchant
Konsumption	consumption

Kraft	force
Kunstfertigkeit	skill
Künstler	artisan, artist
künstlich	artificial
Lage der Dinge	circumstances
Land	country, land
Landbauer	farmer
Landesgeld	national currency
Legalität	lawfulness
Lehnverfassung	feudal system
Lehre	doctrine
Leichtsinn	frivolity
List	cunning, cunning ruses, ruses
Macht	might, power
Meinung	opinion
Menge	a great many, mass, multitude, quantity
Mensch	human, human being, man
Mißverhältnis	disparity
mitteilen	communicate, impart
Mittel	means
Moralität	morality
nachbilden	copy
Nachdenken	reflection, thought
Nachteil	disadvantage
Nahrung	nourishment
Nahrungszweig	branch of agriculture
Nation	nation
Naturstand	state of nature
Notdurft	bare necessity
notdürftig	absolutely necessary, meager, with only the bare necessities

Notfall	emergency
nützlich	useful
Oberherr	sovereign
Obrigkeit	authority
Operation	operation
ordnen	regulate
Ordnung	order
Organisation	organization
pekuniarisch	pecuniary
Pflicht	duty
Politik	political thought, politics
Politiker	politician
politisch	political
Potenz	power
Produkt	produce, product
produktiv	productive
produzieren	produce
Publikum	public
Rat	council
Rechenschaft	account
Recht	Right
Rechtens	right
rechtgläubig	orthodox
rechtlich	just, rightful(ly)
rechtlicherweise	rightfully
rechtmäßig	rightful
Rechtsanspruch	rightful claim
Rechtsbegriff	concept of Right
rechtsbeständig	rightfully existing
Rechtsbeständigkeit	justification
rechtsgemäß	in accordance with Right

Rechtsgesetz	law of Right, rightful law
Rechtsgrund	basis of right, rightful basis
rechtswidrig	contrary to Right
Regelmäßigkeit	regularity
Regierung	government
rein	pure
Repräsentation	representation
richtig	correct
Sache	concern, matter at hand, thing
Satz	proposition
Schätzung	appraisal, estimation, value
Schlichtung	resolution
schließen	close
Schließung	closure
selbständig	independent, self-sufficient
sichtbar	visibly
sinnlich	sensual
Sitte	custom, morals (pl.), practice
Staat	state
Staatskasse	state funds, state treasury
Staatsrecht	Right of state
Staatswirtschaft	political economy
Stand	estate, position
stattfinden	take place
Stellvertreter	representative, substitute
Stiftung	institution
Störung	disruption, disturbance
Strafgesetz	penal law
Streit	conflict
Subsidie	subsidy

Subsistenz	sustenance
Summe	quantity, sum
System	system
Tatsache	fact
Tausch	exchange, trade
Tauschhandel	barter
Tauschmittel	means of exchange
Teil	part, portion, share
Teilhaber	partner
teilhaftig	partaking
teilnehmen	participate
Teilnehmer	participant
Teilung	division
Tendenz	tendency
Überfluß	abundance
Übergewicht	superiority
umlaufend	circulating, in circulation
umsetzen	convert
umwandeln	transform
unabhängig	independent(ly)
unaufführbar	incapable of being carried out
unbegrenzt	unlimited, without limit
unbestimmt	indefinite, indeterminate
Ungefähr	chance
ungerecht	unjust
Ungerechtigkeit	injustice
unheilbar	incurable
unmittelbar	direct(ly), immediate(ly)
Unrecht	injustice, not right
unrechtlich	unjust

Unsicherheit	insecurity, uncertaintly
untergeordnet	subordinate
Unterhalt	sustenance
Unterricht	instruction
Unterstand	sub-estate
Untertan	subject
ursprünglich	indigenous, original(ly)
vaterländisch	patriotic
verabreden	agree on, negotiate
verarbeiten	labor on, subject to workmanship, use as raw materials
Verarbeitung	manufacture
verbessern	improve
verbieten	ban, forbid
verbinden	bind, oblige
Verbindlichkeit	obligation
Verbindung	nexus
veredeln	refine
vereinigen	agree, combine, unify, unite
Verfassung	constitution
verfertigen	manufacture
Verhältnis	circumstance, proportion, ratio, relation
verhältnismäßig	proportionately, relative(ly)
verhindern	hinder, keep, prevent
Verkehr	commerce
verkehren	engage in commerce
Verletzung	injury
Verlust	loss
vermeiden	avoid
vermitteln	mediate

Vermögen	ability, wealth
Vernuft	reason
vernünftigerweise	reasonably, reasonably speaking
vernunftmässig	rational
Vernunftstaat	rational state
vernunftwidrig	contrary to reason
Verordnung	ordinance
Verpflichtung	obligation
verschließen	close (off), close off, lock, shut
verschmelzen	amalgamate
verteilen	distribute, divide
Vertrag	treaty
vertragen	negotiate treaties
Verwaltung	administration
verwandeln	change (into), turn into
verwenden	apply, expend
Verzicht	renunciation
Visitation	inspection
Volk	people
von Rechtswegen	by Right
voraussetzen	presume, presuppose
vorhanden	available, existing, given
vorhergegangen	preceding, previous
Vorkehrung	provision
vorläufig	for the time being, in advance, preliminary, provisionally, to begin with
Vorrecht	prior right
Vorschlag	proposal
Vorschrift	prescription
vorstellen	represent

Vorteil	advantage, benefit
vorteilhaft	advantageous
Vorurteil	prejudice
Vorwand	pretext
Vorwurf	objection, reproach
Vorzeit	past
Wahrheit	truth
wahrscheinlich	likely, probable
wandelbar	variable
Ware	commodity, good, ware
Warenlager	stock-hold
Weltgeld	world currency
Welthandel	world trade
Weltteil	continent, part of the world
Wert	value, worth
Widerstand	resistance
Widerstreit	conflict
Willkür	free license, pleasure, something arbitrary
wirklich	acting, actual(ly)
Wirklichkeit	reality
Wirksamkeit	effectiveness, effects
Wirkung	effect
Wirkungskreis	circle of efficacy
Wirkungssphäre	sphere of efficacy
Wirtschaft	economy
Wissenschaft	science
Wohlleben	good living, luxury
Wohlsein	well-being
Wohlstand	prosperity, state of prosperity
Zahl	number, size

Zeichen	sign
Zeitalter	age, generation
Zeitgeschichte	history of the present time
zerstreuen	disperse, distract, scatter
zerteilen	divide into pieces
zu Grunde gehen	be ruined, perish
zu Grunde richten	destroy
zueignen	appropriate, dedicate
Zufall	accident, chance
zur Verarbeitung	as raw materials
Zustand	state, state of affairs, state of existence
Zweck	end, goal, purpose
zweckmäßig	expedient, purposeful, serve (someone's) purposes
Zweig	branch
zwingende Gewalt	power of coercion

Index

JC 181 .F6 2012
The closed commercial state
101675